Corporate Learning with Moodle Workplace

Explore concepts, implementation, and strategies for adopting Moodle Workplace in your organization

Alex Büchner

BIRMINGHAM—MUMBAI

Corporate Learning with Moodle Workplace

Commissioning Editor: Pavan Ramchandani
Acquisition Editor: Pratik Tandel
Senior Editor: Hayden Edwards
Content Development Editor: Aamir Ahmed
Technical Editor: Deepesh Patel
Copy Editor: Safis Editing
Project Coordinator: Kinjal Bari
Proofreader: Safis Editing
Indexer: Manju Arasan
Production Designer: Jyoti Chauhan

First published: November 2020

Production reference: 1261120

Published by Packt Publishing Ltd.
Livery Place
35 Livery Street
Birmingham
B3 2PB, UK.

ISBN 978-1-80020-534-5

www.packt.com

Packt>

Contributors

About the author

Alex Büchner is the co-founder of the Premium Moodle Partner and Platinum Totara Partner Synergy Learning. He has been administering and configuring learning management systems of all shapes and sizes since their advent on the educational landscape.

Alex holds a Ph.D. in computer science and an MSc in software engineering. He has authored over 50 international publications, including four books, and is a frequent speaker on Moodle, Totara, and related open source technologies. His first three books on Moodle administration by Packt Publishing have become the de facto standard on the topic.

The best learning experience in Moodle Workplace is provided when communication and collaboration is utilized. The same applied to writing this book, which would not have been possible without the Packt editorial team's support.

I want to thank Gavin Henrick for his constructive feedback provided during the reviewing process. This book would not be the same without your comments and suggestions. I would like to thank Emilio Lozano, Product Lead of Moodle Workplace, for his insights into what truly has become a fantastic piece of software. I would also like to thank Marina Glancy, Technical Lead of Moodle Workplace, for her support with any technical queries.

Last but not least, I have to thank my family for their support and patience while I have been hiding away writing yet another book. I will make up for it. Promise!

About the reviewer

Gavin Henrick is a learning technology consultant based in Dublin who has years of experience assisting organizations with their teaching and learning strategies. Gavin is the CEO and co-founder of Brickfield Education Labs, which provides an accessibility platform for Moodle using institutions to effectively manage the accessibility and usability of their course materials.

Gavin started his own consulting firm in 2011, Learning Technology Services, working with colleges, universities, corporates, and semi-states on Moodle deployments, training, and customizations. Gavin is an active member of the Moodle community, and he has worked for more than 14 years with Moodle Partners and Moodle HQ, in addition to running the UK and Ireland MoodleMoot.

Having co-authored *Moodle 2.0 for Business Beginner's Guide*, *Moodle Administration Essentials*, and *Moodle Add-Ons*, Gavin has also published a number of whitepapers on Moodle and some educational guides, including the *Moodle 2 Toolguide* and the *Moodle Universal Design for Learning Guide*.

Packt is searching for authors like you

If you're interested in becoming an author for Packt, please visit `authors.packtpub.com` and apply today. We have worked with thousands of developers and tech professionals, just like you, to help them share their insight with the global tech community. You can make a general application, apply for a specific hot topic that we are recruiting an author for, or submit your own idea.

Table of Contents

6
Onboarding and Compliance

7
Skills and Incentives

8
Generating Custom Reports

9
Seminar Management

10
Mobile Learning

11
Corporate Identity

12
Migrations

Appendix A –
Moodle Workplace Web Services

Other Books You May Enjoy

Index

Preface

Since its launch in 2002, Moodle has become the benchmark that every learning management system is measured against. It has won a wide range of international accolades and has established itself as an ecosystem for a large number of educational tools and services.

Moodle Workplace has been designed for corporate and organizational training, resulting in a powerful and flexible platform for workplace learning. Moodle Workplace has grown into a mature, sophisticated, and complex software system, covering a wide range of topics. A fun way to demonstrate the various subjects is in the form of a tube / subway / metro / underground map, where any icon(ic) stations represent Moodle Workplace-only features (more languages available at www.openumlaut.com):

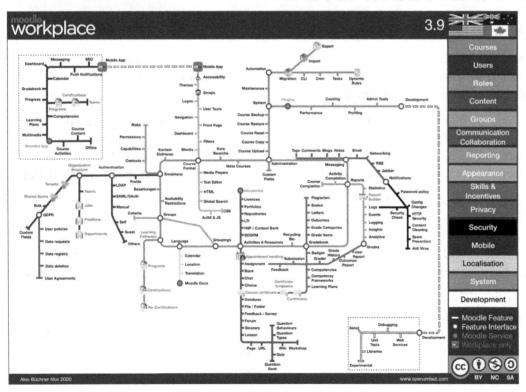

Moodle Workplace is a set of tools built on top of Moodle. This book is a complete, practical guide for managing Moodle Workplace.

The author, who has been at the cutting edge of Moodle since its advent, has adopted a problem-solution approach to bring the content in line with your day-to-day operations. The practical examples will help you to set up Moodle Workplace for large organizations and small commercial entities alike.

Who this book is for

This book is written for administrators managing an entire Moodle Workplace site or a single tenant, managers who lead teams, and learners who use Moodle Workplace for their continuous professional development. Whether you are dealing with a small-scale Moodle Workplace instance or a large-scale multi-national system, this book will assist you with any administrative tasks.

Some basic Moodle knowledge would be helpful but is not essential.

What this book covers

Part I: Basic Concepts

Here you will learn about the main purpose and basic concepts of Moodle Workplace. You'll familiarize yourself with the Workplace terminology and its user interface. This part comprises the following chapters:

Chapter 1, *What Is Moodle Workplace?*, is an introductory chapter to give you an overview of Moodle Workplace and its various new key features. This new kid on the Moodle block will be compared with its little sibling, standard Moodle, and its main rival, Totara Learn. You will also explore Moodle Workplace's business model and its versioning policy.

Chapter 2, *Working with Moodle Workplace*, will cover essential elements that you will be using when working with Moodle Workplace and also throughout the book. You will learn about the key players in Workplace, their roles, their responsibilities, and what functions they have in your setup. Also, you will learn about important user interface interactions, and finally, you will become familiar with different help sources, both built-in and external.

Chapter 3, *Exploring Moodle Courses, Users, and Roles*, is a short primer on Moodle courses, users, and roles. It covers the basics of the three key concepts and demonstrates how the three core elements are inherently intertwined.

Part II: Data, Processes, and Workflows

Learning in enterprise environments is driven by data, processes, and workflows such as induction programs, compliance training, and controlling based on reporting. There is a plethora of new tools in Moodle Workplace to model organizational data, map out processes, and optimize learning management workflows. This section comprises the following chapters:

Chapter 4, Tenants, Organizations, and Teams, is all about setting up and managing the structure of your user-related data. Tenants are entirely isolated entities with their own look and feel, structure, users, and learning entities. Each tenant is modeled using organizations with multiple hierarchical department and position frameworks. Based on job positions and reporting lines, teams are a key feature that lets managers see the learning progress of their staff.

Chapter 5, Automation and Dynamic Rules, covers the definition and execution of centralized and automated rules using an "if this then that" conditional approach to trigger actions when certain conditions are met. Dynamic rules allow you to automate a wide range of steps you would otherwise have to work through manually.

Chapter 6, Onboarding and Compliance, deals with two powerful features of Moodle Workplace, namely programs and certifications. Programs allow you to establish learning pathways for your employees by adding a combination of courses or a hierarchical sequence of courses. Certifications allow you to validate learning paths by offering certifications for recurring programs.

Chapter 7, Skills and Incentives, covers three Moodle Workplace tools to reward staff: certificates, competencies, and badges. You will learn how to create and issue certificates in different contexts. We will then briefly introduce competencies, which describe the learner's proficiency or level of understanding in specific subject-related skills. Finally, we will cover the basics of badges, which are a good way of celebrating achievement and showing learning progress.

Chapter 8, Generating Custom Reports, focuses on the Moodle Workplace custom report builder, which allows you to create site-wide reports that are then distributed to users, such as managers and trainers, so that they can review and manage employee training programs.

Chapter 9, Seminar Management, will equip you with the knowledge to organize and manage face-to-face training events using the appointment booking activity.

Part III: Technical Tools

Moodle Workplace is a highly modular and adaptive learning management system that can be tailored according to your (mobile) workforce and customized to reflect your corporate identity. Furthermore, it supports the exchange of all Workplace elements via migrations and provides an abundance of web services to facilitate integration with other systems in your technical infrastructure. This part comprises the following chapters:

Chapter 10, Mobile Learning, is all about the dedicated Moodle Workplace app. You will learn how to prepare and use the app, and we will cover some relevant configuration options.

Chapter 11, Corporate Identity, tells you how to adapt your Moodle Workplace system to bring it in line with the corporate branding of your organization. To achieve this, you will be given an overview of Moodle designs, before we brand individual tenants as well as the mobile app.

Chapter 12, Migrations, is all about moving various data and elements between tenants and sites. Moodle Workplace's powerful migration tool expedites and simplifies importing and exporting processes. We will then apply the migration tools via its versatile CLI to demonstrate HR synchronization processes.

Appendix A, Moodle Workplace Web Services, looks at ways to integrate Moodle Workplace with other systems via web services. We will provide information about the basic concepts of Moodle web services before exploring the differences between migrations and web services. You will also find a helpful reference of Moodle Workplace-specific web services.

To get the most out of this book

All you require is administrator access to a Moodle Workplace system. The book is based on the latest version at the time of writing (3.9.2), but any newer version will also suffice.

Software/hardware covered in the book	OS requirements
Administrator access to a Moodle Workplace system	Windows, macOS X, or Linux (any)

Moodle Workplace is not being distributed in the same way as standard Moodle. Moodle Workplace is only available via Moodle Premium Partners (moodle.com/workplace).

Conventions used

There are a number of text conventions used throughout this book.

`Code in text`: Indicates code words in text, database table names, folder names, filenames, file extensions, pathnames, dummy URLs, user input, and Twitter handles. Here is an example: "If no tenant is specified in the URL, the settings for a default tenant (`tenantid=1`) will be applied."

A block of code is set as follows:

```
/* Change color of drawer button & give it a bit of a curve */
#page-wrapper >.fixed-top >div>.drawer-toggle-button {
   background: #E54F11;
   border-top-right-radius: 1em;
}
```

Bold: Indicates a new term, an important word, or words that you see onscreen. For example, words in menus or dialog boxes appear in the text like this. Here is an example: "To expedite this refreshing process, clear your caches at **Site administration | Development | Purge caches**."

> **Tips or important notes**
> Appear like this.

Get in touch

Feedback from our readers is always welcome.

General feedback: If you have questions about any aspect of this book, mention the book title in the subject of your message and email us at `customercare@packtpub.com`.

Errata: Although we have taken every care to ensure the accuracy of our content, mistakes do happen. If you have found a mistake in this book, we would be grateful if you would report this to us. Please visit `www.packtpub.com/support/errata`, selecting your book, clicking on the Errata Submission Form link, and entering the details.

Piracy: If you come across any illegal copies of our works in any form on the Internet, we would be grateful if you would provide us with the location address or website name. Please contact us at copyright@packt.com with a link to the material.

If you are interested in becoming an author: If there is a topic that you have expertise in and you are interested in either writing or contributing to a book, please visit authors.packtpub.com.

Reviews

Please leave a review. Once you have read and used this book, why not leave a review on the site that you purchased it from? Potential readers can then see and use your unbiased opinion to make purchase decisions, we at Packt can understand what you think about our products, and our authors can see your feedback on their book. Thank you!

For more information about Packt, please visit packt.com.

1
What Is Moodle Workplace?

Here it is, a comprehensive guide to the new kid on the block: **Moodle Workplace**. You are invited to join this exciting journey through the latest variant of the most-used **Learning Management System (LMS)**, Moodle.

Without further ado, let's get started. In this chapter, we will introduce Moodle Workplace and cover its various new key features. We will then compare this newly updated software with its little sibling, standard Moodle, and with Totara, the other popular Moodle distribution for learning in organizations and businesses. Then, we will explore Moodle Workplace's business model and its versioning policy.

So, we will cover the following topics in this chapter:

- Introducing Moodle Workplace
- Comparing Moodle Workplace and standard Moodle
- Comparing Moodle Workplace and Totara Learn
- Understanding Moodle Workplace's business model
- Understanding Moodle Workplace versions

Introducing Moodle Workplace

According to moodle.com/workplace, Moodle Workplace empowers "*your team with an effective learning solution for training and development.*"

Moodle Workplace, or **Workplace** for short, is an open source LMS that has been developed by Moodle Pty Ltd. Workplace is based on standard Moodle and has extra features specially designed for corporate and organizational training, resulting in a powerful and flexible platform for workplace learning.

The main targets for Workplace are companies – from small to medium enterprises, all the way to global corporations and governments (regional and national), as well as public sector and non-governmental organizations, such as charities, foundations, and healthcare providers. However, Moodle Workplace is not limited to these entities: a university might make use of Moodle Workplace for the training and development of its employees, while using standard Moodle as their LMS for students.

The key features of Moodle Workplace are as follows:

	Multi-tenancy This allows you to create different tenants in the same Workplace installation. These are completely isolated from each other, with their own look and feel, structure, users, and learning entities. There might be multiple hospitals belonging to the same trust, but each with their own individual corporate identity, and their own employees organized in their local department structure. There is likely to be learning content unique to the hospital's specialism, but also courses that are shared across hospitals.
	Organization structure This allows you to model your organization with multiple hierarchical departments and position frameworks, and define reporting lines assigning jobs to your staff, giving managers visibility on learning progress. The departments of a heart clinic might be Cardiac Imaging and Testing, General Cardiology, Heart Rhythm/Electrophysiology, Interventional Cardiology, and Peripheral Vascular Disease Treatment. Typical positions include cardiologists, electrophysiologists, and cardiac nurses. A job assignment would assign the user Joe Flutter to the position of cardiac nurse in the Electrophysiology Department, which is managed by user Joanne Ticker.

	Report builder This allows you to build and customize your own reports with drag and drop, instant preview, inline column editing, groupings, aggregation, and restrictions to specific audiences from various data sources, including the internal Workplace datastore. A typical report would display all staff who have completed the *Clinical Documentation* course and can be filtered by department and position.
	Dynamic rules These allow you to define and execute centralized and automated rules using an "if this, then that" conditional approach to trigger actions when certain conditions are met. A sample rule might stipulate that upon completion of the *Clinical Documentation* course, a message is sent to the user's manager, and a certificate of completion is issued alongside a badge.
	Programs These allow you to establish learning pathways for your employees by adding a combination of courses or a hierarchical sequence of courses. You have the tools to control what learners need to complete to progress and ensure a deep understanding of subjects by defining different completion criteria at the program and set levels. A typical program comprises a number of courses that make up an onboarding program for a particular audience, for instance, nursing apprentices. Assignment to a program can take place via dynamic rules, and reporting shows the progress of all recent hires.
	Certifications These allow you to validate learning paths by offering certifications for recurring programs. Ensure your staff are compliant with regulatory demands by enabling certification expiry and re-certification pathways. Certifications are used for compliance training. Typical compulsory training topics with a validity period in the context of a hospital include health and safety and hygiene sessions.

	Certificates Certificates are issued to learners or teams in any context: site-wide, per tenant, by category, or by course. The creation of diplomas takes place in a built-in certificate designer supporting digital signatures. A dedicated course activity accompanies the certificate tool to issue certificates from within courses. Certificates can either be used as incentives for hospital employees, or they become part of the staff's employment record, in particular when there is a legal requirement to complete a course, program, or certification.
	Appointment bookings These allow you to create one-to-one meetings or seminars with multiple sessions through the internal booking system. Session management supports bulk event creation, attendance handling, and waiting-list features. A ward manager might schedule regular 1:1 sessions with all nurses to discuss any issues in the facility. Both scheduling and attendance recording take place via the Appointments module.
	Migration The migration tool offers the capacity to export different parts of a Moodle Workplace instance and import them to the same or a different site. A clinic might join an existing cluster of hospitals. Instead of setting up the new tenant from scratch, key elements from the existing sites will be re-purposed using export and import migrations. Additionally, the powerful migration CLI will be used to automate nightly synchronizations between the clinics' HR systems and Moodle Workplace.
	Mobile app This allows you to provide your employees with a seamless learning experience across devices and allow your learners to fit learning around their lives. A fully branded Workplace app supports your corporate identity for a fully customized experience.

Now that you are familiar with the key features of Moodle Workplace, let's compare it with its little brother, standard Moodle.

Comparing Moodle Workplace and standard Moodle

The usage of the term Moodle – both as a noun and a verb – has been synonymous with the leading open source LMS. However, there are multiple components in the Moodle product family, and the one almost everyone refers to as *Moodle* is technically called **Moodle Core**. The high-level components can be seen in the following diagram:

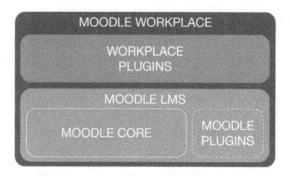

Figure 1.1 – Moodle Core versus Moodle Workplace

Let's have a closer look at each of the components in the preceding diagram.

Moodle Core or standard Moodle

Moodle Core is the original open source LMS, which has become the de facto standard worldwide in educational settings, particularly in schools, colleges, and universities. Since its inaugural launch in 2002, Moodle Core has become the benchmark that every LMS is measured against. It has won a wide range of international accolades and established itself as an ecosystem for a large number of educational tools and services.

> **Important note**
> Throughout the book, we are going to refer to Moodle Core as **standard Moodle** for simplicity and better readability.

Standard Moodle contains facilities for formative and informal assessment, synchronous and asynchronous communication and collaboration, grading, competencies, and much more. Various standards, such as SCORM, LTI, and IMS, have been adopted, and integration via numerous standard protocols is available, including SOAP and REST web services, Active Directory, and SAML.

A key ingredient to the success story of Moodle is its flexibility and customizability. In addition to hundreds of application configuration options, various elements can be tailored to your needs, including the look and feel of the LMS to represent the corporate identity of your organization. Think of Moodle as a massive box of Lego bricks, where you can either follow pre-built sets or build your own individual system. A major contribution to the latter is Moodle plugins.

Moodle plugins and Moodle LMS

While standard Moodle is a powerful and comprehensive LMS, very few sites solely rely on the base system. Instead, add-on modules are used to supplement the feature set of standard Moodle to customize the platform to individual requirements. These add-ons are called **Moodle plugins** and are mostly community-contributed additions to standard Moodle, extending its functionality for a specific use case. At the time of writing, there are over 1,750 (!) entries in the official Moodle plugins database at `moodle.org/plugins`.

There exists a plethora of third-party Moodle plugins that add new functionalities, fix problems, or integrate Moodle with external systems and cloud services. This also covers add-ons for commercial software popular in workplace settings, such as the following, for example:

- **Office systems**: For instance, Microsoft has developed a suite of plugins to allow Microsoft Office 365 usage within Moodle. This includes logging in via OpenID, access to OneDrive, integration with Office resources, and Outlook calendar synchronization.

- **Web conferencing**: Various commercial web conferencing suppliers provide plugins for their system to be used from within a Moodle course. Examples are WebEx, Zoom, and BigBlueButton.

- **Video platforms**: Streaming is a highly effective way to transport video content, which is already supported via basic integrations with YouTube and Vimeo. The Moodle functionality of the latter can be nicely enhanced using the popular Video Time plugin. Additionally, dedicated video platforms, such as Kaltura, also provide suites of plugins for smooth integration with Moodle.

Moodle LMS is effectively standard Moodle plus – optionally – one or many Moodle plugins.

Workplace plugins

Moodle Pty Ltd – the company behind Moodle – has developed a set of **Workplace plugins** that contain the key features of Moodle Workplace that sit on top of Moodle LMS. These plugins are the main focus of this book. All Moodle plugins still work in Moodle Workplace, with the rare exception of features that conflict with Workplace functionality.

Some of the Moodle Workplace plugins will make their way into standard Moodle over time, so Moodle LMS users can benefit from the investment that has gone into the Enterprise Edition of Moodle. The priority and timing will be determined through a collaborative approach with the Moodle community and Moodle Partners.

This section gave you a brief overview of the delta between standard Moodle and Moodle Workplace. Since Workplace is an extension of Moodle LMS, the differences are clear cut. This is different when it comes to Totara Learn, which we will cover in the next section.

Comparing Moodle Workplace and Totara Learn

Totara LMS is a subscription-based Moodle distribution that was launched in 2010 by Totara Learning (`www.totaralearning.com`). Initially, it was an extension to standard Moodle, plus some plugins, that was kept in lockstep with Moodle's releases until version 2.9. Moodle introduced competencies and learning plans in version 3.1, which conflicted with their counterparts in Totara. Totara LMS was renamed to Totara Learn, and new versioning was introduced that is currently at release 13 (see `www.totaralearning.com` for details).

Totara Learn is now part of a product family—**Totara Experience Platform** (**TXP**)—that comprises the following three interlinked components:

- **Totara Learn**: An LMS for training and development

  Totara Learn is Totara's flagship product and has been the only serious contender among the open source Moodle LMS distributions for the commercial sector, until Moodle Workplace arrived on the scene. Totara Learn is the product in the Totara suite that is used for comparison with Moodle Workplace in this chapter.

  Key features include online learning design and delivery, offline seminar management, assessment and certification, learning plans, program management, adaptive learning, and reporting.

- **Totara Engage**: A **Learning Experience System** (**LXP**) focused on social learning

  Totara Engage provides a secure social space powered by people, where learning comes recommended and self-directed, and not just mandated by the organization. Totara Engage is an LXP that supports day-to-day workplace communication, knowledge sharing, and discovery.

  Key features include peer-to-peer content creation and sharing, collaborative workspaces, integration with Microsoft Teams and Slack, informal learning, messaging, discussion, recognition, pulse surveys, and action lists.

- **Totara Perform**: A performance management tool supporting various HR activities

  Totara Perform is a flexible performance platform that allows organizations to proactively manage staff performance in order to operate more effectively and achieve their goals.

  Key features include appraisals, check-ins, goals, OKRs, 360° feedback, competencies, evidence banks, and reporting dashboards.

There might be additional products added to the mix in the future, but for now, these are the available components. All three products make use of the same underlying core business logic represented in a shared services layer.

Totara Learn and Moodle Workplace target the same audiences and are effectively competing products. You may ask what the differences are between the two available offerings. Generally, these dissimilarities can be grouped into the following three categories:

- Features unique to Moodle Workplace

- Features unique to Totara Learn

- Features that exist in both products but are implemented differently

Let's take a look at these in more detail.

Features unique to Moodle Workplace

There are several features that only exist in Moodle Workplace that are not offered by Totara Learn. An example is dynamic rules, where automation can be achieved via "if this, then that" rules to trigger actions when certain conditions are met. For instance, when a course has been completed, a certificate will be issued, and a notification will be sent to the user and also to the responsible manager.

Totara Learn comes with so-called dynamic audiences, which support similar workflows, but are nowhere near as comprehensive and flexible as Workplace's dynamic rules.

Another example is the migration tool, which supports the export and import of various Workplace elements into other Workplace instances.

Features unique to Totara Learn

Equally, some features are unique to Totara Learn. For instance, seminar management is a component covering room and equipment management, manager approval, sign-ups to the course catalog, and much more.

Moodle Workplace contains the appointments feature mentioned earlier, which covers some of the same use cases, but to date, it is no match for Totara's seminar management functionality.

Another example is the highly customizable course catalog offered by Totara Learn. It allows users to browse, search, and filter courses, programs, and certifications. Moodle Workplace currently doesn't have a catalog feature.

Features that exist differently in both products

Competencies and learning plans have already been mentioned as two features that exist in both products but have been modeled and implemented very differently.

Another good example is the way managers are modeled. In Totara Learn, a manager has a 1:1 relationship with a user; that is, one user is the manager of another user. Both users belong to one or many organizations. In Moodle Workplace, a user belongs to a department, and a manager is responsible for this organizational entity. Every user that belongs to the same department reports to the manager in charge. The result – one user is the superior to one or many other users – is the same in both systems, but their implications when implementing user profiles and synchronizing HR data are significant.

There are plenty of features that belong to this category but a full comparison is beyond the scope of this treatise. Instead, we offer some pointers on how to decide which is the better product for your setup.

So, which is the better product?

The only way to answer this question is that *it depends on the project at hand and its requirements*. For instance, if your organization only provides sporadic face-to-face training, Moodle Workplace is likely to suffice. However, if you require full-blown seminar management, Totara Learn might be the better option. A thorough evaluation of each element and how it responds to your requirements is highly recommended to make an informed decision.

It has to be noted that both systems continue to grow organically at a breakneck pace. Also, both products' architects look sideways to see what the other side is doing, and we all know that competition is good for business!

Both Moodle and Totara offer their services through global partner networks. While the principles behind the partner models are similar, the business models are very different. Moodle's business model is discussed in the following section.

Understanding the Moodle Workplace business model

60% of Moodle's revenue comes from the sectors that are targeted by Moodle Workplace, that is, commercial, not-for-profit, and government. Well-known examples of organizations that run Moodle include global enterprises such as Google, Cisco, Coca-Cola, Shell, Intel, and Bridgestone, but also large organizations such as the United Nations, which relies on Moodle as its LMS.

Moodle's main stream of revenue comes from **Moodle Partners** (Standard, Premium, and Integration), who pay **royalties** on all Moodle work. **Customers** who (hopefully) engage with a Moodle Partner pay **fees** for the **services** provided, such as consultancy, hosting, support, custom development, theme creation, and integration work. These high-level revenue streams are displayed in the following diagram, showing the overall Moodle business model:

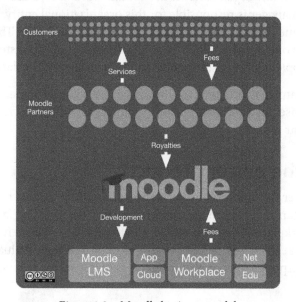

Figure 1.2 – Moodle business model

Moodle HQ employs a global team of staff who develop and maintain a range of offerings, comprising the following six products (see moodle.com/products for more details):

- **Moodle LMS**: Standard Moodle plus Moodle plugins (as was covered earlier in the chapter).

- **Moodle App**: This includes the Moodle app, the Moodle Workplace app, and related chargeable branding services. We will deal with the Workplace app in *Chapter 10, Mobile Learning*.

- **MoodleCloud**: A Moodle **Software-as-a-Service** (**SaaS**) offering of Moodle LMS and Moodle Workplace (see further in this section for details). There is a free basic plan for small Moodle LMS projects; all other packages are paid-for offerings.

- **Moodle Workplace**: Well, you know what this is…

- **MoodleNet**: An open source social media platform for educators, integrated with Moodle and focused on collaboratively curating collections of open content.

- **Moodle Education**: The **Moodle Educator Certification** (**MEC**) program is a comprehensive teaching and learning curriculum designed to help you develop transferable knowledge and skills to be effective educators in today's growing digital workplace.

Both standard Moodle and Moodle Workplace are open source under the GNU Public License 3.0. However, unlike standard Moodle, which is available from the download section of moodle.org, Moodle Workplace is currently only available through Premium Moodle Partners (www.moodle.com/partners). Workplace can either be hosted in the data center facilities of a Moodle Partner or on-premises. The latter requires you to sign a three-way agreement between Moodle HQ, your Moodle (Premium) Partner, and your company. You need to agree to the Moodle Workplace License, which outlines your responsibilities as the customer.

The purpose of the aforementioned arrangement is to protect Moodle's significant investment in Moodle Workplace and to ensure that the Workplace source code is not distributed to any third parties.

The other option for utilizing Moodle Workplace in your business is via **Workplace on MoodleCloud**, a SaaS offering from Moodle HQ. It is a turnkey solution for sites of up to 1,000 users that includes a video conferencing tool (BigBlueButton) as well as access to content from GO1. However, Workplace on MoodleCloud does not allow you to install plugins or themes, and certain features and configuration settings cannot be changed. Depending on the chosen package, different Workplace features are limited, for instance, the number of tenants allowed or the number of custom reports that can be created. For more details and pricing, contact your Moodle Partner.

Now that you are familiar with Moodle's business model and its primary revenue streams, let's have a look at the Moodle Workplace versions, which differ slightly from the release schedule of standard Moodle.

Understanding Moodle Workplace versions

Moodle Workplace versions are based on the releases of standard Moodle, so Moodle Workplace 3.9.2 is based on standard Moodle 3.9.2. **Minor versions** of Workplace are released the day after their standard Moodle counterparts, which typically takes place on the second Monday of odd months (January, March, May, July, September, and November). The same applies to unscheduled releases in the case of a severe security issue or serious regression being fixed. **Major versions** of Workplace are released 1-2 weeks after the respective major version of standard Moodle. The release frequency is twice a year (the second Mondays of May and November).

> **Important note**
>
> Moodle Workplace is always based on the official update (minor version) that does not have a "+" sign.

Currently, backporting to older releases is not supported by Workplace, even if the standard Moodle counterpart is still under support. However, this is likely to change in the future. The following timeline diagram demonstrates the interdependence between standard Moodle and Moodle Workplace releases:

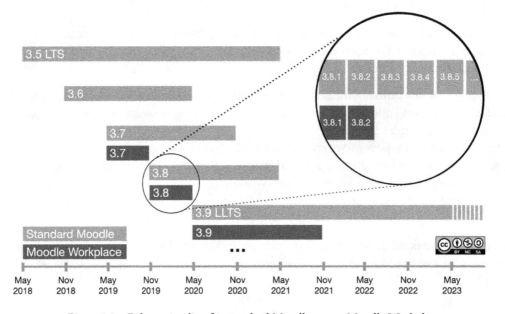

Figure 1.3 – Release timeline for standard Moodle versus Moodle Workplace

Version 3.7 was the first (mostly internal) version of Moodle Workplace. This book is based on version 3.9.2, which is the most up-to-date release at the time of writing. Standard Moodle 3.5 and 3.9 are **Long-Term Support** (**LTS**) releases that will be supported for 3 and 5 years respectively. The next major release of standard Moodle will be version 4.0, to be released in November 2021.

For more information on standard Moodle releases, check out `docs.moodle.org/dev/Releases`. You can find the release notes of Moodle Workplace at `docs.moodle.org/en/Moodle_Workplace_Release_notes`.

Each Moodle Workplace release is a full distribution that contains standard Moodle, all Workplace plugins including the Workplace theme, and several core modifications that can be either future core fixes or Workplace-only patches that allow Workplace plugins to hook into the Core functionality. That is, when installing Moodle Workplace, you do not have to install standard Moodle first and then add plugins or apply Core patches.

This section has provided you with an overview of the Moodle Workplace release schedule and its relationship with the standard Moodle releases. This timetable should be taken into account when planning updates and upgrades, as this is likely to involve maintenance work as well as some downtime.

Summary

In this chapter, you have been introduced to the key features of Moodle Workplace, such as multi-tenancy, dynamic rules, reports, and many more. You have learned about the divergence between standard Moodle and Moodle Workplace, which is a powerful extension of the base product. The design and development of this delta between the two products is quite a technical masterpiece, maintaining 100% compatibility with standard Moodle while adding a plethora of features that can be used consistently throughout the system.

We have also covered the popular Totara product suite and explained the dissimilarities between Moodle Workplace and Totara Learn, both in terms of functionality and commercials. This led nicely into Workplace's business model, showing its main revenue streams and stressing the importance of Moodle Partners. Finally, you have been given some insight into the Workplace versioning policy and its dependencies on standard Moodle.

Understanding the information we have covered in this chapter is important in order to acknowledge the depth and breadth of Moodle Workplace and the impact it is likely to have when you provide your team with such a powerful learning solution for training and development. Yes, Moodle is a bit late to the party, but when it finally turned up, it brought a superstar of a guest along.

Now, equipped with this knowledge, it is time to give you a more detailed overview of Moodle Workplace. Let's start in the next chapter with the basic concepts and terminology that are crucial when working with Workplace.

2
Working with Moodle Workplace

Moodle Workplace is 100% compatible with standard Moodle, also known as Moodle Core. The focus of this book is the delta between Workplace and Core, plus a range of critical concepts that you need for setting up and managing a professional learning environment for workplace learning.

Before we get started, it is helpful to cover some essential elements that you will be using when working with Moodle Workplace and also throughout the book. You will learn about the key players in Workplace, their roles, their responsibilities, and what functions they have in your setup. Also, you will learn about the important user interface interactions, and finally, you will learn about different help sources, both built-in and external.

While Moodle Workplace is very intuitive, it is highly recommended that you familiarize yourself with the basic workings since they are used consistently throughout the book.

We will cover the following topics:

- Knowing your Workplace stakeholders
- Interacting with the Workplace user interface
- Getting help

Knowing your Workplace stakeholders

In a typical Workplace learning environment, you have the following key players and their responsibilities (roles) in Moodle Workplace:

Stakeholder	Moodle Workplace	Responsible for...
Site admin	Admin	the entire site and all tenants
Sub-admin	Tenant admin	a single tenant
Employee	Learner	participating in online and offline learning activities
Manager	Manager and department lead	employees of a region or a department
Coach	Non-editing trainer	individual courses
Author	Trainer	learning content and organization

Most of the preceding stakeholders should be self-explanatory. However, there are two roles that deserve some further explanation due to their Moodle-esque idiosyncrasies: manager and trainer:

- **Manager** is a role in Moodle that is distinct from the aforementioned general and department managers. Users with the manager role can access courses and modify them; they usually do not participate in these courses. **Manager** and **department lead** are extra permissions granted in positions, which are explained in detail in *Chapter 4, Tenants, Organizations, and Teams.*

- Moodle distinguishes between a trainer with editing rights (content authoring) and a trainer without editing rights (content delivery). For legacy reasons, these roles are called **trainer** and **non-editing trainer**, respectively.

In addition to the preceding general roles, Moodle Workplace comes with several additional specialist roles that are automatically created during installation:

- **Certification manager**: Allows the creation and management of certifications within the current tenant and allocates users to them.

- **Dynamic rules manager**: Allows the creation and management of dynamic rules within the current tenant.

- **Organisation structure manager**: Allows the creation and management of jobs, positions, and departments within the current tenant.

- **Program manager**: Allows the creation and management of programs within the current tenant and allocates users to them.

- **Report builder manager**: Allows the creation and management of custom reports within the current tenant.

- **Tenant administrator**: Assigned automatically to the tenant admin in the context of their course category.

- **Tenant administrator in course category**: This is effectively the tenant manager role, which is assigned automatically to the tenant admin in the context of their course category.

- **Tenant user**: Assigned automatically to all tenant users in the context of their course category.

Additionally, it is, of course, possible for the site admin to create entirely new roles – for instance, a seminar manager who is responsible for creating and managing face-to-face training (appointment bookings), or a role for the ever-so-popular external auditor. However, this is only required when the function exists in your organization and you have a dedicated role in your LMS setup.

You are now familiar with the key stakeholders of a typical Moodle Workplace environment. Now, let's look at how the different types of users will work with the Workplace user interface.

Interacting with the Workplace user interface

If you are familiar with standard Moodle, you will feel in familiar territory when using Moodle Workplace. However, Moodle has developed a more advanced and modern user interface for Workplace, which you will see in this section.

Once logged in or authenticated with Workplace, the dashboard is shown. As always in Moodle, functionality is only available when it is activated and configured, and the respective user has the correct permissions to make use of the feature. Here, you see a sample dashboard where the user has completed 33% of the **Onboarding Marketing** program and hasn't commenced with the **Health & Safety 01** course:

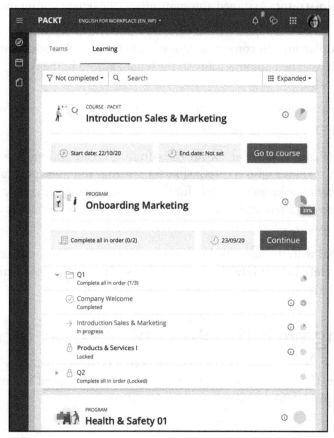

Figure 2.1 – Sample dashboard

There are four important types of elements you should familiarize yourself with, since these are used throughout Moodle Workplace:

- General user elements and actions
- Header elements
- Dashboard
- Course navigation

Let's take a look at each one in more detail.

General user elements and actions

Moodle Workplace has a hugely improved user interface that has been designed from the ground up. A list of icons used throughout the LMS is shown in the following table:

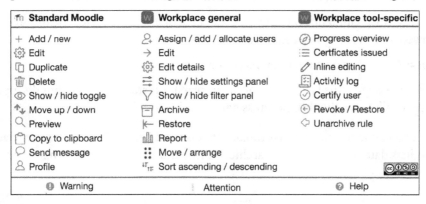

Figure 2.2 – Moodle Workplace icons

Most of the general Workplace icons should be self-explanatory. Some tool-specific icons are unique to Moodle Workplace and their purposes will be explained in more detail when they are used in a particular context – for instance, inline editing in the built-in reporting tool or manually certifying a user.

Every time you see a table, list, or any other set of elements that can be ordered, such as the activities in a course, Moodle Workplace lets you re-arrange the items via drag-and-drop using the Move icon.

Now, let's move on to the different types of status messages you will come across when working with Moodle Workplace:

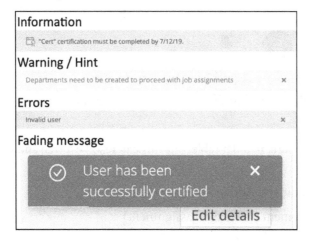

Figure 2.3 – Moodle Workplace status updates

You will see the following four status messages throughout Moodle Workplace:

- **Information**: Some advice about the current situation. Some information boxes remain on the screen; others can be hidden via the little **x** on the right.

- **Warning/hint**: Guidance on how to use a particular feature. Once the hint has been followed, the warning will disappear.

- **Errors**: A fault has occurred that has to be investigated.

- **Fading message**: This is a variant of the information status message but disappears automatically once the thin progress bar at the bottom has run down.

The last general element unique to Workplace that is used heavily is an interactive data view, which lists data in tabular or hierarchical form, and usually offers a range of actions for each row:

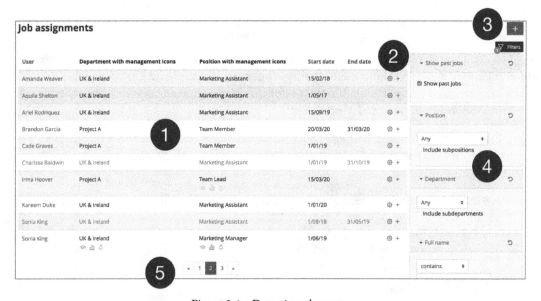

Figure 2.4 – Data view elements

The preceding example screenshot shows job assignments and contains all the key elements of data views:

1. The actual data (here, in a flat table, but this can also be a tree and can support ordering)

2. Actions (here, Edit and Add)

3. Adding a new element (here, a job assignment)

4. Filters to be applied to the data shown

5. Pagination to navigate between pages of data

If you are technically minded and want to know what is happening under the bonnet of data views, Moodle Workplace has added an interesting current query feature, where you can view the SQL query and associated parameters of the shown data. To enable the current query feature, the Moodle administrator has to change the **Debug messages** setting in **Site administration | Development | Debugging** to **NORMAL**, **ALL**, or **DEBUG**:

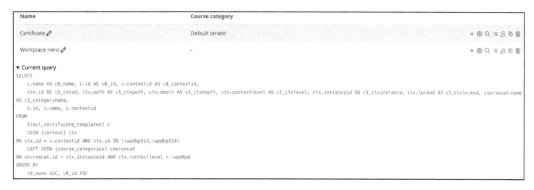

Figure 2.5 – Current query sample

Next up in the list of important user interface elements is the header of Moodle Workplace.

Header elements

The Moodle Workplace header comprises different navigational elements, as shown here:

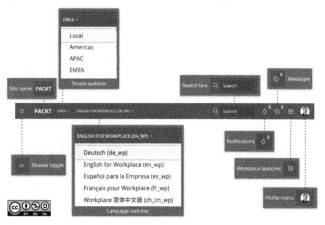

Figure 2.6 – Moodle Workplace header

The different navigational elements include the following:

- Drawer toggle to open and close the sidebar on the left
- Name of your site (here, it is **PACKT**)
- Tenant switcher (this is only visible if you have access to multiple tenants)
- Language switcher (this is only available when configured in the language settings)
- Search box (global search has to be activated by the administrator)
- Notifications indicator and notification menu toggle
- Messaging indicator and messaging toggle drawer
- Workplace launcher (details explained in the paragraphs to follow)
- Profile menu (details explained in the paragraphs to follow)

As the administrator, you can add additional menu items via the **custommenuitems** setting in **Site administration | Appearance | Themes | Theme settings**. You can add links to both internal Workplace pages and external web sites. The custom menu mechanism supports sub-menus and also delimiters.

There are two menu items that we want to take a closer look at.

First, the **Workplace launcher** gives you, as an administrator, direct access to all the key Moodle Workplace features (see the screenshot on the left in the following figure). If a user only has restricted access to certain features – for instance, a manager – the number of elements in the Workplace launcher is reduced accordingly (see the screenshot on the right):

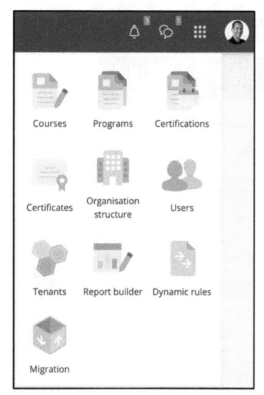

Figure 2.7 – Workplace launcher

The icons in the workplace launcher should look familiar as they were used in the introductory chapter when key features were described. With the exception of courses and users, each icon represents a major unique functionality of Moodle Workplace. Each feature will be described in greater detail in the book; most have an entire chapter dedicated to them.

There is an alternative view of the Workplace launcher. Instead of showing it as a pop-up window, the launcher can be shown as a modal dialog box. To change this, toggle the **Workplace launcher as modal** switch in **Site administration | Appearance | Themes | Workplace**. The modal view improves usability on some mobile devices and is also a matter of personal preference.

Second, we are going to have a closer look at the profile menu, which contains some extra features compared to its standard Moodle counterpart:

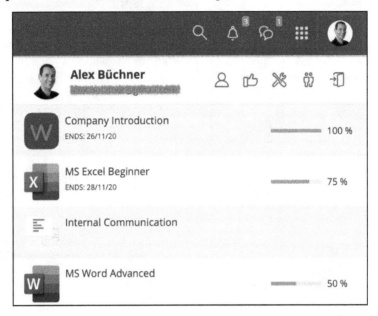

Figure 2.8 – The profile menu

In the first row, the following options are available:

- User image, full name, and email address.
- Access to the user profile, where information such as course details, certificates, and ongoing learning is displayed.
- The grades of the user can be viewed. This is rarely used in Workplace contexts.
- Access to user preferences – for instance, to change the password or configure messaging or notification settings.
- The option to switch roles with another user (mainly for the administrator).
- The log-out option.

As the administrator, you can add and remove existing options (except profile, switch role, and logout) via the **customusermenuitems** setting in **Site Administration | Appearance | Themes | Theme settings**.

Each of the rows underneath displays information about up to five most recent courses. The data that is displayed (from left to right) is the course logo, course name, end date (if set), and progress (if course completion has been activated). To jump directly to one of the up-to-five courses, the user has to click on the respective row.

Next up is the dashboard, which acts as a front page for most users on your system.

Dashboard

Moodle Workplace contains a dashboard that is different to standard Moodle's equivalent – there are significant differences, both in terms of functionality and usability. You already saw the expanded dashboard earlier on; now here is its collapsed version:

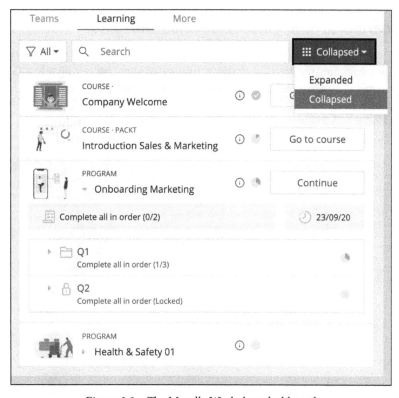

Figure 2.9 – The Moodle Workplace dashboard

The dashboard contains up to three tabs:

- **Teams**: Displays information about team members of managers or department leads.
- **Learning**: Displays information on the user's courses, programs, and certifications.

- **More**: A customizable dashboard, identical to the one in standard Moodle. If a user has permission to change the layout of the dashboard via the **Add a block** option in the side drawer, the selection of the blocks, their individual configuration options, and the placement options (content and right) can be modified. However, the content will only be displayed in the mobile app (refer to *Chapter 10, Mobile Learning*). This also means that the tab will only show while a user is customizing the dashboard (via the **Customize this page** button).

The **More** tab of the preceding dashboard should be self-explanatory and is not described in more detail. If you need more instructions, check out the official Moodle Docs at `docs.moodle.org/en/Dashboard`. The other two tabs – **Learning** and **Teams** – will be described next.

The dashboard Learning tab

The **Learning** tab displays progress information about any courses, programs, and certifications. For each item, a circular progress indicator is shown alongside a **Go to course** or a program **Continue** button. To the left of those two elements, you can see a small info icon. When you select this, a modal window will pop up to display details about the respective item. Here, you see the information about our **Onboarding Marketing** program; the detail box for courses looks almost identical:

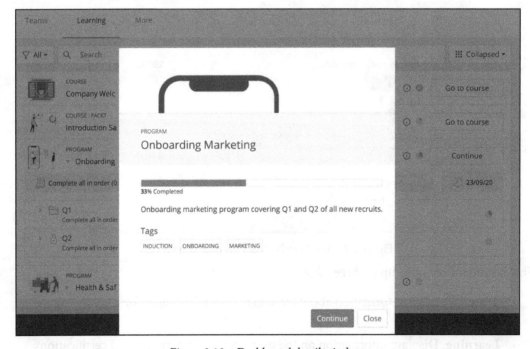

Figure 2.10 – Dashboard detail window

Programs are packages of modules that allow you to establish learning pathways for your employees by adding a combination of courses or a hierarchical sequence of courses. Certifications are based on programs and allow you to validate learning paths by offering certifications for recurring learning, usually in the context of compliance training. Details on programs and certifications will be described in greater detail in *Chapter 6, Onboarding and Compliance.*

The dashboard Teams tab

The **Teams** tab displays information about all team members of a department manager or global manager. Filters can be applied (in the following example, only marketing assistants from the UK and Ireland are shown) and details for each team member can be expanded and collapsed:

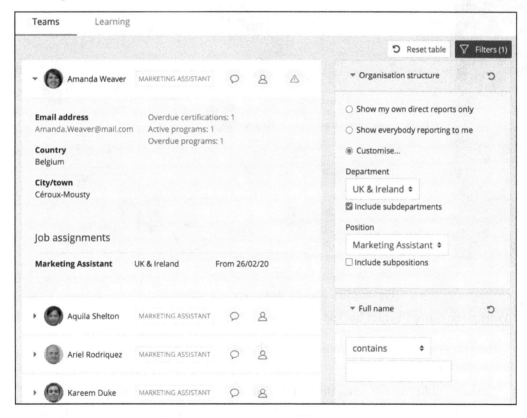

Figure 2.11 – The dashboard Teams tab

The **Teams** tab provides information about and actions for each team member. Details on teams will be described in more detail in *Chapter 4*, *Tenants, Organizations, and Teams*, and *Chapter 8*, *Generating Custom Reports*.

Now that you are familiar with the header elements and the dashboard, let's go one step further and investigate navigating a Moodle Workplace course.

Course navigation

Moodle has given Workplace a very modern-looking and intuitive course format, without losing any of standard Moodle's features and functionalities. A sample course snippet is shown in the following screenshot of the **MS Word Advanced** course:

Figure 2.12 – Moodle Workplace course format

The Workplace course format has the following main features:

1. The side drawer should be familiar since this is very similar to the arrangement in standard Moodle.

2. The same holds for the navigation in the form of a breadcrumb trail.

3. The content part allows users to expand and collapse topics. Progress for each topic is visualized by a thin progress bar. Activity completion is recorded to the left of the activity or resource name. Restricted activities auto-update without page refresh when activities are completed. Details for locked items will be shown when clicked.

4. The blocks are displayed on the right and can be re-arranged once the editing mode has been activated.

The Workplace theme contains new icons that are in line with the Moodle Workplace branding. Apart from the **Appointment booking** and **Course certificate** activities (starred in the following screenshot), all other activities and resources are identical to standard Moodle:

Figure 2.13 – Moodle Workplace activities and icons

Popular activities in a commercial learning setting are **Appointment booking** (refer to *Chapter 9, Seminar Management*), **Feedback** (surveys for training participants), **Quiz** (assessments), and **SCORM package** (commercial learning content and assessment).

It has to be mentioned that the described Workplace theme has various customization options. These are described in more detail in *Chapter 11, Corporate Identity*.

Information Box

If the Moodle Workplace default theme has been replaced on your site, some user elements and colors are likely to look different from the ones presented here.

This completes the last category of Moodle Workplace user elements. Now, let's move on to getting help in case you get stuck when working with the LMS.

Getting help

There are a number of sources where you and your users can get assistance when working with Moodle Workplace. By default, a number of "user tours" have been configured that are displayed the first time a user navigates to certain pages. For instance, you will see the following message when you visit the dashboard for the first time:

Figure 2.14 – Moodle dashboard tour

As an administrator, you have the ability to create your own user tours. More details on this standard Moodle feature can be found at docs.moodle.org/en/User_tours.

Throughout Moodle Workplace, you can see the little Help icon beside individual configuration options. Upon selection, a little balloon will pop up displaying context-sensitive help, like so:

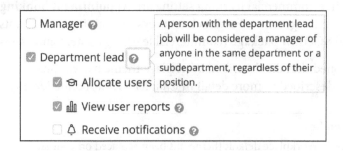

Figure 2.15 – Moodle built-in help

The Moodle community is growing continuously and, at the time of writing, has well over 1 million registered users (yes, 1 million!), of which over 5% are active. If you cannot find a solution to any of your Moodle problems using the preceding facilities, use the **Search** functionality at the top of the screen at `moodle.org`.

The entire Moodle documentation is online at `docs.moodle.org` – the earlier-mentioned help page on user tours is a good example. The landing page for the Workplace-related documentation is located at `docs.moodle.org/en/Moodle_Workplace`.

Information on how to get help is provided there for the (hopefully rare) situations when you need some assistance with Moodle Workplace.

Summary

In this chapter, we covered some essential elements that you will be using when working with Moodle Workplace and also throughout the book. You learned about the roles and responsibilities of the key stakeholders in Workplace. You further became familiar with the Workplace user interface, namely general user elements and actions, header elements, the dashboard, and course navigation. Finally, you learned about different help sources, both built-in and external.

Throughout this chapter, several core concepts, such as users, courses, and roles, among others, were mentioned without further explanation and, to a degree, taken for granted. If Moodle is all new to you, do not worry. You will be learning the key concepts of users, courses, roles, and any associated constructs in the Moodle primer in the next chapter. Once this has been dealt with, we can finally start working with the Moodle Workplace-specific features.

3
Exploring Moodle Courses, Users, and Roles

The objective of this chapter is to give you a quick rundown of the core concepts and features of Moodle that are available in all Moodle distributions, including Moodle Workplace.

The underlying foundation of Moodle is based on courses, users, and roles. The three concepts are inherently intertwined, and any one of these cannot be used without the other two. We will deal with the basics of the three core elements in this Moodle primer and show you how they work together. Let's see what they are:

- **Moodle courses** are central to Workplace as this is where the actual learning takes place. You will be introduced to courses and how they are organized in categories. You will also learn about the key ingredients of courses, namely activities and resources.

- **Moodle users** are the individuals accessing your Workplace system. We will cover the basic concepts of authentication – how to get access to Moodle – and enrollment – how to get access to a course – before briefly dealing with two different types of user collections: cohorts and groups.

- **Moodle roles** are effectively permissions that specify which features users are allowed to access and, also, where and when (in Workplace) they can access them. Typical roles are learners and trainers, but there are also others, such as managers, authors, auditors, and guests – and the administrator, of course. You will become familiar with the concepts of roles, contexts, and capabilities, which are essential for controlling permissions in Moodle.

If you are already familiar with Moodle, you can run through this chapter very quickly or skip this chapter altogether. If you are looking for a more in-depth guide to the content covered in this chapter, I recommend either the Moodle Docs at `docs.moodle.org` or *Moodle 3 Administration* by Packt Publishing, from which some parts have been borrowed for this primer chapter.

We will cover the following topics:

- Getting started with a high-level overview
- Exploring Moodle courses
- Exploring Moodle users
- Exploring Moodle roles

Getting started with a high-level overview

To give you an overview of courses, users, and roles, let's have a look at *Figure 3.1*. It shows nicely how central these three concepts are and also how other important features are related to them. Again, all of their intricacies will be dealt with in due course, so for now, let's just start getting familiar with some Moodle terminology:

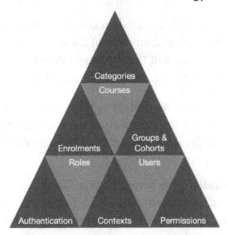

Figure 3.1 – Core Moodle concepts

Let's start at the bottom-left and cycle through the pyramid in a roughly clockwise fashion. Users have to go through an **Authentication** process to get access to Moodle. They then have to go through the **Enrolments** step to be able to participate in **Courses**, which themselves are organized into **Categories**. **Groups** and **Cohorts** are different ways to group users at a course level or site-wide, respectively. Users are granted Roles in particular Contexts which are ring-fenced Moodle areas. Which role is allowed to do what and which isn't depends entirely on the **Permissions** set within that role.

The diagram also demonstrates a chicken-and-egg situation. If we start with users, we have no courses to enroll them onto; if we start with courses, we have no users who can participate in them. Not to worry, though. Moodle Workplace lets us go back and forth between any administrative areas and, often, perform multiple tasks at once.

Now that you have been given a high-level overview, let's start with the first corner of our triangle, dealing with courses.

Exploring Moodle courses

Courses are central to Moodle as this is where content is presented to learners and where the vast majority of learning and collaboration takes place.

Resources and activities

Moodle stores resources and manages activities in courses:

- **Resources** are learning elements where the learner is passive; for instance, a PDF document can be read, a URL can be navigated to, a podcast can be listened to, or a video can be watched.

- **Activities** are learning elements where the learner is active and more engaged; for example, posting to a discussion forum, responding to a feedback questionnaire, attending a face-to-face appointment, collaborating with others in the authoring of an FAQ, or answering questions in a SCORM-based quiz.

> **Important Note**
> You already saw the list of Moodle Workplace's default activities in the *Course navigation* sub-section in *Chapter 2, Working with Moodle Workplace*.

Resources and activities can be arranged in any order and dependencies can be specified via a combination of access restrictions and activity completion criteria. To illustrate the workings of the sequencing versus non-sequencing of content, let's have a look at a sample blended learning course. In our example, this comprises three phases (called topics in Moodle), but any other structure would be possible: **preparation** (pre-seminar), **face-to-face** (seminar), and **follow-up** (post-seminar):

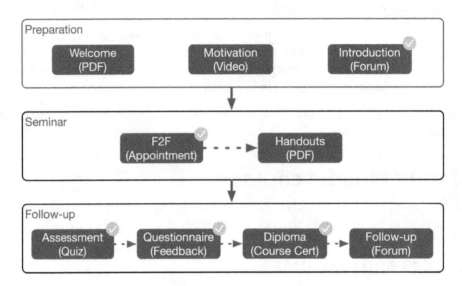

Figure 3.2 – Sample course content

During the preparation section, participants are welcome to read the provided PDF document and watch a motivational video. They are also asked to introduce themselves in a forum, so attendees can start networking prior to the event. While the first two activities are optional, the introduction is compulsory and a pre-requisite to attending the seminar. The face-to-face activity has to be marked off by the trainer before access to the handouts is granted. The follow-up part comprises four activities: a certain percentage has to be achieved in the quiz to complete the assessment and the feedback questionnaire has to be submitted before the diploma will be issued. Access to the alumni forum will only be granted when all three activities have been completed.

Course categories

Categories act as containers for courses. They can have sub-categories, which can have sub-sub-categories, and so on. The hierarchical arrangement is similar to that of files and folders on your computer, where categories are like folders and courses are like files:

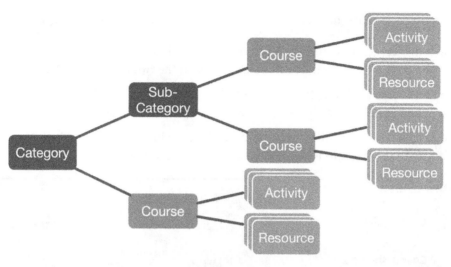

Figure 3.3 – Categories, courses, activities, and resources

Workplace comes with a default category called **Default tenant**, reflecting the support for multi-tenancy. In standard Moodle and most other Moodle distributions, this category is called **Miscellaneous**.

Information Box

A course always belongs to a category. It cannot belong to multiple categories and also cannot be without a category.

Creating a Moodle course

The quickest way to access the management of courses and categories is via the **Courses** icon in the Workspace launcher:

Figure 3.4 – Courses and categories launcher

To begin with, let's create the first course. To do so, run through the following steps:

1. Click the **Create new course** button. You will be directed to the screen where course details have to be entered. For now, let's focus on the two compulsory fields.

2. Enter a course full name (here, we used `Manual Handling Operations Regulations`), which is displayed at various places in Workplace.

3. Enter a course short name (here, we used `MHOR`), which is used by default to identify the course and is also shown in the breadcrumb trail:

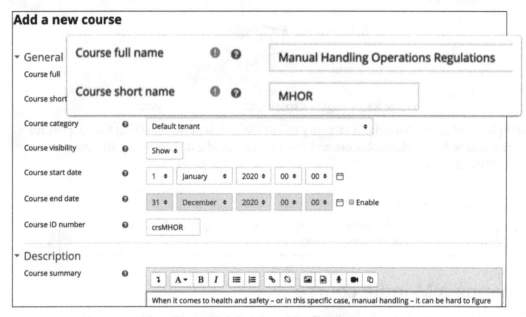

Figure 3.5 – Creating a Moodle course

You can also see the already-mentioned default course category, **Default tenant**. To change its name or add other categories and sub-categories, you need to go back to the previous page where course categories are managed.

For now, we will leave all the other fields empty or at their default values and save the course by clicking on the **Save and display** button at the bottom. The screen that is displayed shows enrolled users, if any. Since we just created the course, there are no participants present in the course yet.

So, we leave the course without participants for now and add some users, before coming back to this screen.

Exploring Moodle users

Each user in Moodle is represented as a **user account**, which contains information about the person's profile.

Authentication and enrollment

Before we start, it is vital to understand the difference between authentication and enrollment. Users have to be authenticated in order to log in to Moodle. **Authentication** grants your users access to the system through a login where a username and password have to be given. Moodle supports a significant number of authentication mechanisms, such as MS-AD, LDAP, and SAML. For now, let's work with so-called manual authentication to simplify the overall user management.

Enrollment happens at a course level. However, a user has to be authenticated to the system before enrollment on a course can take place. The house and key analogy might help: you need a key (authentication) to the house (Moodle), and you then need a separate key (enrollment) for each room (course).

So, a typical workflow is as follows (there are exceptions as always, but this will do for now):

1. Create your courses (and categories).
2. Create user accounts.
3. Associate users with courses and assign roles.

Again, this sequence demonstrates nicely how intertwined courses, users, and roles are in Moodle. Another way of looking at the difference between authentication and enrollment is how a user will get access to a course. Please bear in mind that this is a very simplistic view that ignores supported features such as external authentication, guest access, and self-enrollment:

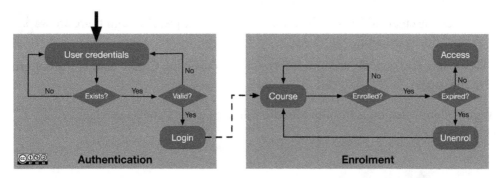

Figure 3.6 – Authentication and enrollment

During the authentication phase, a user enters their credentials (username and password), or they are entered automatically via single sign-on. If the account exists locally – that is, within Moodle – and the password is valid, the user is granted access. If the account is held externally – for instance, in an active directory – the check will be carried out remotely.

Once this is successful, the next phase is enrollment. If the user is enrolled and the enrollment hasn't expired, access is granted to the course where resources and activities can be worked through. As mentioned before, this graphic only shows the very basics, but for now, it hopefully demonstrates the difference between authentication and enrollment.

Adding a user account

Select the **Users** icon in the Workplace launcher to get to the Workplace users, or rather, their user accounts:

Figure 3.7 – The Users launcher

To add a user account manually, run through the following steps:

1. Select the **Add a new user** button at the bottom. As with courses, we will only focus on the mandatory fields, which should be self-explanatory.

2. Provide a *unique* username.

3. Set a new password. If a password policy has been set, certain rules might apply.

4. Enter the user's first name and surname.

5. Provide the email address of the user. It has to be unique, although there are ways around this restriction.

6. Make sure you save the account information by selecting **Create user** at the bottom of the page.

If any entered information is invalid, Moodle will display error messages right below the field:

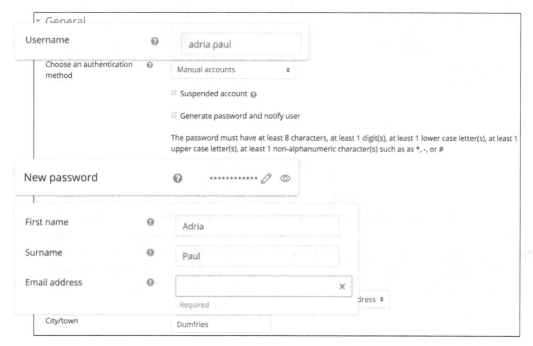

Figure 3.8 – Adding a Moodle user account

I have created a few more accounts (via batch upload); to see who has access to your Moodle system, select the **Users** icon in the Workplace launcher again, where you will see all users:

First name / Surname	Email address	City/town	Country	Last access	Edit
Adria Paul	Adria.Paul@mail.com	Dumfries	United Kingdom	Never	🗑 👁 ⚙
Adrienne Griffith	Adrienne.Griffith@mail.com	Rio Negro	Argentina	Never	🗑 👁 ⚙
Alex Büchner	▬▬▬▬▬▬▬▬	Heidelberg	Germany	48 secs	⚙
Alexandra Wagner	Alexandra.Wagner@mail.com	Apeldoorn	Netherlands	Never	🗑 👁 ⚙
Amanda Weaver	Amanda.Weaver@mail.com	Céroux-Mousty	Belgium	Never	🗑 👁 ⚙
Amy Payne	Amy.Payne@mail.com	Tourcoing	France	Never	🗑 👁 ⚙
Anton Richter	Anton.Richter@mail.com	Köln	Germany	Never	🗑 👁 ⚙
Aquila Shelton	Aquila.Shelton@mail.com	Trochu	Canada	Never	🗑 👁 ⚙
Aspen William	Aspen.William@mail.com	Eugene	United States	Never	🗑 👁 ⚙
Autumn Brennan	Autumn.Brennan@mail.com	Milford Haven	United Kingdom	Never	🗑 👁 ⚙
Basil Terry	Basil.Terry@mail.com	Lummen	Belgium	Never	🗑 👁 ⚙
Beverly Savage	Beverly.Savage@mail.com	Ollolai	Italy	Never	🗑 👁 ⚙

Figure 3.9 – Moodle user accounts

Now that we have a few users on our system, let's go back to the course we created earlier and manually enroll new participants onto it.

Enrolling users

To achieve this, go to **Courses** via the Workplace launcher, select the **Default tenant** category again, and select the created course. Underneath the listed course, details will be displayed alongside a number of options (on large screens, details are shown to the right). Here, select **Enrolled users** from the available options:

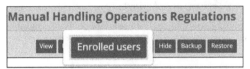

Figure 3.10 – Enrolling users I

As expected, the list of participants is still empty. Click on the **Enrol users** button to change this. A pop-up window will appear, where you select one or many users via the **Search** field. If you are already familiar with standard Moodle, you will realize that this screen looks very different in Moodle Workplace. It is one of many places where the usability and user experience has been significantly improved in the Workplace edition:

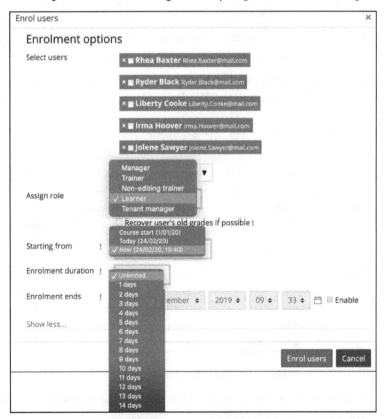

Figure 3.11 – Enrolling users II

We will leave all the timing-related fields at their defaults. Some of those parameters will be set automatically by some Workplace tools, such as programs and certifications. You have probably spotted the **Assign roles** dropdown below the list of selected user accounts. This is where you select what role the selected user(s) will be granted, which leads us to the third part of the pyramid: roles. However, before we deal with roles, let's have a quick look at the last missing user-related piece in our triangle: cohorts and groups.

Using groups and cohorts

Cohorts are global groups, which are used to logically cluster related users. They can either be in the System, that is, site-wide context or limited to a Category context. In standard Moodle, cohorts are frequently used to group users that belong to the same team or department. As we will see, there are better ways to deal with organization-related users in Moodle Workplace, and so cohorts are mainly used for groups where membership is not tied to positions and departments – for example, all first aiders or data protection officers.

To create a new cohort, go to **Site administration | Users | Accounts | Cohorts** and select **Add a new cohort**. Name the cohort and select the **context**; the **cohort ID** and **description** are optional, but it is good practice to provide these values:

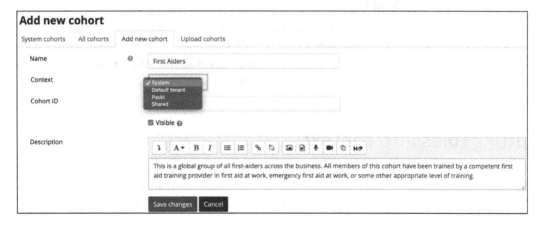

Figure 3.12 – Adding a new cohort

Once you have saved the changes, the cohort will be created but doesn't contain any members yet. To add users to the cohort, select the **Assign** icon beside the cohort details. You can then select users from the list on the right and add them to the list of cohort members on the left.

So, what can you do with cohorts? The main purpose is to enroll all members onto courses in a single operation or synchronize their enrollment with a course. To stay with our first aiders example, when a new member is added, the user will be enrolled automatically to all first aid-related courses; when membership is removed, the user will be unenrolled.

Groups are used at a course level to organize participants into smaller groups. As a member of a group, you learn and work in your own group. There are two group modes: visible and separate. When you are a member of a **visible** group, you can see the other groups; that is, they are in read-only mode. When you are a member of a **separate** group, you cannot see the other groups; that is, you are not even aware that there are other groups. The visible mode is great for team-working exercises, whereas the separate mode is often a requirement to ensure confidentiality.

Moodle Workplace makes use of groups in programs where courses are shared across tenants. Users from different tenants will then be added to separate groups – another great example of where a Workplace tool makes use of a standard Moodle feature.

Now that we have dealt with users, cohorts, and groups, let's have a closer look at the third vertex of our triangle: roles.

Exploring Moodle roles

Roles define what users can or cannot see and do in your Moodle system. Workplace comes with a number of predefined roles – we already saw **Learner** and **Trainer**, as well as various managerial roles, such as **Department manager**, **Certification manager**, and **Tenant administrator in course category** – but it also allows us to create our own roles (for instance, for auditors or external suppliers).

Putting roles into context

Each role has a specific scope (called its **context**), which is defined by a set of permissions (expressed as **capabilities**). For example, a trainer is allowed to create a feedback form, whereas a learner isn't. Or, a participant is allowed to submit the feedback form, whereas a trainer isn't.

Information Box

A role is assigned to a user in a context.

Okay, so what is a context? A context is a ring-fenced area in Moodle where roles can be assigned to users. A user can be assigned different roles in different contexts, where the context can be a course, a category, an activity, a user, a block, the front page, or Workplace itself. For instance, the **Administrator** role is assigned for the entire system, but additionally, the admin might be assigned the **Trainer** role in any courses they are responsible for; or, an employee will be given the **Learner** role in a course, but might have been granted the **Trainer** role in a forum to act as a (temporary) moderator.

Defining roles

To give you a feel for how a role is defined, let's go to **Users | Permissions,** where roles are managed, and select **Define roles**. Click on the **Trainer** role and, after some general settings, you will see a (very) long list of capabilities:

Figure 3.13 – Roles, permissions, and capabilities

For now, we only want to stick with the example we used earlier in the chapter. Now that we know what roles are, we can slightly rephrase what we have done. Instead of saying, "We have enrolled the user Adria Paul in our MHOR course as a trainer," we would say, "We have assigned the trainer role to the user Adria Paul in the context of the MHOR course."

Roles are critical when granting and denying permissions to users. However, when you get started, try sticking with the pre-configured roles in Moodle Workplace, since they have proven to be sufficient in most setups. You can always adjust roles at a later stage, if and when required.

Summary

In this chapter, we briefly introduced the concepts of Moodle courses, users, and roles. We also saw how central they are to Moodle Workplace and how they are inherently intertwined. Any one of these concepts simply cannot exist without the other two, and this is something you should bear in mind throughout.

Just to recap, the three key takeaways from this chapter are as follows:

- Courses comprise activities and resources, and this is where your employees' learning takes place. Courses are organized hierarchically in categories.

- Users are represented by an account; access is granted to the system by authentication and to courses by enrollment. Users can be clustered into cohorts, which usually spawn across courses and groups, which are limited to courses.

- Roles grant permissions for certain features to certain users in certain contexts, such as courses.

If you haven't fully understood any of the three areas, don't worry. The intention was only to provide you with a high-level overview of the three core components and to touch upon the basics. Going forward, we will concentrate on Workplace-specific features, which is the focus of this book. When standard Moodle features are needed to facilitate or accompany a Workplace tool, we will briefly cover the principles of that feature in a sidebar and also provide references for more detailed assistance.

Now that you have learned about the basic concepts of Moodle courses, users, and roles, let's start with the first Workplace-specific features that make use of these: tenants, organizations, and teams.

4
Tenants, Organizations, and Teams

Tenants, organizations, and teams are three notable features of Moodle Workplace and are the first of many key differences from Moodle core. This chapter is all about setting up and managing the structure of your user-related data.

Tenants are entirely isolated entities with their own look and feel, structure, users, and learning entities. They are critical for when you wish to represent multiple self-contained business entities in your enterprise. You will learn about the fundamentals of tenants and how to manage them in Moodle Workplace.

Each tenant is modeled using **organizations** with multiple hierarchical department and position frameworks. Departments and positions are vital to defining reporting lines and assigning jobs to your staff. You will gain knowledge of all the aspects of organizations, including departments, positions, and job positions.

Teams are a key feature that let managers see the learning progress of their staff. You will learn how to set up teams within Workplace and how to represent different types of structures, including matrix organizations.

In this chapter, we will cover the following three topics:

- Managing tenants
- Managing organizations
- Managing teams

Let's get started with the feature that most Moodle aficionados have been waiting for a very long time: tenants.

Managing tenants

One of the masterpieces of Moodle Workplace is the introduction of **multi-tenancy** and its consistent application throughout. We define multi-tenancy as a single instance of Moodle that serves multiple client organizations (tenants), where its data and configuration are virtually partitioned and each client organization works with a customized virtual application instance.

In the context of Moodle Workplace, this means the ability to enable the configuration for multiple tenants with different themes and permissions, keeping them separated so that users in one tenant cannot see the users in another. Each tenant has its own users (an admin, supervisors, and employees), hierarchies, roles, dynamic rules, theme settings, reports, and learning entities (courses, programs, and certifications).

Not all the elements in Workplace are multi-tenant-aware; that is, some features can only be configured globally and not at the tenant level. For example, at the time of writing, plugins can only be configured site-wide and cannot be customized at the tenant level. As a consequence of this limitation, it is, for instance, not possible to authenticate users in different tenants against different authentication sources. However, it has been announced that some critical features, such as authentication, will be supported by Workplace very shortly, so watch this space.

Important Note

As a rule of thumb, all tools in the Workplace launcher can be configured at the tenant level. All other features cannot (yet).

For demonstration purposes, we will use a hypothetical company (`tenant = Packt`) in this chapter, as well as two sub-contracting businesses (`tenant1 = imPackt` and `tenant2 = comPackt`).

Let's get started with setting up our first tenants in Moodle Workplace.

You can access the management of tenants via **Site administration | Users | Manage tenants** or directly via the **Tenants** icon in the Workplace launcher, shown here:

Figure 4.1 – Tenants in the Workplace launcher

In this comprehensive section, we will be covering the following topics:

- Understanding tenant basics
- Tenant settings
- Adding new tenants
- Configuring tenants
- Archiving and deleting tenants
- Limiting the number of tenants
- Allocating users to tenants in batch mode
- Sharing content across tenants

First of all, let's deal with the basics of tenants.

Understanding tenant basics

You can already see a **default tenant** that has been created during installation and at least one user has already been assigned to it (your admin account). There are two critical rules—some may call them restrictions—when dealing with users and tenants in Workplace:

> **Important Note**
>
> A user is always assigned to a tenant; that is, an account cannot be tenantless.
>
> A user cannot be assigned to more than one tenant; an account always belongs to a single tenant and a single tenant only.

When a new user account is created, whether by self-registration, manual entry, batch upload, or via web services, it is always attached to the default tenant, unless specified otherwise. The following diagram illustrates how users are assigned to tenants:

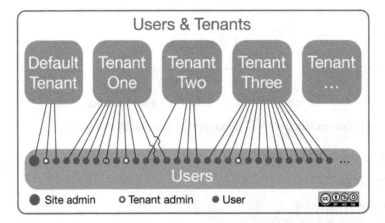

Figure 4.2 – Users and tenants

You can see, in the diagram, that each user belongs to exactly one tenant. Each tenant can have zero, one, or many tenant administrators. By default, a tenant admin has permission to manage tenant users, manage tenant roles, and adjust the tenant theme settings. These will be discussed in more detail later.

You can also see a **Default tenant** item in the list of active tenants. Each tenant can have a course category attached to it, which has to be a top-level course category.

Important Note

A course category can only be attached to a single tenant.

If a course category is selected, the tenant administrator is automatically assigned the tenant manager role in this category; this means they have permission to create courses, assign roles, and so on. Each user in this tenant is automatically assigned a tenant **User** role in this category.

Tenant settings

Now that you are equipped with the basics of tenants, let's edit the default tenant (using the cogwheel on the right) and change the settings according to your setup. The tenant parameters can be seen here:

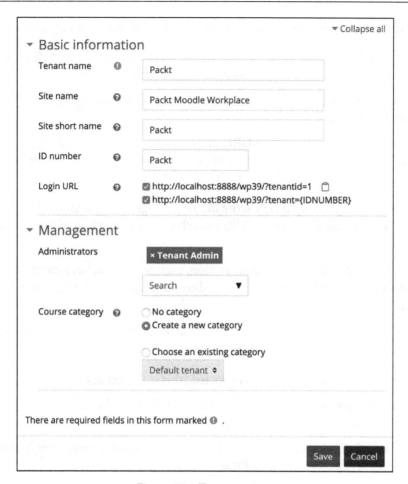

Figure 4.3 – Tenant settings

There are a couple of things to consider when configuring a tenant.

Tenant name is precisely that—the name of the tenant. While it is possible for multiple tenants to have the same name, it is highly recommended that you use different names for different tenants.

Site name and **Site short name** are effectively the same as the full site name and the short name for the site settings used for the front page in **Site administration | Front page settings**. Once a tenant is active (either by selecting it via the tenant switcher or when a user belongs to a tenant), the tenant settings will override the site settings.

ID number is a unique name for your tenant and has the following three purposes:

- Matches against external systems—for instance, connecting to your HR system via web services (see *Appendix A, Moodle Workplace Web Services*).

- Uses the upload user tool (see the *Provisioning your users* section in *Chapter 12, Migrations*).

- Is used as a parameter for **Login URL**. As you can see in the preceding screenshot, there are two selections available: one containing the ID number and the other an internal numeric tenant ID (the default tenant always has ID=1).

When users log in using the login URLs, the theme settings are applied to the login screen. This is not the case for the main URL, which uses the branding of the default tenant.

As seen in the *Understanding tenant basics* section, each tenant can have multiple tenant administrators that have to be chosen via the **Administrators** search, which only contains tenant users.

Courses that belong to a particular tenant have to be located in a tenant category. There are three options for the **Course category** choice:

- **No category**: No tenant category is selected (this is the default).

- **Create a new category**: A top-level course category with the same name as the tenant name is created.

- **Choose an existing category**: All top-level categories that are not already assigned to any other tenants are available for selection.

Moodle Workplace supports courses that are shared across tenants. We will deal with this special case at the end of this section.

Adding new tenants

Once you select the **+New tenant** button, you will be presented with the same screen as in the previous screenshot, but with two notable differences:

- The internal tenant ID is not available during tenant creation. As a consequence, the login URLs are displayed as tenantid={ID} and tenant={IDNUMBER}, respectively.

- The choice to select tenant administrators is not available, which makes sense since no users have been assigned to the tenant yet.

> **Important Note**
> Moodle Workplace does not support sub-tenants.

Once you have created one or more tenants, you will see a list of all the active tenants. The following is a sample of my three tenants: **Packt**, **comPackt**, and **imPackt**:

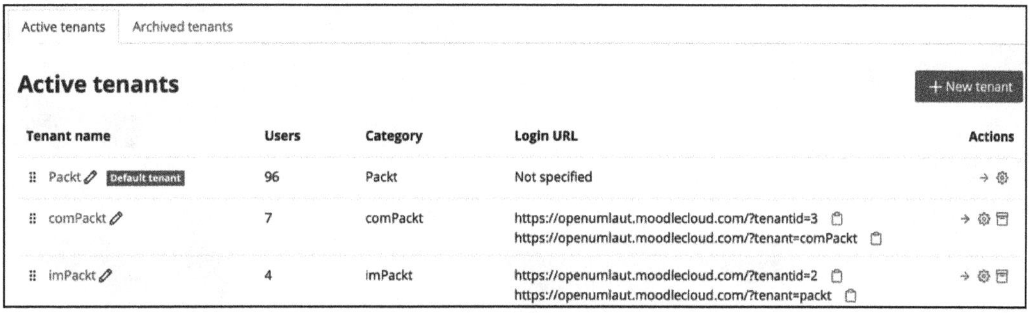

Figure 4.4 – Tenant listing

Now that we have created some tenants, let's look at how we configure them.

Configuring tenants

As a site administrator, you can configure tenants using the right-arrow icon. As a tenant administrator, you can get to the same screen via **Workplace launcher | Tenant**. Once selected, you have the following four tabs at your disposal:

- **Users**: Manages tenant users

- **Roles**: Manages tenant roles

- **Appearance**: Configures the tenant's look and feel

- **Details**: Displays tenant information

Let's go through them one by one.

Managing users

You can manage (that is, modify and delete) all tenant users and also add new users to the tenant in the **Users** tab. The required capability is `tool/tenant:manageusers`. Using the drop-down menu at the bottom, a tenant administrator can suspend or unsuspend users. The site administrator is presented with the ability to assign or unassign selected users with the tenant administrator role:

Figure 4.5 – Tenant user management

If multiple tenants exist on your site, a user with the `tool/tenant:allocate` capability can move selected users to another tenant. None of their data, such as courses or certification completion, will be affected by this.

As a tenant administrator, you can also batch upload users via the standard **Upload users** Moodle feature, by going to **Site administration | Users | Accounts | Upload users**. The new users will be added automatically to the current tenant.

The manual enrollment method has been modified in Moodle Workplace, so the user picker only displays users from the current tenant.

Managing roles

The **Roles** tab is where the available roles and their assignment to users in the current tenant are displayed. Three roles are created automatically during the Workplace installation and are assigned automatically to the following users:

- **Tenant administrator**: Assigned to the tenant administrator (in the system context).

- **Tenant administrator in the course category**: Assigned to the tenant administrator (in the context of the course category of the tenant). Also known as tenant manager.

- **Tenant user**: Assigned to all tenant users (in the context of the course category of the tenant).

You cannot delete these three roles, nor can you change their assignments. However, as a site administrator, you can modify these roles if necessary.

Customizing appearance

The **Appearance** tab lets you customize the look and feel of the tenant (the required capability is `tool/tenant:managetheme`). The three main categories are **Images**, **Colours**, and **Advanced**. We will deal with appearance and design issues in *Chapter 11*, *Corporate Identity*.

Displaying details

In the **Details** tab, the meta-information about the tenant is displayed. Tenant administrators do not have access to the main tenant list, so this is the place where they can view data about the following fields: **ID number**, **Site name**, **Site short name**, **Login URL**, **Administrators**, and **Course category**.

Archiving and deleting tenants

Moodle Workplace supports the archiving of tenants via the corresponding icon. Archiving a tenant performs the following two actions:

- All users are moved to the default tenant.

- The tenant is made unavailable throughout the site.

> **Important Note**
> The default tenant cannot be archived or deleted.

The **Archived tenants** tab gives you access to all non-active tenants. Here, you can either restore or irrevocably delete a tenant. A restored tenant keeps all its settings, roles, and theme variables. It even moves users back from the default tenant to the restored tenant! This reallocation does not apply to users who have already been moved out of the default tenant:

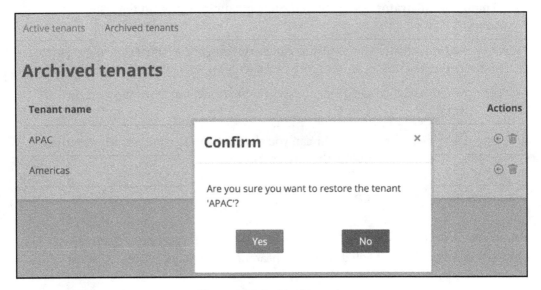

Figure 4.6 – Archived tenants

Next up is the option to limit the number of tenants, which also includes archived tenants.

Limiting the number of tenants

By default, you can create as many tenants in Moodle Workplace as you wish. You can change the limit, however, using the **Tenant limit** (`tool_tenant_tenantlimit`) setting in **Site administration | Advanced features**. First, you have to enable the **Tenant limit** feature via the **tool_tenant_tenantlimitenabled** setting:

Enable tenant limit tool_tenant_tenantlimitenabled	☑ Default: No If this is enabled it's possible to limit number of tenants on this site.
Tenant limit tool_tenant_tenantlimit	10 Default: 1 Maximum number of tenants allowed in the system, both active and archived tenants are counted. Save changes

Figure 4.7 – Tenant limit

Your system administrator can also fix the tenant limit using the following two variables in `config.php`, located in the main directory of your Moodle system (`$CFG->dirroot`):

```
$CFG->tool_tenant_tenantlimitenabled = true|false;
$CFG->tool_tenant_tenantlimit = <VALUE>;
```

> **Important Note**
> The maximum number of tenants allowed includes both active and archived tenants.

By default, Moodle Workplace is prepared for multi-tenants. The `moodle/category:viewcourselist` capability is removed from the roles of **Authenticated user** and **Guest**. If you disable the multi-tenancy functionality, you may consider allowing this capability.

For completeness, there are two more tenant-related limitation settings that can only be set in `config.php`:

- The number of custom reports (see *Chapter 8, Generating Custom Reports*) can be restricted per tenant via the `$CFG->tool_reportbuilder_tenantlimit` setting.
- The number of dynamic rules (see *Chapter 6, Onboarding and Compliance*) can be restricted per tenant via the `$CFG->tool_dynamicrule_tenantlimit` setting.

The next part of the tenant section explains how to allocate users to tenants in batch mode using CSV files.

Allocating users to tenants in batch mode

Once you have created tenants manually, you can specify them in the user CSV file. A tenant is matched by its tenant ID number.

The following is a sample CSV file, adding three users to two different tenants (in bold):

```
username,firstname,lastname,email,tenant
cogea,Aileen,Cogé,a.coge@mail.com,imPackt
bittnerh,Helmut,Bittner,h.bittner@mail.com,imPackt
henrickl,Lea,Henrick,l.henrick@mail.com,comPackt
```

The user who uploads the file has to be able to use the **Upload user** tool. If the user also has the `tool/tenant:allocate` capability, they will be able to specify a tenant when uploading users (both when creating new users and updating existing ones). If the user does not have this capability, users can only be created and updated in their own tenant.

Since a user cannot be tenantless, it is impossible to remove tenant allocation. However, you can move a user from one tenant to another by replacing the old tenant in the CSV file with the new value.

The final part of the tenant section deals with sharing content across tenants.

Sharing content across tenants

So far, all Workplace-only tools, such as programs, certifications, dynamic rules, and reports, have been tied to a single tenant. Also, it was emphasized that users belong to one tenant and one tenant only. So, how can you share content across tenants?

There are two ways that content sharing across tenants can be facilitated:

- Shared courses
- Shared space

We are going to cover these two options next.

Shared courses

As described earlier in this section, each tenant has its own course category and hence its own courses. However, there are scenarios where an enterprise might want to have courses shared among tenants—for instance, an introductory course providing an overview of the business.

To guarantee full compatibility with standard Moodle, the following constraint has been imposed on sharing courses: all users (learners and trainers) enrolled in a course will see users from other tenants while browsing the course. This behavior applies to all activities—core or third-party—that contain user data, such as forums, the gradebook, or the list of course participants.

> **Important Note**
> Multi-tenancy does not apply to course content. When enrolling users from multiple tenants to a course, this course effectively becomes a shared course.

While this approach might appear very restrictive, it actually gives you a high degree of flexibility when sharing courses across tenants:

- By enrolling users from multiple tenants, you decide who can access the content and who cannot. That is, if only users from two tenants should get access to a course, you only enroll those users. Users from other tenants are not even aware of the existence of the course.

- If the organization wants staff from different entities to learn together or a trainer from one tenant to be the trainer for all learners regardless of their tenant, no additional configuration is needed, as this is supported as the default behavior.

- If the organization wants staff from different entities to learn independently, the users must belong to different groups in separate group mode (preferably forced). Make sure any trainer roles in the course do not have the `accessallgroups` capability, and trainers are also allocated to the relevant groups. Allocation to separate groups is done automatically when a shared course is part of a program or certification. We will deal with this scenario in *Chapter 6, Onboarding and Compliance*.

Shared courses provide you with a powerful vehicle to share content with users from different tenants. Let's compare this to its big sibling: shared space.

Shared space

Shared space enables the sharing of entities **across all tenants**. It works like a special tenant where users can create supported entities to be available in other tenants. At the time of writing, supported entities are programs, certifications, and certificates.

> **Important Note**
> Shared space is a special tenant to share Moodle Workplace entities and content among *all* tenants.

The site administrator has to enable the shared space feature once using one of these two options:

- Choose **Shared space** from the tenant switcher and select **Enable Shared space**. If you select the **Not now** button, the option will be removed from the tenant switcher, and enabling the feature will only be possible from the tenant menu (as follows).

- Go to the tenant menu (via the Workplace launcher) and select **Enable Shared space**. As before, the shared space will be created, and the option will reappear in the tenant switcher.

> **Important Note**
> Enabling the **Shared space** feature cannot be undone. Once enabled, always enabled!

So, what happens when you switch to shared space? Any supported entities created will be available in all tenants. For instance, when you create an onboarding program to welcome new staff, this will be available in the list of programs in every tenant. We will deal with shared programs and certificates in more detail in *Chapter 6, Onboarding and Compliance.*

When you are in the shared space, the following features are unavailable and have also been removed from the Workplace launcher: report builder, dynamic rules, and organization structure. It wouldn't be a big surprise, however, if the former two will be supported by the **Shared space** feature in the not-too-distant future.

Shared space is a special tenant and does count toward the number of tenants. You need to consider this if you have activated the tenant limit in the previous sub-section.

This concludes the first part of this chapter, and hopefully, you have gathered a good understanding of how to make use of tenants in your setup. Now that you are equipped with the knowledge of how to handle tenants, let's move on to the second key feature in Workplace: organizations.

Managing organizations

Organization structure is a combination of three Moodle Workplace features: **departments**, **positions**, and **jobs**. You deploy department and position hierarchies to represent your organization structure and define reporting lines by assigning job assignments to employees in any department with any position.

Once created, a site or tenant administrator can utilize an organization structure to perform the following operations:

- Create dynamic rules to automate specific steps based on a user's position or department; for instance, all employees who belong to the R&D department will be enrolled in the newly introduced ethics course.

- Create custom reports that show the data of a specific department or position as their audience; that is, the same report only displays data depending on where in an organization the viewer is based.

- Create team managers by assigning jobs with different types of positions to users, effectively creating reporting lines.

- Filter and/or search lists of users within a company based on their position and department, thereby allowing certain drill-down operations.

> **Important Note**
>
> An organization structure always belongs to a tenant and cannot spawn across tenants.

The following diagram provides a high-level overview of the three Workplace components—departments, positions, and job assignments:

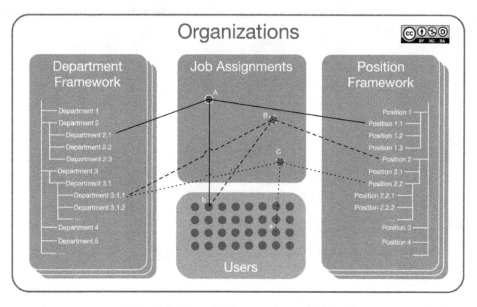

Figure 4.8 – Organization structure – high level

We will spend the remainder of this section dealing with department frameworks, position frameworks, and job assignments. For now, let's get a feel for Workplace's approach to model organizations by looking at the two users, **a** and **b**, in the preceding high-level diagram:

- User **a** has been assigned to job assignment **C**. Job assignment **C** is linked to **Department 3.1.1** and **Position 2.2**. So, user **a** works in **Department 3.1.1** and has **Position 2.2**.

- User **b**, on the other hand, has been assigned to two job assignments: **A** and **B**. **A** is linked to **Department 2.1** and **Position 1.1**; **B** is linked to **Department 3.1.1** and has position **Position 2**. User **b** not only has two jobs in the organization but is also likely to be the manager of user **a**! Do you see why this is the case? They both work in the same department and the position of user **a** is located below the position of user **b** in the position framework.

To shed more light on the abstract example just given, let's take a more detailed look at departments, positions, and job assignments. By default, these three areas can be managed by users within the admin, tenant admin, or organization structure manager roles, respectively.

You access the management of organizations via **Site administration | Users | Organisation structure** or directly via the **Organisation structure** icon in the Workplace launcher, shown here:

Figure 4.9 – Organisation structure in the Workplace launcher

In this section, we will be covering the following topics:

- Departments and department frameworks

- Positions and position frameworks

- Job assignments

First, let's deal with departments and department frameworks, which are managed via the **Departments** tab.

Departments and department frameworks

Departments are organized into department frameworks. A framework is effectively a container that related departments are grouped in. In most settings, a single framework is sufficient, but some scenarios justify multiple department frameworks. They are as follows:

- Frameworks can represent sub-divisions of large organizations with a high degree of autonomy—for example, at a regional or country level.

- Frameworks can be used when you have external organizations as customers. For instance, a training provider might want to offer a personalized learning environment to different clients and also offer client tools to manage their own users and pull individual reports.

- When representing a matrix organization, you can create completely isolated sets of departments; for example, one framework could be based on physical location and another one on a product team within the organization. We will look more at matrix organizations when we have a closer look at teams.

Department structures can be hierarchical; however, it is more likely that only one of the structures in an organization is hierarchical and the others are flat.

When adding a department framework (via the usual **+ New framework** button), you are required to give it a descriptive name. The **ID number** and **Description** fields are optional, but it is recommended that you fill those in:

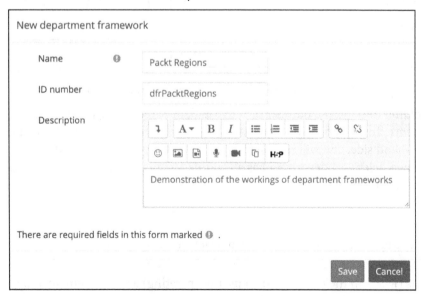

Figure 4.10 – Adding a department framework

Once you have created a department framework, you should start populating the structure with departments, sub-departments, and so on. Select the + icon to the right-hand side of the framework to create your first department. The input screen is identical to the one for adding department frameworks; only the heading is different.

Once you have created some departments, you can create sub-departments by selecting the + icon next to a department; alternatively, use the built-in drag-and-drop functionality. In our demonstration system, we created two separate department frameworks: one hierarchical (by region) and one flat (by function), which are shown in the following side-by-side screenshots:

Figure 4.11 – Two department frameworks – one hierarchical and one flat

The **Jobs** column displays the number of active and, in parentheses, the number of past job assignments. This will become clearer when we deal with jobs later in this chapter. On the right-hand side, you will see the familiar **Actions** options for each department. Be careful when deleting a department as all sub-departments will also be removed—this action cannot be undone!

> **Important Note**
> A department can only be deleted when no jobs are assigned to it.

Departments (*where* in the organization a user is operating) are complemented by positions (*what* a user's function is), which we will cover next.

Positions and position frameworks

Positions and position frameworks are managed via the **Positions** tab, which we will cover in this section.

Positions are organized into position frameworks. A framework is effectively a container that related positions are grouped in. Positions are structured in the same way as departments but have two additional properties, called **Manager** and **Department lead**. These are effectively permissions that are tied to their respective positions:

- **Manager**: This is the manager of anyone in a lower position, regardless of their department. This is not to be confused with Moodle's manager role.

- **Department lead**: This is the manager of anyone in a lower department or sub-department(s), regardless of their position.

When you add a new position using the standard + button, you will be presented with the following pop-up screen:

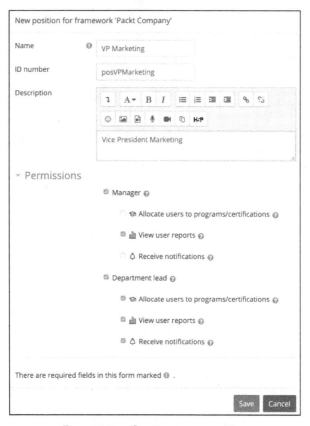

Figure 4.12 – Creating a new position

For both the **Manager** and **Department lead** options, the following three permissions are available:

- **Allocate users to programs/certifications**: This setting grants permission to assign users to programs and certifications. This feature will be used in *Chapter 6, Onboarding and Compliance*.

- **View user reports**: Workplace contains a powerful built-in reporting tool. This option allows managers to view reports containing progress data about their staff. Reporting will be dealt with in depth in *Chapter 8, Generating Custom Reports*.

- **Receive notifications**: Various Workplace features support features that notify managers or leads—for instance, when the due date has passed for a compliance training or when a colleague has been booked onto a face-to-face seminar. If this option is selected, managers will receive alerts when configured appropriately.

Once you have created your position hierarchy (or flat list), a tree-like structure is displayed, as follows:

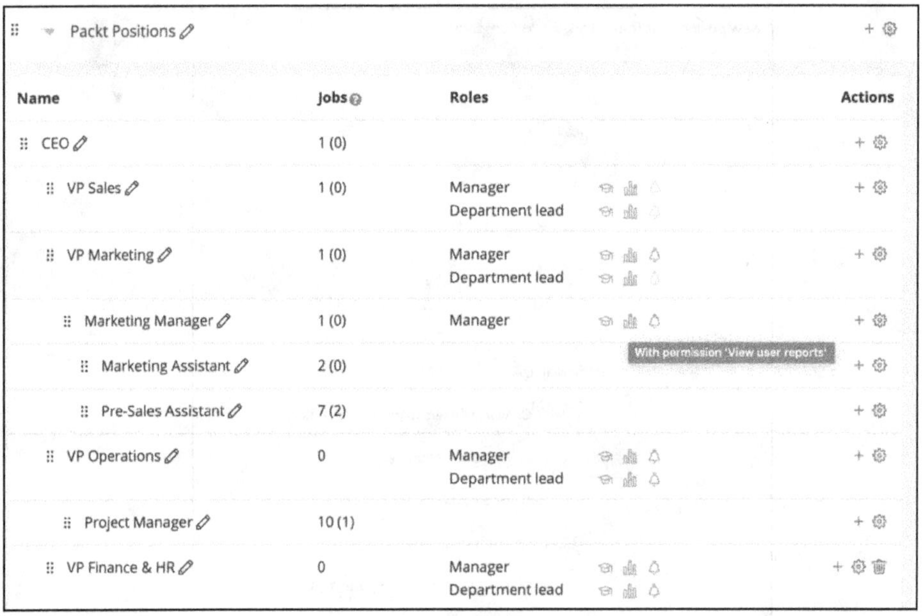

Figure 4.13 – Position hierarchy

You can see the familiar layout (displaying the **Name**, **Jobs**, and **Actions** columns), which is identical to its departments counterpart. What is different is the additional **Roles** column, which shows the manager permissions with icons, as we have just discussed.

Now that we have set up our departments and positions, let's bring everything together and cover Workplace's job assignments.

Job assignments

A job assignment, or job for short, connects a department and a position to a user and adds some auxiliary data—namely the start and end dates.

Important Note

Departments and positions need to be created to proceed with job assignments.

For each job, you have the **Select users**, **Position**, and **Department** options. If you select multiple users, you effectively create multiple jobs with the same position, department, start date, and end date for each employee.

The default **Start date** option is today's date. It is not possible to leave **Start date** empty. This is slightly controversial since this piece of information is not always available. However, the **Start date** and optional **End date** options are used to decide whether a job is current or whether it is a past job.

When you add a new job assignment, using the standard + **New job** button, you will be presented with the following pop-up screen:

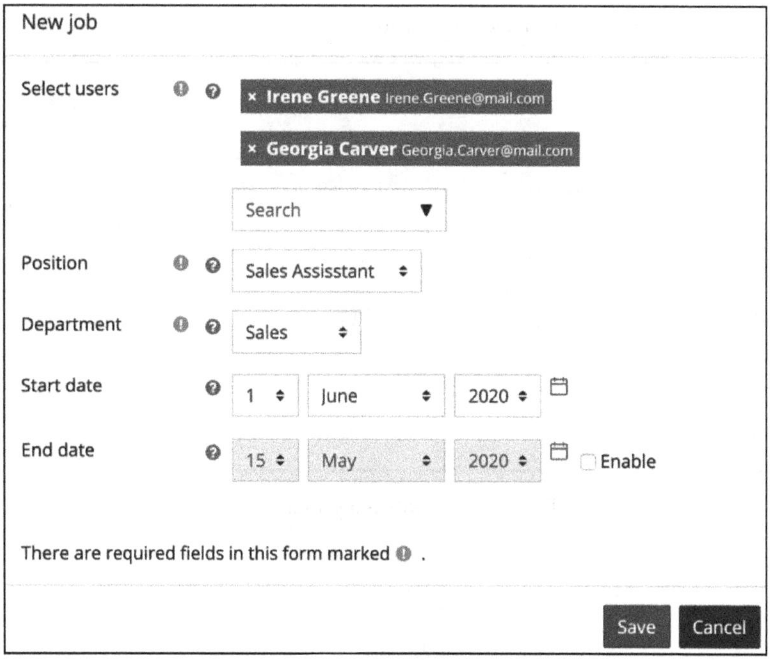

Figure 4.14 – Adding a new job assignment

Moodle Workplace deliberately does not perform any checks on overlapping jobs. This is to facilitate scenarios where one employee holds two or more positions in the same company. If you need to create a second job for a user, you can use the + icon beside the user entry to perform this operation without having to select the user again. This is a small but useful shortcut, especially when you have to create multiple entries manually.

Note that once you have created a job assignment for a user, you cannot change the position nor the department. You can only modify the start and end date. If you entered an incorrect position or department, you have to delete the job assignment and re-create it.

> **Important Note**
> It is not recommended that you delete job assignments unless they were created by mistake. Instead, you should set the end date of the current job and create a new job in the new position or department to guarantee a complete and consistent job and learning history of all users.

In the following example, you can view a number of job assignments in the marketing department, both present and past. The latter entries are grayed out. Unfortunately, it is currently not possible to sort this table by department or position, but you can apply filters to narrow down the number of entries displayed:

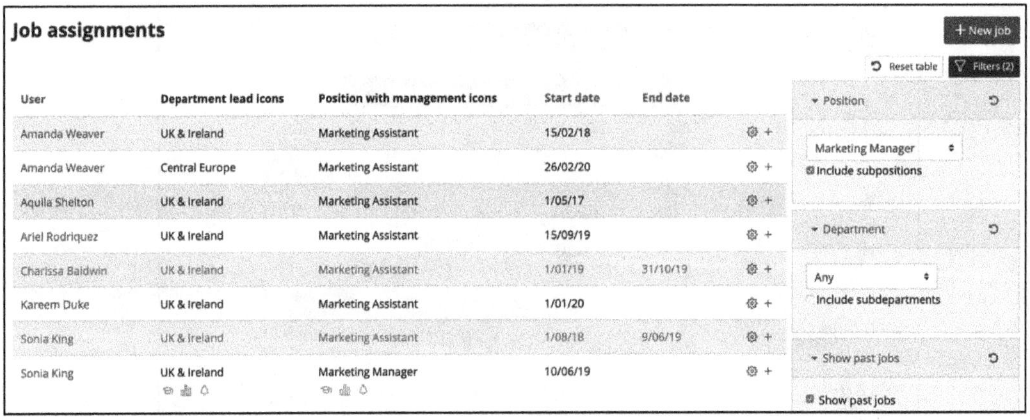

Figure 4.15 – Job assignments

The preceding screenshot shows users holding different jobs and demonstrates how several features in Moodle Workplace handle job assignments. Here, we have narrowed down the number of displayed employees to marketing positions only and also listed past jobs. **Charissa Baldwin** and **Sonia King** both no longer work as marketing assistants, which is indicated by the end date and the grayed-out font. Unless **Charissa Baldwin** has moved on to a non-marketing position, she must have left the organization. **Sonia King**, on the other hand, has been promoted to the position of marketing manager in the same department. **Amanda Weaver** holds two positions simultaneously in two different regions (departments).

Sonia King is the manager of anyone in her department and any department underneath, regardless of their position. She has permission to allocate users to programs and certifications, view user reports, and receive notifications, as indicated by the three icons underneath the department name.

> **Important Note**
> Managers are assigned indirectly via positions, not directly to an employee.

What exactly does this mean? Well, instead of stating that **Sonia King** is the manager of **Amanda Weaver** and three others, we assign all five staff to the **UK & Ireland** department. Since **Sonia King** is the department manager, she is automatically the manager of the other four staff. So, every user that belongs to the same department is reporting to the manager in charge and is automatically part of the same **team**.

Unless you are modeling a hippie commune, there will be managers who are in charge of a department at different levels of the organizational hierarchy. All staff belonging to a department or jointly working on a product/service are represented by Moodle Workplace as teams. Managing teams will be the topic of the third section of this chapter. But first, let's close off the section by looking at assigning jobs in batch mode via CSV files.

Assigning jobs in batch mode

By working your way through this section, you might have realized that manually assigning job assignments is a daunting task and potentially prone to errors. While this approach might be acceptable in small institutions, it is untenable in larger and more complex organizations.

In addition to adding tenants via CSV files, assigning jobs is also supported by Moodle Workplace. Job assignments are supported via the following four new self-explanatory variables:

- `jobdepartment`
- `jobposition`
- `jobstartdate` (optional)
- `jobenddate` (optional)

Each variable has to have a numeric postfix to support multiple job assignments. Just like tenants, departments and positions are matched by their respective ID numbers. For any date field, use the `YYYY-MM-DD` ISO standard format, which will then be properly localized during the upload process.

In addition to permission to upload users, the `tool/organisation:assignjobs` capability is required to create jobs for users or to modify existing ones.

The following is a sample CSV file, adding two job assignments and changing an existing one (in bold). When a user already has a job in a department and position, the dates will be modified without creating a new job:

```
username,firstname,lastname,email,jobdepartment1,jobposition1,
jobstartdate1,jobenddate1

cogea,Aileen,Cogé,a.coge@mail.com,depCentralEurope,
posMarketingManager,2020-02-26,

bittnerh,Helmut,Bittner,h.bittner@mail.com,depCentralEurope,
posMarketingAssistant,,2020-12-31

henrickl,Lea,Henrick,l.henrick@mail.
com,depUKIRE,posMarketingManager,2020-01-01,
```

The example CSV file demonstrates nicely the importance of providing meaningful ID numbers for departments and positions, respectively. Bear in mind that it is not possible to delete a job assignment via the user upload feature.

Let's recap what tools we have added to our toolbox in this section. You are now able to represent the structure of your organization in Moodle Workplace. This includes departments (where users are located in the organizational hierarchy) and positions (what functions users have). Job assignments link individual users to departments and positions to effectively represent both current and past employment. Superiors are assigned via manager and department lead permissions, respectively, implicitly creating teams, which is the next section's topic.

Managing teams

You might recall the **Teams** tab on the dashboard, which we mentioned in the overview chapter. Now that we have dealt with departments, positions, and job assignments, we can look at the different facets of how Moodle Workplace handles teams.

In this section, we will be covering the following topics:

- Managerial rights and responsibilities
- Teams versus cohorts
- Modeling different types of organizations

Managerial rights and responsibilities

With great power comes great responsibility. As we have already seen in the *Job assignments* section, users with managerial positions can do the following:

- Allocate team members to programs and certifications.
- View custom reports on team members (according to configured report audience settings).
- Receive notifications about completions and activities that are overdue.

Having a manager position further means that the team list is displayed on the dashboard. The **Teams** tab displays information about all the team members of a manager or department lead. Let's zoom in on the **Teams** tab from *Chapter 2, Working with Moodle Workplace*, where we briefly looked at the dashboard while logged in as the superior of the following two marketing managers:

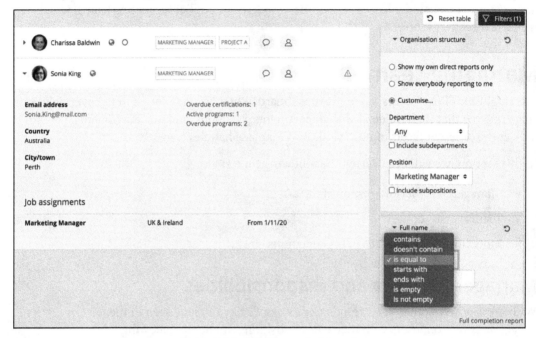

Figure 4.16 – The Teams dashboard

The **Teams** tab provides the following information and actions for each team member, respectively:

- Their full name

- An indicator, in the shape of a globe, if the colleague is a manager

- An indicator, in the shape of a circle, if the colleague is a department lead

- The position(s) the team member holds

- An action icon to send a direct message to the person

- An action icon to view the user's profile

- A warning icon if a program or a certification is overdue

You can expand and collapse the view for each user to display the following additional data:

- An email address (if allowed in the user profile), the country, and the city (if specified in the user profile).

- Job assignment details.

- Certified, expired, or overdue programs and certifications, including links to the progress report, which provides detailed information about the user's current progression (see *Chapter 6, Onboarding and Compliance*). At the bottom of the page, you can also navigate to a full completion report.

If a team comprises more than 10 members, the standard pagination is shown below the table. Alternatively, you can apply filters to **Organisation structure** and **Full name**. The former lets you choose between the following three options:

- **Show my direct reports only**

- **Show everybody reporting to me**

- **Customise…**, where you can select departments and positions including their sub-elements

In our example, only marketing managers have been selected without sub-positions. We could have achieved the same by only showing direct reports.

We will come across teams and managers every so often throughout this book—for example, when dealing with programs, certifications, or reporting. For now, let's look at the difference between teams and cohorts.

Teams versus cohorts

One question that comes up regularly is whether teams replace cohorts. The answer depends on how cohorts have been used so far.

If you have grouped users belonging to the same department or position as a cohort, it is strongly recommended that you replace these with teams as they offer more flexibility in terms of dynamic allocation and support for hierarchical organization. For instance, if you have organized all the users of a particular division into a cohort, it is more logical to model the division as a department and assign its staff via job positions. They'll automatically become a team with one or more managers.

If, on the other hand, you have used cohorts for global groups of users related to a subject that is not reflected by either departments or positions, then it makes sense to retain those cohorts. An example may be all the first aiders in the organization; they belong to a single group but are not represented in any organizational hierarchy.

The beauty of Moodle Workplace is that teams and cohorts can happily co-exist side by side. Being a member of a team does not prevent you from being a member of a cohort and vice versa.

Modeling different types of organizations

Different companies are structured in different ways. While there might be similarities, there are almost always some idiosyncrasies, depending on the size, geographical spread, industry, and personal preferences of the executive team. We are going to cover three types of organization structures, which are representative of most organizations out there:

- Organization structure hierarchy based on departments
- Organization structure hierarchy based on positions
- Matrix organizations

Let's kick things off with a department-based topology.

Organization structure hierarchy based on departments

An organization structure based on departments is modeled around where in the business staff are located, as opposed to what their function is. In this type of organization, departments represent different divisions and teams inside the company. Their structure is almost always hierarchical.

The **Regions** department framework shown earlier was an example of such an organization structure. The department hierarchy is then accompanied by a position framework with staff and department leads. When users get assigned jobs in different departments, the manager(s) will be able to see everybody from their department as their team.

Organization structure hierarchy based on positions

An organization structure based on positions is modeled around what the functions of staff are, as opposed to where in the business they are located. In this type of organization, the company chooses to store its hierarchy in a position tree.

In the position hierarchy shown earlier on, the CEO has the top position, and underneath are the VPs for sales, marketing, operations, finance, and HR, respectively. The managers of several teams are located under the marketing VP and the members of these teams are positioned under these managers. This means that there might be marketing managers operating in different parts of the company, but while they are all part of a (different) local team, they are reporting to the (same) marketing VP.

In this structure, all positions that have sub-positions have manager permissions. This allows users who hold jobs in these positions to see everybody in the positions below them as their team. In our scenario, the CEO does not need to receive notifications from their subordinates, but they need to see reports on them.

Matrix organizations

In a matrix organization, some individuals report to more than one supervisor or manager. A data scientist might report to the R&D manager for their day-to-day activities but also report to a project manager for a particular project they are working on. Conversely, a manager might be responsible for multiple cross-functional or cross-business teams.

Moodle Workplace fully supports multi-dimensional arrangements, as depicted in the sample matrix organization here:

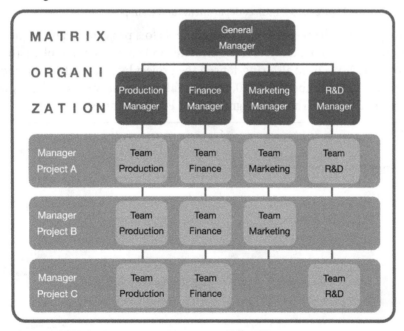

Figure 4.17 – Matrix organization

This diagram shows a typical matrix and is a combination of the two organizational structures just described, one based on departments (production, finance, marketing, and R&D) and one based on positions (creatively named **Project A**, **Project B**, and **Project C**).

So, what is needed to model the described matrix organization? We already have the department and position structure in place for the vertical dimension of the matrix, representing production, finance, marketing, and R&D, as well as any associated positions (such as **Packt Functions**). What is missing is the horizontal dimension representing projects and all that is required are two additional flat structures: a department framework (**Packt Projects**) with the three departments (**Project A**, **Project B**, and **Project C**) and a position framework (**Packt Teams**) with the two positions (**Team Member** and **Team Lead**). In our case, the team lead is a department manager with the related permissions. The two small frameworks are shown here:

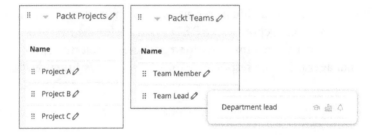

Figure 4.18 – Project departments and team positions

Once you have assigned the respective job assignments to a project, a team might comprise a team lead (in our example, **Irene Greene**) and some team members (here, five current and one past). We have also ring-fenced the project by time and set the end date of all job assignments to December 31, 2020, except **Wallace Montoya**, who already left the project on January 31, 2020. The job assignments of **Project A** are shown here:

Job assignments

User	Department lead icons	Position with management icons	Start date	End date	
Georgia Carver	Project A	Team Member	1/01/20	31/12/20	⚙ +
Ignacia Curtis	Project A	Team Member	1/01/20	31/12/20	⚙ +
Irene Greene	Project A	Team Lead	1/01/20	31/12/20	⚙ +
Liberty Cooke	Project A	Team Member	1/01/20	31/12/20	⚙ +
Rose Briggs	Project A	Team Member	1/01/20	31/12/20	⚙ +
Ryder Black	Project A	Team Member	1/01/20	31/12/20	⚙ +
Wallace Montoya	Project A	Team Member	1/01/20	31/01/20	⚙ +

Figure 4.19 – Job assignments of Project A

The beauty of this approach is that there is no limit in terms of dimensions and the matrix is effectively created automatically. For example, let's take a closer look at **Irene Greene**, who is **Team Lead** of **Project A**. In her day job, she is also **Project Manager** in the **Production** unit (department). Her start date was back in 2018, and no end date has been set. The job assignments of **Irene Greene** are shown here:

User ↑⚌	Department lead icons	Position with management icons	Start date	End date
Irene Greene	Production	Project Manager	1/01/18	
Irene Greene	Project A ☜ 🏛 ⌂	Team Lead	1/01/20	31/12/20

Figure 4.20 – Job assignments of a team lead

The two job assignments illustrate nicely how multiple dimensions of a matrix organization can be modeled and concludes this exciting part about handling organizations. If your organizational setup requires more complexity, it is possible to create even more intricate structures with hierarchies in both positions and departments and also positions that are both managers and department leads.

Summary

Phew, that was a lot to take in! In this chapter, we covered three fundamental concepts, namely tenants, organizations, and teams.

You first learned how to manage different facets of multi-tenancy. You then became familiar with organization structures, which covered departments, positions, and job assignments. Finally, you acquired new knowledge about managers and teams, as well as different types of organization structures, including matrix organizations.

You might still be unsure about when to model a business entity as a tenant, as a framework, or as a department. While there are no clear-cut rules about when to use which structural elements, there are the following rules of thumb:

- Tenants represent self-contained business units with a high degree of autonomy, an individual look and feel, and separate structural elements.

- Frameworks act as containers for departments and positions and are usually part of the same business entity, managed centrally.

- Departments are individual units, organized either hierarchically or as a flat list.

This chapter was all about setting up and managing the **structure** of your organization. In the next chapter, we want to focus on **processes** in the form of dynamic rules.

5
Automation and Dynamic Rules

Dynamic rules allow you to define and execute centralized and automated rules using an "if this then that" conditional approach to trigger actions when certain conditions are met. This powerful feature of Moodle Workplace allows you to automate a wide range of steps you would otherwise have to work through manually. For example, for each user who successfully completes a course, the following steps have to be carried out: issue a certificate, award a competency, notify the user's manager, and enroll them in the follow-up course.

In this chapter, you will be learning all the ins and outs of dynamic rules, which always comprise three parts: the rule header, rule conditions, and rule actions. You will further learn about rule enablement, processing, reporting, archiving, and deleting. All these operations will equip you with the knowledge required to create automation workflows in Moodle Workplace.

To put your learned skills into action, we have created a dedicated section on automating processes, providing you with some sample Workplace workflows and dynamic rules tips, including performance considerations.

In this chapter, we will be covering the following topics:

- Managing dynamic rules
- Automating Workplace processes

The main goal of this chapter is to acquire the skills to handle dynamic rules and put them into action in your Moodle Workplace setup. Without further ado, let's get started with the management of dynamic rules.

Managing dynamic rules

In this first part of the chapter, we are going to cover all the intricacies of dynamic rules. Before we get started, let's deal with some of the basics of dynamic rules. A rule comprises a rule header and a rule body. The **rule header** contains information about the rule, while the **rule body** contains two parts: **conditions** and **actions**. The basic statement that is applied to every active user in the tenant that the dynamic rule belongs to is as follows:

```
IF <Conditions> = TRUE THEN execute <Actions>
```

Each <Conditions> clause comprises a single condition or multiple conditions, where all conditions are connected via AND operators; that is, all conditions must be met for <Conditions> to be true. <Actions> is a series of actions to be executed on all users that <Conditions> applies to.

In the context of Workplace, both conditions and actions are always applied to users. Conditions are matched against all users in the tenant, whereas actions are applied to a subset of all users, namely the ones that satisfy the conditions. This basic flow is depicted in the following diagram:

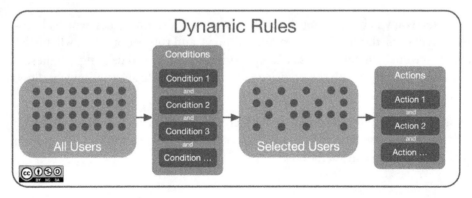

Figure 5.1 – Conditions and actions

A sample rule could be as follows:

```
IF user has position Marketing Assistant AND completed course
Onboarding I
THEN send message to the user's manager AND trigger enrollment
to course Onboarding II
```

Enough of the theory, let's get started by creating our first dynamic rule.

You can manage dynamic rules by going to **Site administration | Dynamic rules** or directly via the **Dynamic rules** icon in the Workplace launcher:

Figure 5.2 – The Dynamic rules icon in the Workplace launcher

Moodle Workplace lists all active rules in the same format—each rule has a **Name**, a set of **Conditions**, and a set of **Actions**. Additionally, you will see a switch indicating whether a rule is enabled or disabled, as well as the usual icons (Edit, Details, Duplicate, Report, and Archive) for each rule:

	Name	Conditions	Actions	
	Welcome	User is allocated to department 'UK & Ireland' Sub-departments: Included On or after: 26/02/20	Enrol in course 'Company Welcome' Role: Learner Group: None	→ ⚙ ⧉ ⬚ 🗂
	UK & Ireland	User is allocated to department 'UK & Ireland' Sub-departments: Not included Users who have completed course 'Company Welcome' Users who have completed course 'Products & Services I'	Send notification 'Well done' to users Issue certificate 'Seminar participation' to users	→ ⚙ ⧉ ⬚ 🗂
	Marketing	User has position 'Marketing Manager' Sub-positions: Included Users that have status 'Completed' in program 'Onboarding Marketing'	No actions on this rule	→ ⚙ ⧉ ⬚ 🗂
	Project A	User is allocated to department 'Project A' Sub-departments: Not included User has position 'Team Member' Sub-positions: Not included	Allocate users to program 'Health & Safety' Program start date: '29/11/20'	→ ⚙ ⧉ ⬚ 🗂

Active   Archived

Active rules   + New rule

Figure 5.3 – Active rules

In this section, we will be covering the following topics:

- Adding a rule header
- Exploring dynamic rule conditions
- Rule enablement and processing
- Rule reporting
- Rule archiving and deletion

First of all, let's deal with rule headers.

Adding a rule header

As outlined in the introductory section, a rule comprises a header and a body. The rule header, which will be covered in this sub-section, acts as a descriptive rule wrapper that is applied to all elements of the rule body.

Creating a new rule can be done using the + **New rule** button in the dynamic rule area of Moodle Workplace. Before we can specify conditions and actions, we need to give the rule a name. The name doesn't have to be unique, but it is recommended you give each rule a unique and meaningful label. The rule header settings that are shown in the following screenshot will be used throughout this section in our in-depth explanations:

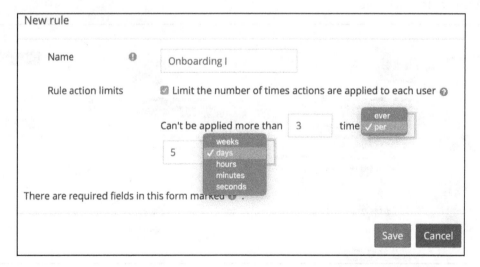

Figure 5.4 – Creating a new dynamic rule

By default, rule actions are applied to users when conditions are met. If **Rule action limits** are enabled, the rule application is limited to the number of times you have selected per your desired period. We will also refer to rule action limits to matching frequency. Rules will be executed as an ad hoc task during each **cron** run.

SIDEBAR - cron

Moodle Workplace has to perform several background tasks regularly, usually every 60 seconds. The maintenance script that performs these tasks is known as a **cron** script and is executed by the system's **cron** process. An entire page has been dedicated to this in the Moodle documentation; you can find it at `docs.moodle.org/en/Cron`. The cron process must be set up correctly by the system administrator; otherwise, any timed Workplace features, such as scheduled backups, sending notifications, dynamic rules processing, and so on, will not work.

END SIDEBAR

Once the rule action limits setting has been activated, you have two options to limit the number of times the matching process is performed:

- Can't be applied more than X times **ever**
- Can't be applied more than X times **per** Y **seconds/minutes/hours/days/weeks**

The rule action limits diagram in the following figure demonstrates all three available modes, where **e1–e4** symbolizes events when matching is successful. If rule action limits have not been enabled, all four events will, as expected, trigger the configured action. **e1** and **e2** will be actioned almost immediately, while **e3** and **e4** will be executed with a short delay since the condition was met while the cron process was already running.

When rule action limit **ever** has been chosen (here, the time value is set to 8), **e1** and **e2** will be actioned, while **e3** and **e4** will never be reached.

When rule action limit **per** has been selected (with a **times** value of 3 and a **per** value of 4), **e1** will be actioned straight away, while **e2** and **e3** will be actioned with a delay. **e4** will not be executed at all because the number of durations has already been exceeded.

The three matching options and four events have been arranged in the following diagram. A dash on the timeline represents the time interval, as specified in the cron process:

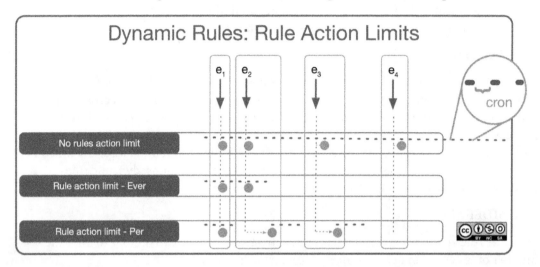

Figure 5.5 – Matching frequency in dynamic rules

When do you use which type of frequency matching? Two types of criteria should be applied when creating a dynamic rule:

- **Functionality**: No rule action limits is the default and should be used when you cannot predict when conditions are met and when quasi-real-time actions are expected. An example is the successful completion of courses that staff can sign up to themselves, which consequently triggers an award of a competency or a badge.

  The **ever** matching mode is preferred when you know that a condition will only be met a certain number of times. An example is the one-off issuing of a certificate to all users who completed an already archived course after migrating historical data.

  The **per** matching mode is useful if a delay in executing the action part of the rule is acceptable. For instance, notifying the manager after a team member has participated in a face-to-face seminar does not have to take place instantaneously and is usually sufficient once a day.

- **Performance**: Functionality permitting, you could keep rule action limits mode disabled all the time. However, this is likely to have a negative impact on the performance of your Workplace system. Applying rule action limits reduces the strain on each cron process. More on this later in this chapter, when we cover the impact of dynamic rules on performance.

Now that you have created the rule header, let's get going with the two components of the rule body: conditions and actions.

Exploring dynamic rule conditions

Conditions represent the IF part of a dynamic rule and will be the subject of this section.

On the **Conditions** tab, you will find a list of predefined conditions for each entity, which can be evaluated to trigger one or many actions. To add the first condition, you have to pick an element from the list on the left; for instance, in our screenshot, **Course completed**:

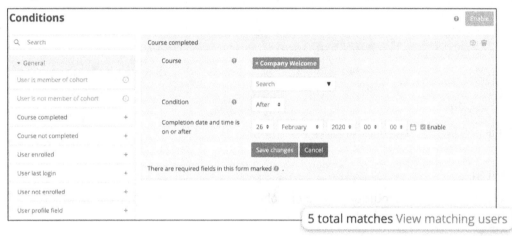

Figure 5.6 – Adding conditions to a rule

Each condition has its own editable properties; for example, using the drop-down menu lets you select a course that has to be completed, as well as the completion date and time parameters.

Grayed-out conditions cannot be selected – in our case the first two cohort membership clauses. This is always the case when it is not possible to define the conditional part of the dynamic rule. In our Moodle Workplace site, no cohorts have been defined yet, which prevents the selection thereof.

Once you save the changes, you can add more conditions if needed. You can always come back later and modify or delete these settings via the edit or delete icons in the top-right corner.

At the bottom of the tab, you can check how many users would meet these conditions. By clicking on the **View matching users** link, you can view a complete user listing.

> **Important note**
> Each condition can be used multiple times in a rule.

There are scenarios where it makes sense to use the same condition multiple times in the same rule; for example, if a requirement is that users must have completed multiple courses. Workplace does not check for contradictions in rules, so if you have one condition that requires users to hold a particular position and another condition requiring the exact opposite, this is perfectly fine for Workplace, even though the rule never matches any users.

Currently, Workplace provides conditions for the following categories:

- General
- Certifications
- Organization structure
- Program

Let's have a closer look at each of these condition types.

General

This category contains conditions based on cohort membership, course completion and enrolment, and user-related criteria.

Cohort conditions

A lot of Workplace conditions come in opposing pairs; for instance, **User is member of cohort** and **User is not member of cohort**:

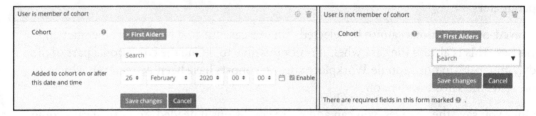

Figure 5.7 – Cohort conditions

The positive condition contains an optional date and time parameter, which wouldn't make any sense in the negative condition. You will come across this type of condition pair quite frequently; for instance, in course completion, which is up next.

Course completion and enrolment

You have already come across the **Course completed** condition and all its properties when we looked at how to create a new rule, and there is a **Course not completed** condition to complement it. It only comprises a single compulsory property, namely the course that a user must not have completed to meet the condition. The rule only applies to users who are enrolled on a course, not all users in the tenant.

Another condition pair is **User enrolled** and **User not enrolled**, which provides criteria about whether users have been enrolled on a course or not:

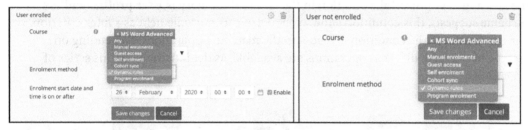

Figure 5.8 – User enrolment conditions

In both conditions, you have to select a course and an enrolment method. The latter lists all the enabled enrolment methods, including an option that is unique to Moodle Workplace: **Dynamic rules**. This method will be used later when we execute an action that automatically enrolls users in a course.

The **User enrolled** condition provides an additional, optional (and hopefully self-explanatory) property, called **Enrolment start date and time is on or after**.

User conditions

A very useful user-related condition for creating dynamic rules is **User last login**:

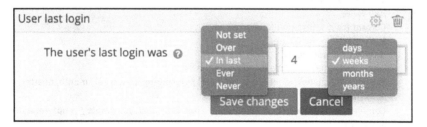

Figure 5.9 – User last login condition

There are several options to choose from:

- **Not set**: The initial setting, which cannot be selected or saved

- **Over**: The number of days, weeks, months, or years

- **In last**: The number of days, weeks, months, or years

- **Ever**: When the user has logged on sometime in the past

- **Never**: When the user has an account but has never logged in to Workplace

The last, and very powerful, condition in the **General** category is **User profile field**. As the name suggests, this condition allows you to use a user profile field as a filter criterion. A major feature of the condition is type-specific matching operations. Depending on the type of the field, different operations are available, as demonstrated in this series of screenshots:

Figure 5.10 – User profile field condition

The available operations (the values in brackets) for each field type are shown here:

Type	Operations
Checkbox	**Value** (true, false)
Date/Time	**Any value** **Current** (day, week, month, quarter, year) **In the past** / **In the future** **Is empty** / **Is not empty** **Last … days** (number) / **Next … days** (number) **Previous** (day, week, month, quarter, year) / **Upcoming** (day, week, month, quarter, year)
Drop-down	**Selection** (values)
Text	**Contains** (text) / **Doesn't contain** (text) / **Ends with** (text) / **Is empty** / **Is not empty** / **Starts with** (text)

Figure 5.11 – User profile field condition operations

The **User profile field** condition has great potential to be part of flexible automation processes, especially since custom profile fields are fully supported; here, **Visa Status** (a dropdown), **DOB** (date/time), and **External** (checkbox).

Certifications

Certifications allow you to validate learning paths by offering certifications for recurring programs. They are used for compliance courses and other compulsory training. Given the nature of certifications—deadlines, re-certification dates, grace periods, and so on—it explains why this category contains the most conditions. However, all conditions can be grouped into two different types:

- Certification and date: All conditions that have a date attached
- Certification only: All negative conditions

The **Certification certified** and **Certification not certified** pair illustrates the two condition types nicely. This rule only applies to users who are allocated to a certification, not all users in the tenant:

Figure 5.12 – Certification conditions

This table lists all the available certification conditions alongside the date field, if available:

Condition	Certification date
Certification certified	**Certified date on or after**
Certification expired	**Expired date on or after**
Certification not certified	
Certification overdue	**Due date on or after**
Certification suspended	**Suspended date on or after**
Recertification grace period ends	**Recertification grace period ends on or before**
Recertification period started	**Recertification started on or after**
Users allocated to certification	**Allocation date on or after**
Users not allocated to certification	

Figure 5.13 – Certification conditions

The purpose of these conditions will become more evident when we deal with certifications in detail in *Chapter 6, Onboarding and Compliance*.

Organization structure

There are two pairs of conditions that deal with organizational data:

- **User is in department** and **User is not in department**
- **User has position** and **User doesn't have position**

You always have to select a department or position. You also have the option to include sub-departments or sub-positions. The positive conditions further allow you to specify the job start date:

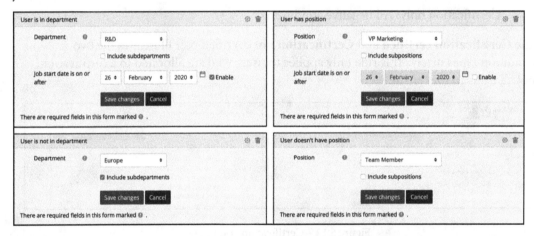

Figure 5.14 – Organization conditions

Organization conditions are very powerful since you can use them to automate processes for staff in individual departments or users who hold a particular position. You might want to combine multiple organization conditions for more flexibility.

Programs

Programs allow you to establish learning pathways for your employees by adding a combination of courses or a hierarchical sequence of courses. They are used for onboarding training and other curricula building. Since programs are closely related to certifications—in fact, certifications are built on top of programs—they can be grouped into the same two types:

1. Program and date: All conditions that have a date attached

2. Program only: All negative conditions

The **Program completed** and **Program not completed** pair illustrates the two condition types nicely. The rule only applies to users who are allocated to a program, not all users in the tenant:

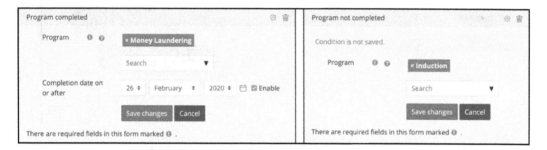

Figure 5.15 – Program conditions

This table lists all the available program conditions alongside the date field, if available:

Condition	Certification date
Program completed	Completion date on or after
Program not completed	
Program overdue	Due date on or after
Program suspended	Suspended date on or after
Users allocated to program	Allocation date on or after
Users not allocated to program	

Figure 5.16 – Program conditions

The purpose of these conditions will become clearer when we deal with programs in detail in *Chapter 6, Onboarding and Compliance*.

This completes the long list of available conditions. Let's move on to the actions part of dynamic rules.

Exploring dynamic rule actions

In the **Actions** tab, you will find a list of actions that will be executed once the previously defined conditions have been met. To add the first action, you have to pick an element from the list on the left; for instance, **Award badge**:

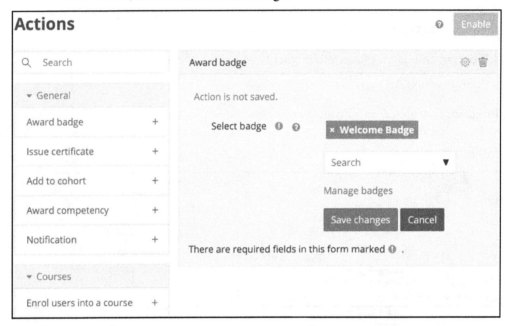

Figure 5.17 – Adding actions to a rule

Currently, Moodle Workplace provides actions for the following four categories:

- General
- Courses
- Certifications
- Program

Let's have a closer look at each of these action categories.

General

There are five items in this action category. You have already seen the **Award badge** action, where you have to select a single badge to be issued. **Award competency** looks and behaves exactly the same as its badge counterpart; the only difference is that you choose a competency instead of a badge. The **Issue certificate** action does exactly what it says on the tin: issues a selected certificate to all users who meet the specified conditions:

Figure 5.18 – Issue certificate action

Competencies and management of certificates will be covered in *Chapter 7*, *Skills and Incentives*. **Add to cohort** is a simple, but powerful action since it lets you dynamically create cohorts based on all available conditions. It only has a single setting, namely the cohort that you need to select.

The **Notification** action is very versatile and deserves a more detailed look. It is also one of the most utilized actions in dynamic rules. In the following screenshot, you can see an example **Notification** action:

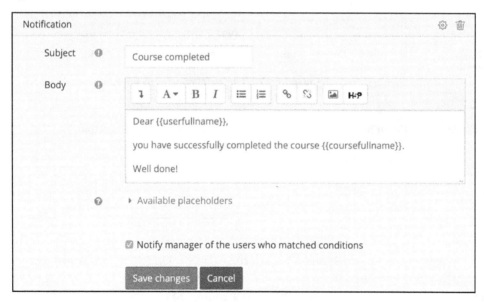

Figure 5.19 – A Notification action

Subject is the title of the notification to be sent out. **Body** is the actual text of the message and can contain any type of HTML formatting supported by the editor, including multimedia content such as images.

There exists a range of placeholders that you can use in the body; these placeholders will be replaced with the appropriate values when the message is sent. All placeholders are enclosed in double curly brackets; for instance, {{**userfullname**}}.

> **Important note**
> The placeholders available in the message's body change depending on the types of conditions that have been selected.

To see the list of available placeholders, you need to expand the **Available placeholders** list. This table shows all the message placeholders, grouped by condition category:

Action category	Placeholder	Description
System	{{sitefullname}}	Full site name
	{{siteshortname}}	Site short name
	{{sitelink}}	Site link
User / Cohort	{{userfullname}}	User's first name and last name
Course completion	{{courseid}}	Internal course ID used in URLs
	{{coursefullname}}	Course full name
	{{courseshortname}}	Course short name
	{{courseurl}}	Course URL
	{{coursecompletiondate}}	Completion date
	{{coursegrade}}	Grade
Program completion	{{programid}}	Internal program ID used in URLs
	{{programname}}	Program name
	{{programcompletedcourses}}	Courses completed in a program, separated by comma
	{{programcompletiondate}}	Program completion date
Certification certified	{{certificationid}}	Internal certification ID used in URLs
	{{certificationname}}	Certification name
	{{certificationdate}}	Certification date
	{{certificationexpirydate}}	Certification expiry date
	{{expirydatetimestamp}}	Certification expiry date timestamp
	N.B. All program completion fields are also available for certifications.	

Figure 5.20 – Notification placeholders

Finally, you also have the **Notify managers of the users who matched conditions** option. For managers to receive messages, the **Receive notifications** permission has to be granted in the **Manager** or **Department lead** options, depending on the position they hold. Details about this feature were discussed in *Chapter 4, Tenants, Organizations, and Teams*.

Courses

There are two actions available in the **Course** category: **Enrol users into a course** and **Unenrol users from a course**. The enrolment action has the following parameters:

Parameter	Description
Course (Required)	Selection of a single course. If you wish to select users to multiple courses, add another **Courses** action.
Role (Required)	Select the course role users will be granted.
End date	If enabled, the **Enrolment ends** setting will be set to the selected value. The **Enrolment starts** setting will be set to the execution date and time of the rule.
Duration	If enabled, the **Enrolment duration** parameter will be set to the specified number of days; otherwise, it will be **Unlimited**.
Group name	If specified, the users will be added to the group as members. The group has to exist; otherwise, the group membership will be ignored.

Figure 5.21 – The enrolment action parameters

The enrolment will be activated immediately after the action has been executed.

> **Important note**
> The **Dynamic rule** enrolment method has to be enabled in the site administration for automatic course enrolment to function.

Figure 5.22 – Enrol users into a course action

The **Unenrol users from a course** action supports two settings, both of which are compulsory:

- **Course**: The name of the course to unenroll users from.

- **Action**: The way the user should be unenrolled from the course. The options are as follows:

  a) **Disable enrolment**: The user's access to the course is disabled, but the course role isn't removed. This is equivalent to suspending the user's enrollment; it still appears in the grade book and completion report, the user just can't access the course anymore.

  b) **Disable enrolment and remove roles**: This is the same as the previous step, plus the user's course role is removed. That way, access to the course is suspended and its appearance in the completion report is hidden, but the user is still enrolled in the course.

  c) **Unenrol user from course**: The user is no longer enrolled in the course and all records, such as the progress report, have been removed.

Certifications and programs

Certifications and programs are closely related as the former is based on the latter. More about these will be covered in *Chapter 6, Onboarding and Compliance*. As you can see in the following side-by-side screenshots, **Allocate users to programs** and **Allocate users to certifications** look and work in exactly the same way; you select a program or a certification that users have to be allocated to, choose the **Start date** (keep the defaults or select a fixed date), and save the changes as usual:

Figure 5.23 – The allocate users to programs and certificates actions

You also have the option to **Deallocate users from programs** and **Deallocate users from Certificates**. However, users can only be unallocated if they were allocated by another dynamic rule; manual program and certification allocations will not be affected. The reason for this restriction is the way the allocation and deallocation of programs and certifications work. A user who has been added manually can only be removed manually; a user who has been allocated via a dynamic rule can only be deallocated via a dynamic rule. This will become clearer once you have worked through some programs and certifications in the next chapter.

This completes the list of actions available in Moodle Workplace. Let's move on to the final step of rule enablement and look at how rules are being processed.

Rule enablement and processing

Once you have finished specifying your conditions and actions, your rule is complete. Well, almost. There is one small step missing, which is the activation of the rule via the **Enable** button. The enablement and consequent execution of a dynamic rule is the topic of this section.

> **Important note**
> A rule requires at least one condition and one action to be enabled.

Before enabling a rule, you are shown a notification to remind you how many users will be affected. Once enabled, rules will be executed as an ad hoc task during the next **cron** run.

Prior to processing a rule, each condition and action is validated for correctness. If at some point in the future a rule fails validation, it will be disabled automatically and flagged as containing an error. An example of such an inconsistency is a course that no longer exists:

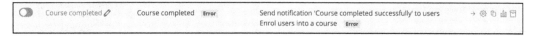

Figure 5.24 – Erroneous condition and action

Validation occurs each time a rule is processed. To re-enable an erroneous rule, it must be edited and corrected. A rule cannot be edited when it is enabled; so, a rule will be disabled automatically before editing can commence. However, you can change the rule header (the name and matching frequency) while a rule is enabled.

Next up is rule reporting, which keeps track of any enabled and processed rules.

Rule reporting

Moodle Workplace keeps an internal log, protocolling every single rule execution. You can view the log of a rule via the standard report icon. For every user that matches the condition, the following information is displayed: **First name**, **Surname**, **Email address**, **Matched time**, and **Unmatched time**. The latter entry takes into account the rule action limit logic described earlier in the chapter, as shown here:

First name	Surname	Email address		Matched time	Unmatched time
Amanda	Weaver	Amanda.Weaver@mail.com		9/02/20, 01:44	9/02/20, 09:44
Aquila	Shelton	Aquila.Shelton@mail.com		9/02/20, 01:44	
Ariel	Rodriquez	Ariel.Rodriquez@mail.com		9/02/20, 01:44	
Amy	Payne	Amy.Payne@mail.com		9/02/20, 09:44	

Comma separated values (.csv)
Microsoft Excel (.xlsx)
HTML table
Javascript Object Notation (.json)
OpenDocument (.ods)
✓ Portable Document Format (.pdf)

Download table data as   Download

Figure 5.25 – Rule report

You also can download the displayed report in various supported file formats, namely CSV, XLSX, HTML, JSON, ODS, and PDF. You can reduce or re-arrange the formats in that list in **Site administration | Plugins | Data formats | Manage data formats**.

Rule archiving and deletion

When a rule is not required anymore, it should be archived or removed entirely; both operations are covered in this section. That way, you keep the active rules list tidy and know which rules are currently being processed and which were processed in the past.

The archiving of a dynamic rule takes place via the standard archive icon beside the rule. Archived dynamic rules are still available for current and future reports, which might be required in an auditing scenario or when an error has occurred. In this screenshot, you can see two archived rules:

Active	Archived	

Archived rules

Name	Conditions	Actions	
UK & Ireland	Users who have completed course 'Our Sales Philosophy' User is allocated to department 'UK & Ireland'	Send notification 'Well done' to users Issue certificate 'Certification' to users	📊 ◇ 🗑
Certifications	User is allocated to department 'R&D' User has position 'Team Member'	Enrol in course 'Post-Sales Activities'	📊 ◇ 🗑

Figure 5.26 – Archived dynamic rules

An archived rule is preserved for future reference and can be unarchived via the standard restore icon. It can further be removed permanently using the standard delete icon.

What's the difference between disabling and archiving a dynamic rule? Technically, you can disable all rules you don't need anymore, but that wouldn't be good practice. As a general rule—pardon the pun—you should disable rules that are currently works in progress or deactivated temporarily. All other rules should be archived or, if neither the rule nor the report is needed anymore, deleted.

Limiting the number of rules

By default, there is no limit on the number of dynamic rules, unless one has been specified. Your site administrator can restrict the number of dynamic rules that can be created per site and tenant by adding the following lines to the config.php site configuration file:

```
$CFG->tool_dynamicrule_limitsenabled = true;
$CFG->tool_dynamicrule_sitelimit = <VALUE>;
$CFG->tool_dynamicrule_tenantlimit = <VALUE>;
```

Beware that archived rules are also counted toward the limit(s). However, rules created automatically by other plugins—for example, programs and certifications— are not counted toward the limit. Omitting this configuration, or setting the tool_dynamicrule_limitsenabled config value to false, indicates that no limit will be applied to the number of dynamic rules that can be created. Note that the tenant limit cannot exceed the site limit; setting values to 0 will effectively disable dynamic rule creation.

This completes the main section about managing dynamic rules in Moodle Workplace. I hope you agree that they provide a great vehicle for optimizing your day-to-day processes and automating your internal learning management system workflows. Particularly for repetitive tasks, you can achieve substantial time savings. To provide you with a few ideas about how dynamic rules can be applied in real-world scenarios, we have created a dedicated section on automating Workplace processes.

Automating Workplace processes

The dynamic rules feature is one of the key differentiators between Moodle Workplace and standard Moodle. Its flexibility and versatility allow the automation of numerous processes within your LMS. The limit to what types of processes you wish to implement is only restricted by your creativity. Oh, and the current set of available conditions and actions, of course.

In this section, we will first outline a number of representative workflows that might be of use to you. We will then conclude the chapter with some tips on dynamic rules, which also includes performance considerations.

Sample Workplace workflows

You probably have a few ideas already about which workflows you wish to optimize. In this section, we have selected three processes that make use of dynamic rules. The sample workflows that are outlined here are the following:

- Promoting new courses
- Keeping your user base current
- Subscription-based courses

We deliberately will not cover some of the more obvious workflows, such as onboarding and compliance processes, since they are described in a later chapter.

Promoting new courses

Let's assume the wiz-kids from your content production department have created two new courses: **Mentoring Basics** and **Mentoring Advanced**. These offerings should now be promoted by the marketing department because there has been negative feedback from some junior members due to a lack of mentoring activity. We propose the following two dynamic rules:

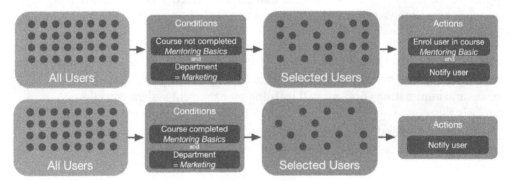

Figure 5.27 – Workflows—promoting new courses

The first rule is targeting all staff from the marketing department who have not completed the **Mentoring Basics** course. They will be automatically enrolled in the basics course and will also receive a notification. The **Conditions** part could be refined further by adding a condition to exclude users who have completed the advanced course and maybe to exclude anybody who holds a senior position, such as the marketing VP.

The second rule is aimed at all marketeers who have completed the **Mentoring Basics** course. The advanced course will be recommended to them in a notification. This type of recommendation is a useful mechanism in other scenarios, too.

Keeping your user base current

If your user data is being managed entirely in Moodle Workplace, keeping your user base current can be challenging. This might also be the case for externals, such as sub-contractors or freelancers, when you store your employee data in an HR system.

Let's assume you aim to send all users in your Workplace system who have not logged in for at least 3 months a reminder message and if no login has taken place within a 1-month grace period, delete them from the LMS. Given the currently available set of conditions and actions, this is only partly achievable using dynamic rules and requires some extra manual steps. The process is shown in the following diagram, where the dotted line denotes a manual step:

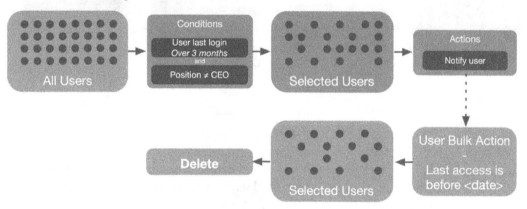

Figure 5.28 – Workflow—keeping your user base current

The automated part of the workflow is relatively straightforward: all users who have not logged in in 3 months will be sent a notification. You might want to reduce the scope of the **Conditions** clause further if you wish (here, we have excluded the position of CEO). We would also set the matching frequency to one run per day or even week.

Ideally, we would create a second rule that would select all users who have not logged in for 4 months (3 months plus the 1-month grace period) and then suspend or delete them. Unfortunately, this action is not available at the time of writing, and we have to make use of the **Bulk user actions** feature in **Site administration | Users**. Here, you enable the **Last access** filter and set the **is before** date to 4 months prior to today. Then, you select all users that satisfy this condition and apply the **Delete** option.

The proposed solution is not ideal, but it demonstrates nicely how to combine dynamic rules with other Moodle tools to semi-automate processes in your Moodle Workplace system.

Subscription-based courses

Let's assume your organization offers access to monthly courses via a subscription. To facilitate this, you have grouped your users into different cohorts, say **P1**, **P2**, and **P3**, where each cohort represents a product offering. You have further arranged courses into programs, where each program contains the three courses of a quarter (for example, **P1Q1**, **P1Q2**, **P1Q3**, and **P1Q4**). Every time a new course is published, it will be added to the appropriate program. To assign customers of product subscribers **P1** to their content, the following dynamic rule is proposed:

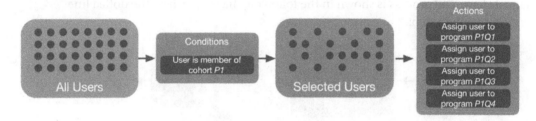

Figure 5.29 – Workflow—subscription-based courses

This workflow assigns every user from the **P1** cohort to the four programs: **P1Q1**, **P1Q2**, **P1Q3**, and **P1Q4**. You might want to consider starting with only the first program and then add the second program to the rule in April, the third program in July, and the last one in October. Otherwise, the subscriber would have access to an empty program that doesn't contain any courses yet.

The three samples provided have hopefully demonstrated the versatility of dynamic rules, but also the limitations that currently exist. New conditions and actions that will be added in future versions will allow more automation of your Workplace processes.

Dynamic rules tips

Managing dynamic rules can be a daunting task at first, so let's look at some common pitfalls when getting started with this topic.

Rule testing

One of the most critical tasks during automating processes is **testing**, as there is no undo button!

> **Important note**
> Actions that have already been taken cannot be undone. Once an action has been executed, it cannot be reversed.

Ideally, you will have a separate test environment that mirrors your production site, where you can test new dynamic rules before implementing them on your live site. Make sure notifications have been disabled to avoid managers receiving emails about their staff running late in a compulsory compliance course when in fact, you are testing out all the notification placeholders (go to **Enable messaging system** in **Site administration | Messaging | Messaging settings**).

Modeling OR logic

Some confusion still exists, since all conditions are logically connected via AND operations. The question of how to implement OR logic arises; for example, how to model the following condition:

```
IF (user completed course1 OR course2 OR course3) AND (user is
member of department1 OR department2) THEN ...
```

You have no choice but to decompose the condition and use the following six separate rules:

```
IF user completed course1 AND user is member of department1
THEN ...
IF user completed course1 AND user is member of department2
THEN ...
IF user completed course2 AND user is member of department1
THEN ...
IF user completed course2 AND user is member of department2
THEN ...
IF user completed course3 AND user is member of department1
THEN ...
IF user completed course3 AND user is member of department2
THEN ...
```

This is far from ideal, especially when there are more cases to be covered and the number of permutations increases significantly. This required decomposition is also likely to have an impact on performance, which we will look at next.

Performance considerations

It is very tempting to automate every possible process that can be automated. However, you should consider the **performance** of your Moodle Workplace system when creating multiple dynamic rules, especially in large-scale implementations.

As mentioned earlier, dynamic rules are processed during the execution of the **cron** process, which is usually scheduled to run every 60 seconds. Now, consider the number of checks (conditions) and potential executions (actions) in a system with a few thousand users. The load on the system will be significant and is likely to have a serious impact on the performance of your LMS.

The following is a list of tips to take into account when managing dynamic rules in Moodle Workplace, some probably more obvious than others:

- Reduce the number of conditions and actions whenever possible.

- Avoid conditions that contradict each other.

- Check whether a rule can be simplified using cohorts instead of multiple conditions.

- Check whether the rule can be implemented as a program; for example, users have to complete course 1 before getting access to course 2 and moving on to course 3.

- Disable rules that are currently not used and archive rules that are not needed anymore.

- Use matching frequency whenever possible to reduce the number of times conditions are checked.

The implementation of dynamic rules in Workplace has been built with performance in mind. However, the overuse of rules, especially when not necessary, can impact any system, no matter how well designed. With that in mind, we have come to the end of this chapter on one of the most exciting features in Moodle Workplace: dynamic rules.

Summary

In this chapter, you have learned how to automate processes in Moodle Workplace using dynamic rules, which comprise the rule body, rule conditions, and rule actions. All three parts have been discussed in great detail before you dealt with the auxiliary topics of rule enablement, processing, reporting, archiving, and deleting. You should now be fully equipped with the tools needed to set up an LMS workflow.

Finally, you have put the skills you have learned into action, acquiring skills for working with some sample Workplace workflows and dynamic rules tips, including performance considerations.

The beauty of dynamic rules is that they are pluggable, which means new conditions and actions can be programmed by Moodle developers when and if required. Expect additional conditions, actions, and properties to appear in future versions of Moodle Workplace and possibly in the plugin database of `moodle.org`.

Two Workplace components have implemented their own dynamic rules feature, namely programs and certifications. These closely related features are the topic of the next chapter, where we will look at onboarding and compliance.

6
Onboarding and Compliance

Programs and certifications are two key features of Moodle Workplace. Programs allow you to establish learning pathways for your employees by adding a combination of courses or a hierarchical sequence of courses. Certifications allow you to validate learning paths by offering certifications for recurring programs.

You may ask what this chapter's title has to do with these two Workplace features. Well, onboarding is the (stereo)typical example usually used in programs, and compliance with certifications. However, neither programs nor certifications are limited to these two use cases; other requirements, such as the building of curricula or constructing multilingual qualifications, can easily be modeled, too.

First, you will learn how to manage programs. After covering program basics, you will create your own program, adding different types of content and providing scheduling information. Next, you will learn how to add users manually and in batch mode before we will cover various reporting options. In addition to automating processes via dynamic rules, we will deal with manual interventions for programs. We will also cover how to share content across tenants via programs.

Second, you will become familiar with certifications, which are built on top of programs. We will cover the foundations of certifications again before you learn all the ins and outs of initial certification paths and recertification.

Finally, you will be able to apply all your acquired skills by modeling a typical onboarding and compliance workflow. This process makes use not only of programs and certifications but also of tools you have already met, such as organizational data and dynamic rules.

So, by the end of this chapter, you will know how to manage programs and certifications and, more importantly, apply the two tools to your onboarding and compliance processes. The chapter comprises three main parts:

- Managing programs
- Managing certifications
- Modeling onboarding and compliance workflows

Managing programs

Before we get started, let's deal with the basic structure of programs. A program consists of courses and sets; both are optional can be arranged in any order. A set contains one or more courses that have to be completed. Interestingly, a set can also contain another set, a great vehicle for creating hierarchical curricula. The recursive structure of programs is depicted in the following diagram:

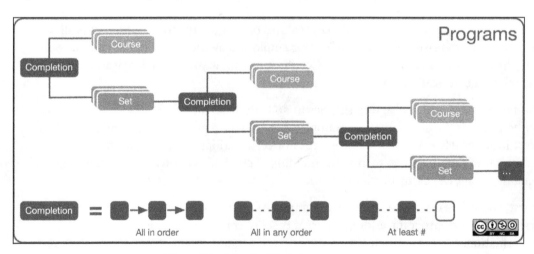

Figure 6.1 – Moodle Workplace programs

An interesting feature is the flexible way that the completion of all elements and completion within sets can be defined. There are three different types of completion you can choose from:

- **All in order**: All courses must be completed in the order specified.

- **All in any order**: All courses must be completed but in no particular order.

- **At least #**: At least # courses must be completed, in no particular order.

For the **Backus-Naur form** (**BNF**) connoisseurs among you, here is the structure of programs in a more formal notation (BNF is used to describe the syntax of languages):

```
<program> = <completion> <content> {<content>}
<content> = course | <set>
<set> = <completion> <content> | <set>
<completion> = All in order | All in any order | At least #
```

OK, enough of the theory; let's put things into practice and create our first program. The remainder of this section comprises the following sub-sections:

- Program details

- Program content

- Program schedule

- Program users

- Program dynamic rules

- Program progress reporting

- Sharing content across tenants

Even if you have no immediate need for programs, you should still read this section, especially if you are planning to implement certifications, which are based on programs.

Program details

You can access the management of programs via **Site administration | Learning | Programs** or directly via the **Programs** icon in the Workplace launcher, shown here:

Figure 6.2 – Programs in the Workplace launcher

You will see a list of active programs. In our example instance, we have already created four programs, one of which is associated with a certification and one is a shared program. To the right of each program, you will see the usual Workplace icons (edit, details, duplicate, show/hide, users, report, and archive):

Figure 6.3 – Active programs

To create a new program, click on the **+ New program** icon on the **Active programs** page. You will then be greeted with a long pop-up screen and a range of program details, as shown:

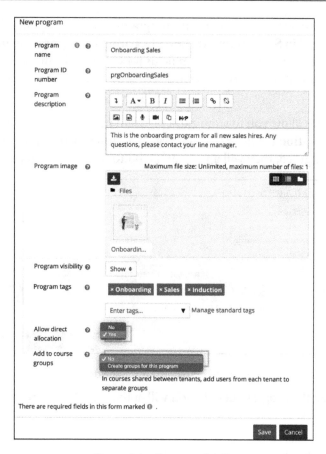

Figure 6.4 – Program details

The following table lists all the program details fields, alongside a short description:

Setting	Description
Program name (Required)	The name of the program which is displayed in the list of active programs and the users' dashboards.
Program ID number	Unique ID number that is used by web services (see *Appendix A*) and Moodle's upload user tool (see *Allocating users to programs in batch mode* section later on).
Program description	Summary of program which is displayed on the users' dashboards.
Program image	Program picture which is displayed on users' dashboards. Supported formats are JPG, PNG, and GIF.
Program visibility	Toggle indicating whether program is shown users' dashboard and if it can be accessed.
Program tags	Tags to be shown on **Active programs** list.
Allow direct allocation	If enabled, users can be allocated directly to this program.
Add to course groups	If enabled, users will be added to a course group when they get enrolled in the course. The name of the group is the same as the program; it will be created automatically when it doesn't exist. This will be covered in more detail later when we deal with sharing programs across tenants.

Figure 6.5 – The program details fields

Moodle Workplace supports custom fields for programs. These user-defined program properties are managed in **Site administration | Learning | Programs customs fields** and they work in exactly the same way as custom fields for courses (for more details, see the Moodle documentation at `docs.moodle.org/en/Course_settings#Course_custom_fields`).

Program custom fields allow you to store extra program information—for instance, **CPD Points, Expected duration (in hours)**, or **Chargeable (internal)?**. If program custom fields have been configured, they will appear at the bottom of the program details form:

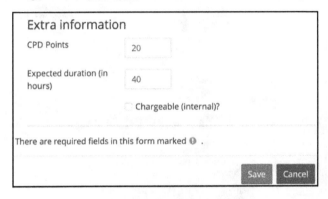

Figure 6.6 – Program custom fields

Once you have saved the program details, you will automatically be directed to the program's **Content** tab.

Program content

The program content contains the courses, sets, and completion types, as described at the beginning of this chapter. Let's start by adding two courses to the program. When you select the + icon at the top right, a drop-down menu will appear with two options. You need to choose the first—**Course:**

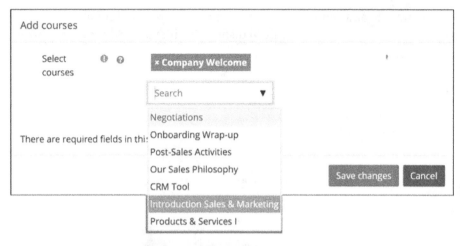

Figure 6.7 – Adding a course to a program

From the course drop-down menu, you can select as many courses as you wish. Each course will be treated as a separate program entry. Save the changes and add a set, using the same + button as before, but this time selecting the **Set** option:

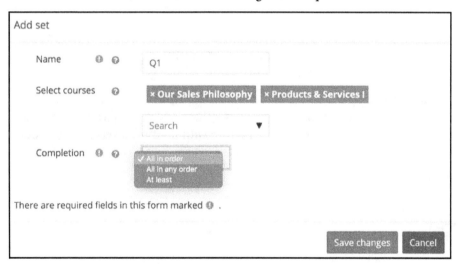

Figure 6.8 – Adding a set to a program

A course set has the following three properties:

- **Name**: Provide the name of the course set.

- **Select courses**: Select one or many courses.

- **Completion**: Pick one of the three completion types—**All in order**, **All in any order**, or **At least**.

You might also want to add some more courses and sets to your program. Once completed, the content of your program will display in a hierarchical form, as shown:

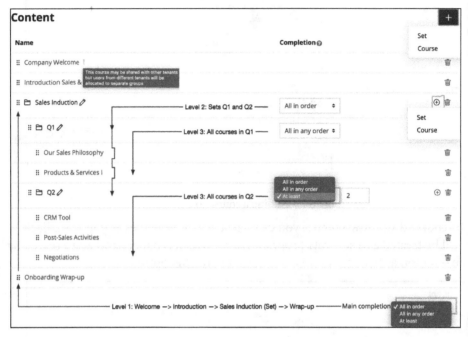

Figure 6.9 – Program content

In this sample onboarding program, you can nicely see which completion type belongs to which set. The preceding screenshot also shows that a set can be part of another set, effectively creating a hierarchical content structure with multiple levels (three, in our example).

To remove any courses or sets, select the delete icon in the same row and confirm the warning shown.

> **Important Note**
> Be careful when you remove a set because all elements in the set—courses and other sub-sets—will also be removed.

SIDEBAR – course and activity completion

There are different ways in which the progress of learning can be tracked. Moodle supports grades, competencies, badges, activity completion, and course completion. Course completion is used by programs to monitor progress and drive progression states, such as **Overdue** and **Completed**.

Course completion is usually based on **activity completion**; for each learning resource or activity, the learner can reach the completion state by fulfilling a pre-defined criterion; for example, successfully finishing a SCORM package. Activity completion criteria are specified in the settings of the respective resource or activity; the conditions depend on the type of activity at hand.

Once all the required criteria have been fulfilled, the course is complete. Additional confirmation might be required by an authorized user; for instance, a manager confirming the knowledge of an on-the-job operation, such as handling credit cards or operating a machine. Course completion is specified at the course level and can be monitored via the **Course completion** status block:

Criteria	Email address	Induction Program	Participants Introduction	Seminar	Assessment	Feedback Questionnaire	Course complete
First name / Surname	Email address						
Charissa Baldwin	Charissa.Baldwin@mail.com	☑	☑	☐	☐	☐	☐
Stone Barlow	Stone.Barlow@mail.com	☑	☑	☑	☑	☑	☑
Hector Barry	Hector.Barry@mail.com	☑	☑	☑	☐	☐	☐
Bianca Bass	Bianca.Bass@mail.com	☑	☑	☑	☑	☐	☐
Flavia Bates	Flavia.Bates@mail.com	☑	☑	☑	☑	☑	☑
Rhea Baxter	Rhea.Baxter@mail.com	☐	☐	☐	☐	☐	☐

Figure 6.10 – Course and activity completion

More details on these two topics can be found at `docs.moodle.org/en/Course_completion` (for course completion) and `docs.moodle.org/en/Activity_completion` (for activity completion).

END SIDEBAR

It is possible to change the structure of a program after users have been assigned to a program and even once it has been successfully completed. The impact of this modification, which is not recommended, is described when the different program statuses are covered later on.

Program schedule

A schedule lets you specify various dates that are relevant to the program. Under the program's **Schedule** tab, you can specify the availability and allocation times for the program. All date values have at least the following two **absolute** options:

- **Not set**: No date has been specified yet (default).
- **Select date**: You explicitly provide a date.

Additional options are **relative** to another date and have the **# days, weeks, months**, and **years** formats. For the **Availability** and **Allocation window** sections, these are as follows.

The **Availability** section defines a start and end date, during which time a user can **access** the program. You can specify the following date parameters:

- **Start date**: The first date that the user can start working on the program. In addition to the two absolute options, there is a single relative setting called **After user allocation date**.
- **Due date**: The time that the user should have completed the program by. In addition to the two absolute options, the available relative settings are **After start date, After user allocation date**, and **Before end date**.
- **End date**: The last date that the user can access the program. The values are the usual two absolute options, plus **After start date, After due date**, and **After user allocation date**.

Allocation window defines when a user can be **allocated** to a program and contains the following values:

- **Start date**: The first day that the allocation can take place (manually, dynamically, or via code).
- **End date**: The last day that the allocation can take place.

The preceding options provide you with a high degree of flexibility to model all feasible scheduling options for your programs. For example, the start date might be immediately after the allocation date, with a due date 1 month later:

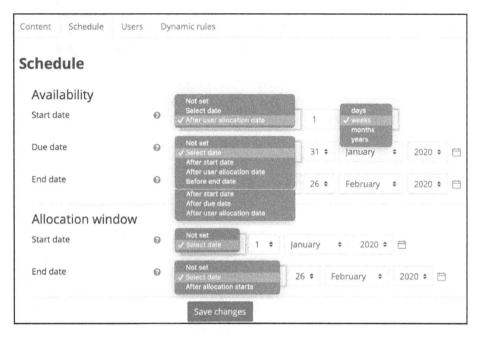

Figure 6.11 – Program schedule settings

So far, we have specified what a program contains (content) and when the program is available and users can be allocated (schedule), respectively. Now, let's actually allocate some users to the program.

Program users

In this sub-section, we are going to look at different options for how to allocate users to programs. In addition to the program schedule, this is the second prerequisite for a user to get access to the program content. There are five ways that users can be allocated to programs:

- **Manually**: See the following sub-section.

- **In batch mode, using Moodle's user upload tool**: See the following sub-section.

- **Automatically via dynamic rules**: We already discussed this option in *Chapter 5, Automation and Dynamic Rules.*

- **Via certifications**: See the *Certifications* section in the second half of this chapter.

- **Programmatically via web services**: Refer to *Appendix A.*

We will only cover the first two items here since the other three variants are dealt with elsewhere in this book.

Manually allocating users to programs

Managers have permission to manually allocate team members to programs; administrators and all users with the `tool/program:allocateuser` capability have the right to allocate all users to programs. Select the **User** tab of a program and use the **Allocate users** button to manually add users to the program. This will present you with a screen where you have to select users (one or many) and choose the status of those users in the program, as shown:

Figure 6.12 – Manually allocating users to a program

The status of every user in the program is either **Active** (by default) or **Suspended**. Why would you suspend a user when you allocate them to a program? You might be preparing for a new batch of interns who are starting next month but shouldn't be able to access the program yet. Once you have saved these changes, you will be shown a table with all the added users. In our example, you can already see the progress (or lack thereof) of each user allocated to the program after they have started working through their content:

Figure 6.13 – The program users

The **Users** tab contains the following textual columns:

Field	Description
Full name	First name and last name
Due date	Date when the user is expected to have completed the program, which is either **Not set** or a date. The date is either driven by the **Due date** in the **Availability** section of the **Schedule** or it has been overridden by the manager. If latter is the case, a warning symbol is displayed beside the date.
Allocation source	The value of this column indicates how the user has been allocated to the program. There are the following three options: • **Manual**: manually as shown above, in batch mode, or via web services • **Dynamic**: via a dynamic rule • **Certification**: as part of a certification
Certification name	If the program is part of a certification, its name will be displayed here. Details in the *Certification* section.
Certification status	If the program is part of a certification, the user's status will be displayed here. Details in the *Certification* section.
Program status	There are five program states a user can have: **Open** — The user has not completed the program yet and the due date has not been reached. **Overdue** — The user is running late in completing the program. **Completed** — The user has successfully finished the program. **Future allocation** — The user's start date is set in the future. **Suspended** — The user's program allocation has been suspended. Its entry in the table will be greyed out. Bear in mind that this is not related to a user's account suspension. Be vigilant when you change the structure of a program after users have successfully completed a program. Once the status of a program for a user has been set to **Completed**, it will not be changed when courses or sets are added or removed.

Figure 6.14 – Program users' details

Additionally, there are five actions that can be performed on each user allocated to a program, each represented by an icon beside the status column in the list of program users.

Editing user allocation

Managers and other users with the `tool/program:edit` capability have permission to manually override the scheduling information of users. This is useful if a team member is unable to complete a program due to a long-term illness or maternity/paternity leave:

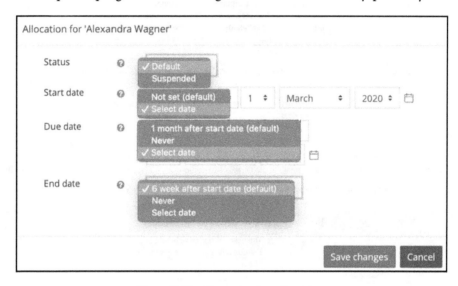

Figure 6.15 – User program allocation

The following scheduling fields can be overridden:

- **Status**: The same values as before, namely **Default** (active) and **Suspended**
- **Start date**: **Default** (as defined in **Schedule**) or a hardcoded date
- **Due date**: **Default** (as defined in **Schedule**), **Never**, or a hardcoded date
- **End date**: **Default** (as defined in **Schedule**), **Never**, or a hardcoded date

Performing a program reset

When this action is carried out, all completion data will be deleted; that is, any course completion data of that user is reset in all courses of the program. This action cannot be undone!

Managers or users with the `tool/program:coursereset` capability are able to reset programs.

The execution of resetting a user's program progress will take place during the next **cron** run and might take a few minutes to complete.

There is a dedicated reporting source called **Course reset for individual user** that provides detailed information about program and certification resets. We will deal with this in detail in *Chapter 8, Generating Custom Reports*.

Viewing the user progress report

As the name suggests, the user progress report provides advancement details for each user allocated to a program. The user progress report offers a detailed breakdown of all the elements in the program:

Onboarding Sales : Knox Irwin
Dashboard / Knox Irwin / Programs / Onboarding Sales

Type	Name	Completion criteria	Parent name	Progress
Set	Q2	Complete at least 2	Sales Induction	0%
Course	Products & Services I	-	Q1	66%
Course	Negotiations	-	Q2	0%
Set	Q1	Complete all in any order	Sales Induction	50%
Course	Introduction Sales & Marketing	-	Base set	100%
Course	Post-Sales Activities	-	Q2	0%
Course	Onboarding Wrap-up	-	Base set	0%
Set	Onboarding Sales (Base set)	Complete all in order	-	42%
Set	Sales Induction	Complete all in order	Base set	25%
Course	Company Welcome	-	Base set	100%

1　2　»

Figure 6.16 – User progress report

The user progress report is of particular interest to managers when monitoring the step-by-step progression of each team member.

Showing the user progress overview

The user progress overview opens a modal window, which is identical to the view on a user's dashboard. Here, an example user progress overview is shown:

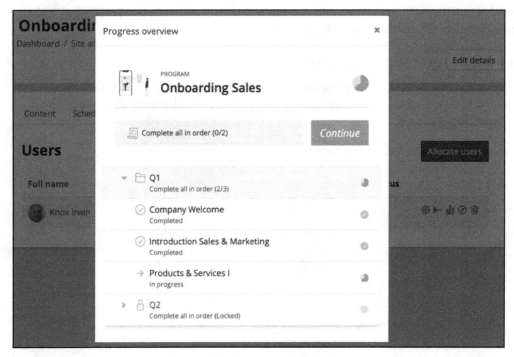

Figure 6.17 – User progress overview

Deleting user allocation

This removes the user and all associated data from the program. This action cannot be undone! This option is only available if **Allocation source** is set to **manual**.

Allocating users to programs in batch mode

Uploading users in bulk allows the importing of multiple user accounts from a text file or the updating of user accounts that already exist in your system. We already used this mechanism to add users to tenants in batches. The CSV file import has been extended to support programs with the following fields (all require a numeric suffix and all dates have to be specified in the YYYY-MM-DD ISO standard format):

- `programstartdate`: The program start date
- `programenddate`: The program end date
- `programduedate`: The program due date

Once you have created your CSV file, go to **Users | Accounts | Upload users** in the **Site administration** section and follow the upload process using your CSV file. The following is a sample CSV file, adding two users to our sales onboarding program:

```
username;program1,programstartdate1,programenddate1,
programduedate1
user1,prgOnboardingSales,2020-02-26,,2020-03-31
user2,prgOnboardingSales,2020-02-26,2020-04-30,
```

The allocation source for allocating users in batch mode is manual; the same holds for allocating users via web services, which has an impact when deallocating users from programs.

Important Note

Users can only be removed from a program at the source of allocation.

So, users with a **manual** allocation source can only be deleted manually, in batch mode, or via web services; users with a **dynamic** allocation source can only be deleted via the **Deallocate users from programs** dynamic rule condition; and users with a **certification** allocation source can only be deallocated within the corresponding certification.

Program dynamic rules

We dedicated the whole of the previous chapter to dynamic rules, and they also feature support for programs both in conditions and actions. Tools can have their own dynamic rules, and programs make use of this mechanism. Local dynamic rules give you quick access to some rules that affect the program and are created by default:

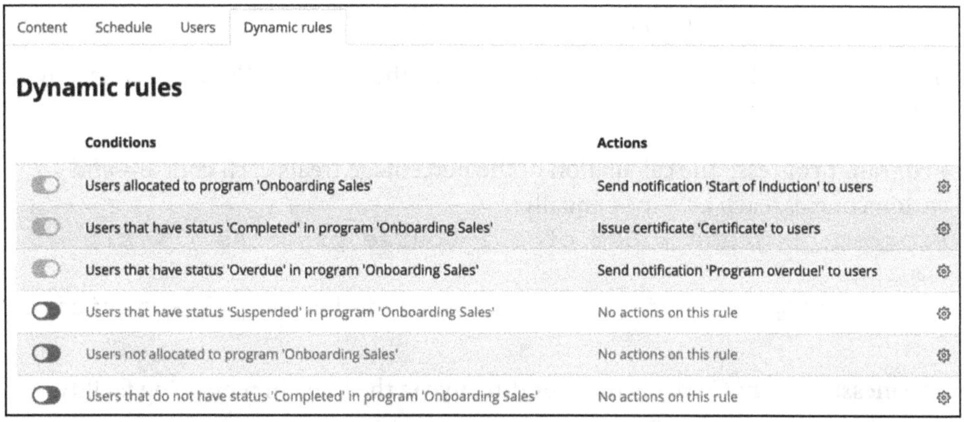

Figure 6.18 – Program dynamic rules

The six entries in the **Dynamic rules** tab are shown in the previous screenshot. The purpose of each condition should be self-explanatory; the **Conditions** part has already been dealt with in *Chapter 5*, *Automation and Dynamic Rules*. You can only change the actions of each rule; the conditions remain fixed. Make sure you enable each dynamic rule that has been configured.

Local dynamic rules save you from having to create lots of global rules and keep everything in a single place, which enhances the user experience when dealing with programs.

Program progress reporting

In addition to the user progress report mentioned previously, Moodle Workplace also offers a program progress report that provides a more detailed view of the data presented so far. You can access the progress report via the report icon on the **Active programs** screen. It looks very similar to the **User** view, except it provides additional information and drill-down options:

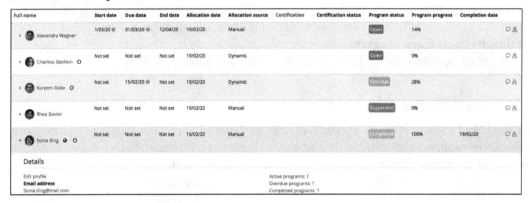

Figure 6.19 – Program progress report

All of the fields should look familiar by now and only the following three columns may require some explanation:

- **Program progress**: The calculation of the percentage treats each course—and within courses, each activity—equally:
  ```
  Program progress = SUM of all Course progress / # all
  courses
  Course progress = # completed activities/# all activities
  * 100
  ```

- **The message icon**: Contacts the user directly via the built-in messaging facility.

- **The profile icon**: Shows the user's profile information.

When a row is expanded, the same information is displayed as in the **Teams** tab on the manager dashboard. When you select any of the links (here, **Active programs**, **Overdue programs**, and **Completed programs**), you will be directed to a report that shows programs filtered by **Program status**:

Figure 6.20 – A user's program progress report

This report doesn't really provide any additional information apart from two familiar links, which are represented as icons in the right-hand side column.

You can also reach the same report(s) for individual participants from the **Learning** section on the user's profile.

Sharing content across tenants

In this sub-section, we will briefly look at two options of how to share content across tenants via programs. There are two dimensions to this, namely sharing courses across tenants in a single program and programs in the shared space. Both variants are covered in the following two sub-sections.

Sharing courses across tenants

You might have spotted the little attention icon in the shape of an exclamation mark next to the first course in our program example. This "company welcome" course is shared across tenants.

As an administrator, it is possible to add the same course to different programs that belong to different tenants. To grant this permission (adding courses to a program that is outside their own tenant's course category) to tenant admins or program managers, you need to assign the moodle/category:viewcourselist capability at the category context. The handling of programs will be the same as before, so program managers need to be vigilant when arranging courses in programs from different tenants.

If a course has been set up using separate groups, the attention icon will be shown. Users will be enrolled in the same course but won't have any visibility of each other. If the course has been configured using visible groups or no groups, the warning icon will be shown. Users from one tenant will be able to see users from other tenants—for instance, in the participants list or in collaborative activities, such as forums.

We introduced the concept of shared courses in *Chapter 4, Tenants, Organizations, and Teams*. All the laid-out principles and restrictions also apply to courses in programs. Make sure any trainer roles in the relevant course(s) do not have the `accessallgroups` capability, and trainers are also allocated to the relevant groups. Allocation to separate groups is done automatically when a shared course is part of a program (or certification).

Programs in the shared space

We introduced Moodle Workplace's shared course feature in *Chapter 4, Tenants, Organizations, and Teams*. We also mentioned that the two supported features are programs and certifications.

When you switch to shared space via the tenant switcher, you as an administrator can create and manage programs (and certifications) in exactly the same way as when in any other tenant. This program will then appear in the list of active programs in **all** tenants with the **Shared space** label displayed:

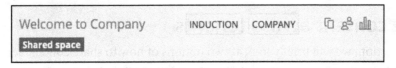

Figure 6.21 – Program in shared space

The range of actions has been restricted to duplicating the programs, allocating users, and accessing the program report. All other actions can only be performed when you manage the program from within the shared space.

This completes this section on one of Moodle Workplace's flagship features: programs. We have already mentioned certifications a few times because they are based on programs. The second part of this chapter deals with certifications and how mandatory compliance training can be modeled.

Managing certifications

Before we get started, let's deal with the basic concept of certifications. A certification comprises a single program or **recurring programs**, both of which expire after a certain amount of time. The renewal of the **initial certification**, known as **recertification**, either uses the same program or another program:

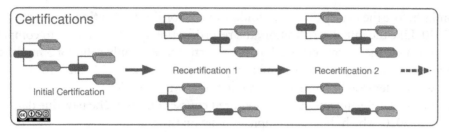

Figure 6.22 – Certifications structure

There are some program properties and actions that have been re-purposed to facilitate certifications, while others have been added:

- **Expiry date**: The time when a program's validity ends

- **Program reset**: Makes use of the reset function to facilitate recertification

- **Due date**: Used for both certification and recertification

We are going to use the certification example depicted in the following timeline to demonstrate the power of Moodle Workplace's certification tool. The example covers a range of typical cases in compliance workflows and demonstrates their implementation in Workplace:

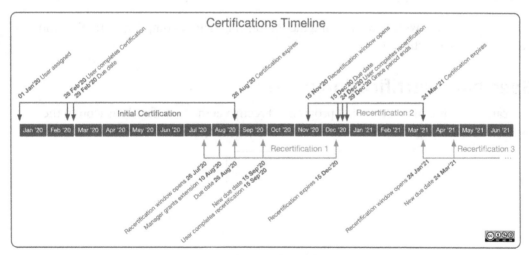

Figure 6.23 – A certification example

Let's take a closer look at the certification example representing a single user. The assignment for **Initial Certification** is January 20, 2020, with 2 months to complete the program. The user completes the task 3 days early, which is when the 6-month certification validity commences, so the expiry date is set to August 26, 2020.

Two months before the expiry date, the window opens for **Recertification 1**, which is on July 26, 2020. Like the initial certification, the recertification grants 2 months to complete the content. Unlike the initial certification, the recertification is only valid for 3 months and also requires the completion of a different program. On August 10, 2020, the manager grants a 3-week extension because their team member will be on leave most of the month and won't be able to complete the required courses on time. The new due date is September 15, 2020, which the user completes bang on time.

The first recertification expires on December 15, 2020, so the **Recertification 2** window opens 2 months before this date. It has been decided that going forward, a grace period of 2 weeks will be set to avoid manually modifying due dates. From now on, any future recertifications will be looked after by Workplace's certification mechanism, without the need for any intervention by the manager.

This section covers the following topics:

- Specifying certification details
- Configuring recertification
- Managing certification users
- Certification dynamic rules

OK, let's get started with implementing the sample mandatory compliance training and creating our first certification.

Specifying certification details

You can access the management of programs directly via the **Certifications** icon in the Workplace launcher or via **Site administration | Learning | Certifications**:

Figure 6.24 – The Certifications icon in the Workplace launcher

The screen showing **Active certifications** looks very similar to the one in **Active programs**, but with two notable differences: The **Program name** column of the initial certification is being displayed instead of **Associated certifications**, and the show/hide icon is not available:

Figure 6.25 – Active certifications

To create a new certification, select the **+ New certification** button and you will be greeted with a pop-up screen with a range of certification details:

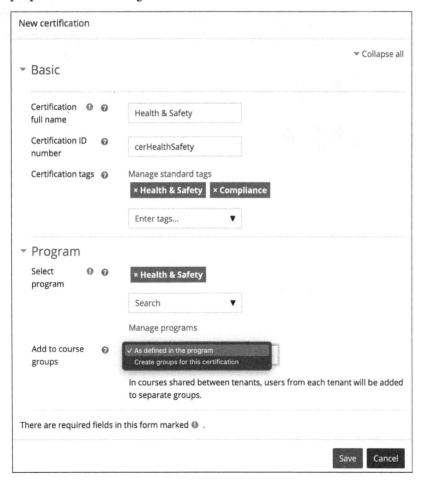

Figure 6.26 – New certification

Like the program, each certification has a compulsory **Certification full name** field, an optional **Certification ID number** field, and **Certification tags**. Additionally, you have to select a program and specify whether you wish to add users to groups **As defined in the program** or **Create groups for this certification**. Once you have saved the certification details, you will automatically be directed to the **Certification** tab, where details of the initial certification path are configured:

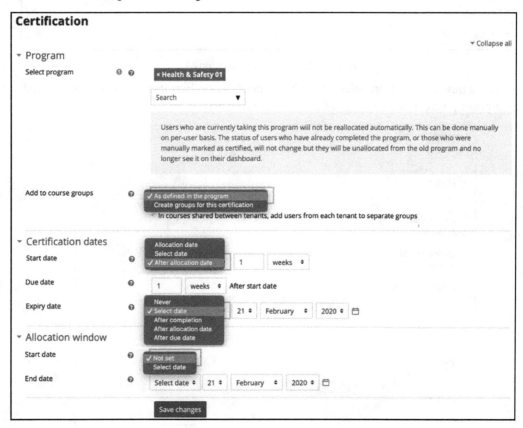

Figure 6.27 – Certification details

The program and group settings are the same as you just entered in the previous screen, but they can be modified at any time. Note the warning that is displayed underneath the chosen program:

> **Important Note**
> Users who are currently taking this program will not be reallocated automatically. This can be done manually on a per-user basis. The status of users who have already completed the program, or those who were manually marked as certified, will not change but they will be unallocated from the old program and will no longer see it on their dashboard.

What does this mean and is it relevant to you? Basically, if there are already users assigned to the certification and you make changes to any parameters, you have to be aware of the fact that the completion records of any certified users will not be affected by those modifications. So, if a user has already achieved a **Completed** status, either by successfully finishing the program or by being marked manually, the status will not change, even if the new certification requirements have not been achieved. This is relevant in a setup where the content of a training program has changed, possibly due to a change in legislation, so users who are already certified won't be affected until their recertification window opens. If they are affected, you will need to change their status manually.

The three values in the **Certification dates** section are effectively identical to their counterparts in the **Availability** section of the **Schedule** tab in programs, except that **End date** has been renamed to **Expiry date** to reflect the terminology of certifications. Equally, the two dates in **Allocation window** are the same as the ones in a program, with the exception that **End date** doesn't have the **After allocation starts** option since this wouldn't make any sense in a certification model.

There are no custom fields for certifications; if you require user-defined properties, you will need to specify these in the program's custom fields.

Configuring recertification

Recertification is the renewal of the initial certification, which we will configure next. By enabling the **Require recertification** parameter on the second tab, you will have to specify details of the recertification:

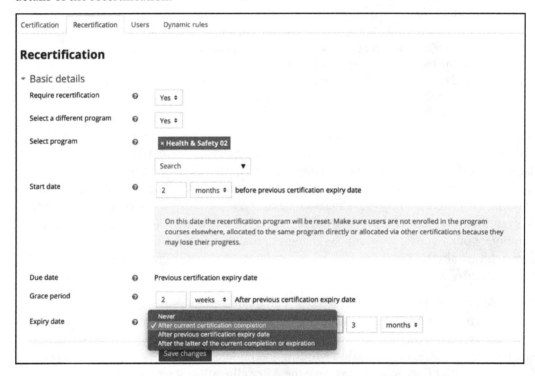

Figure 6.28 – Recertification details

Once recertification has been enabled, you will have to configure a range of parameters:

Setting	Description
Select a different program	If enabled, the recertification path uses a different program from the initial certification path. If disabled (default), the same program will be used.
Start date	This is when the user will be assigned to the program. If the user was previously assigned to the program, all completion records would be reset. Take into account the displayed warning: if users are directly enrolled in any courses outside the program, the resetting will be carried out nonetheless.
Due date	Is always the expiry date of the previous (re)certification. You can see this in the timeline where the last date of the certification *n* is the opening date of the recertification window *n+1*.
Grace period	Extra period of time given to finish the program to get certified after the previous certification expires. This option is only available if the recertification program is different from the initial program.
Expiry date	Same as before, but for the recertification.

Figure 6.29 – Recertification parameters

The values chosen in *Figure 6.28* reflect the requirements laid out in the timeline set out at the beginning of this section; a different program has been selected and the recertification window opens 2 months before the previous expiry date. A grace period of 2 weeks and a validity of 3 months have been specified.

> **Important Note**
>
> For recertification to work, make sure the initial certification is set to expire (not set to **Never**), or set the expiry dates individually.

Now that we have configured the initial certification, as well as the recertification paths, let's start adding users.

Managing certification users

In this sub-section, we are going to look at different options for how to allocate users to certifications. To manage users of the certification, select the **Users** tab. This view looks very similar to the program counterpart, but there are some notable differences:

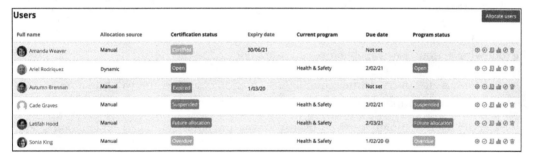

Figure 6.30 – Certification users

In the following table, you can see all the certification settings; a description has been provided for the ones that differ from their program counterparts:

Field	Description
Full name	Same as programs.
Allocation source	Same as programs.
Certification status	There are six certification states a user can have: `Open` Same as program. `Overdue` Same as program. `Certified` User has completed the program associated with the certification. `Expired` Recertification has started but is overdue. `Future allocation` Same as program. `Suspended` Same as program.
Expiry date	Date when current certification expired (date or **Never**).
Current program	Name of the current program; this might be different during initial certification and any recertifications.
Due date	Same as program.
Program status	Same as program.

Figure 6.31 – Certification settings

The following actions are available for each user allocated to the certificate:

- **Edit**: Manually override the schedule information of a user. You will find a more detailed explanation after this list.

- **Certify user**: Manually certify a user. You will find a more detailed explanation after this list.

- **Revoke certification**: Any completion data will be deleted; that is, any course completion data is reset in all courses of the program. This action cannot be undone! The execution of resetting a user's program progress will take place during the next **cron** run and might take a few minutes to complete.

- **Certification activity log**: You can find more details at the end of this sub-section.

- **Progress overview**: Same as programs.

- **Delete**: This removes the user and all associated data from the certification. This action cannot be undone! This option is only available if **Allocation source** is set to **manual**.

Managers and other users with the `tool/certificate:edit` capability have permission to manually override the scheduling information of users via the **Edit** icon. This intervention is useful if a team member is unable to complete a certification due to long-term illness, because of maternity/paternity leave, or any other circumstance that prevents the program from being completed on time. When you manually override a date, the warning icon will be shown beside **Due date** on the list of users:

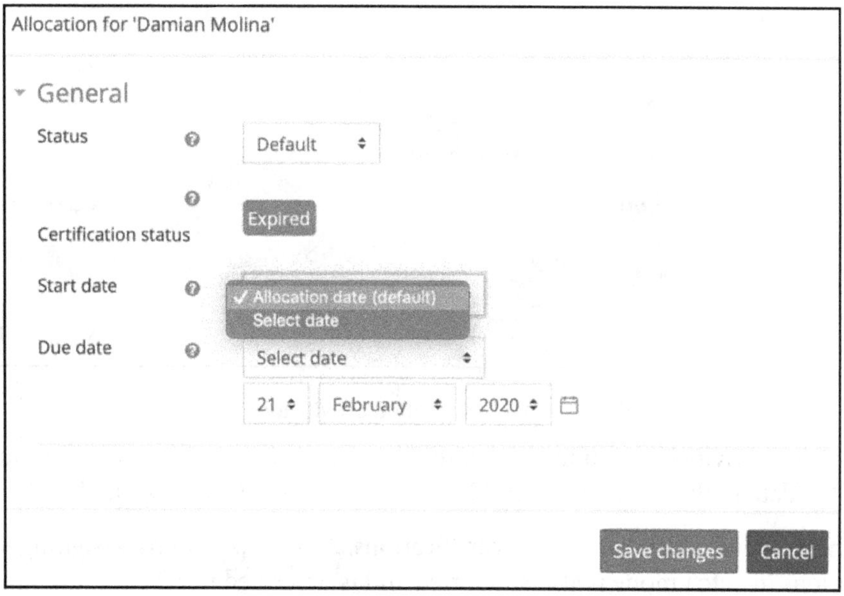

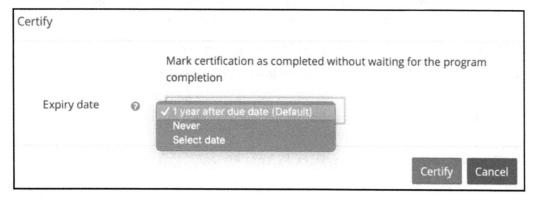

Figure 6.32 – User certification allocation

It is further possible to **manually certify** a user without having to wait for program completion. The **Expiry date** setting has been put on a separate screen where you can choose between the **1 year after due date (Default)**, **Never**, or **Select date** values:

Figure 6.33 – Manually certifying a user

Due to the fact that certifications often contain important information in compliance or mandatory learning settings, Moodle Workplace provides an activity log. The certification activity log is accessed via the logfile icon from the **User** view and shows a user's progress through an allocated certification. In the log shown in the following screenshot, three activities have been recorded, two manually by users and one automatically by the system:

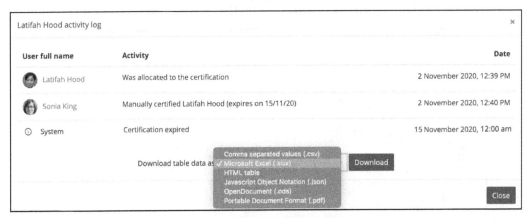

Figure 6.34 – Certification activity log

The certification activity log is an important tool during an auditing exercise. You can download the data in the usual formats: CSV, XLSX, HTML, JSON, ODS, and PDF.

So far, we have added users manually to certifications. As with programs, assigning users to certifications in batch mode is also supported and is described next.

Allocating users to certifications in batch mode

When dealing with large numbers of users, possibly spawning across multiple departments, manually managing certification allocations is not feasible and is prone to errors. As with programs, certifications support different channels to add users to certifications. There are four ways that users can be allocated to certifications:

- **Manually**: This is identical to manually adding users to programs.

- **In batch mode using Moodle's user upload tool**: This will be covered later in this section.

- **Automatically via dynamic rules**: We already discussed this in detail in *Chapter 5, Automation and Dynamic Rules*

- **Programmatically via web services**: Refer to *Appendix A*

We will only cover the second option—bulk upload—here since the other three variants are dealt with elsewhere. The CSV file import of Moodle core has been extended to support certifications with the following fields (all require a numeric suffix and all dates have to be specified in the YYYY-MM-DD ISO standard format):

- `certification`: Certification ID number
- `certificationstartdate`: Certification start date
- `certificationenddate`: Certification end date
- `certificationduedate`: Certification due date
- `certificationexpirydate`: Certification expiry date

Once you have created your CSV file, go to **Users | Accounts | Upload users** in the **Site administration** section and follow the upload process using your CSV file. The following is a sample CSV file, allocating two users to our health and safety certification and one user to the data protection certification:

```
username,certification1,certificationstartdate1,
certificationenddate1,certificationduedate1,
certificationexpirydate18
user1,cerHealthSafety,2020-01-01,2020-02-26,,2020-03-31
user2,cerHealthSafety,2020-02-01,,,
user1,cerGDPR,2020-01-01,,2020-02-29,2021-12-31
```

The same principle for deallocating users in programs applies to certifications: users can only be removed from a certification at the source of allocation. So, users with a **manual** allocation source can only be deleted manually, in batch mode, or via web services, and users with a **dynamic** allocation source can only be deleted via the **Deallocate users from certifications** dynamic rule condition.

Certification dynamic rules

As with programs, certifications also have their own dynamic rules. The eight entries in the **Dynamic rules** tab are shown in the following screenshot. The purpose of each condition should be self-explanatory; the **Conditions** section has already been dealt with in *Chapter 5, Automation and Dynamic Rules*:

Figure 6.35 – Certification dynamic rules

As with programs, you can only modify the **Actions** part of each rule; **Conditions** remains static. Don't forget to enable each dynamic rule after it has been configured.

This completes the section on certifications, and we now want to put it all into action by modeling an onboarding and compliance workflow. In addition to certifications, we will need to make use of a range of Moodle Workplace tools, namely dynamic roles, programs, and reports.

Modeling onboarding and compliance workflows

To finish off this chapter, let's have a look at an onboarding and compliance workflow. While there are many variations in different HR setups, we have picked a typical induction process that can be modified according to your requirements. For simplicity, there are only three main steps in our workflow—registration, learning, and controlling:

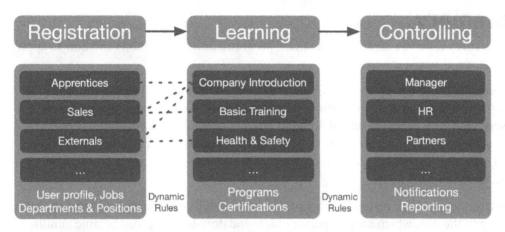

Figure 6.36 – Onboarding and compliance workflow

During the **Registration** process, personal details are stored or synchronized from an HR system (see *Chapter 12, Migration*). These include the user profile details (first name, last name, email, and so on), the position (role of the new recruits), the department (where in the organization new users are located), and the job assignment (relevant dates about their current employment). This setup covers both internal employees (here, apprentices and sales staff), as well as externals (contractors, freelancers, partners, suppliers, and so on).

The **Learning** content to be delivered is represented in courses and packaged in programs (such as company introduction, core training, and health and safety). The latter is represented as a certification since it expires after a pre-defined amount of time and requires a retake. The assignment of users to programs is realized through dynamic rules; for example, if the job position is sales representative and the organization is EMEA, then assign the user to the company introduction and core training programs.

The third part of the workflow has been labeled as **Controlling** and allows managers, HR representatives, and externals facilities to monitor the progress of their team members. This phase comprises a combination of notifications (via dynamic rules) and interactive reports. Reporting will be dealt with in *Chapter 8, Generating Custom Reports*.

This workflow nicely demonstrates that combining Moodle core and Workplace tools allows you to flexibly model internal processes and thereby optimize your day-to-day activities. Onboarding and compliance are ideal candidates for these workflows.

Summary

In this chapter, you learned how to manage programs and certifications and how to apply them to a real-world scenario.

Programs allow you to create flexible collections of courses allotted with multiple dates, which are typical in onboarding scenarios. After covering program basics, you created your own program, added different types of content, and provided scheduling information. You then learned how to add users manually and in batch mode and then dealt with various reporting options. We also covered sharing content across tenants via programs.

Certifications are built on top of programs and add initial certification and recertification paths into the mix, which are compulsory for mandatory training. You became familiar with the foundations of certifications before you learned all the ins and outs of initial certification paths and recertification.

To complete the chapter, you (hopefully) applied all the acquired skills and modeled an entire onboarding and compliance workflow. In addition to programs and certifications, this kind of process regularly consists of the acquisition of competencies, awarding badges, and the issued certificates. These so-called skills and incentives are the topic of the next chapter.

7
Skills and Incentives

Modern talent management is aligned with skills and competency mapping. Skills and incentives are two key ingredients for any human resource strategy. Both concepts are closely tied to intrinsic and extrinsic motivation. The former is driven by internal rewards or self-fulfillment, while the latter is driven by external rewards or to avoid punishment.

Moodle Workplace provides several tools that support both intrinsically and extrinsically motivated tasks, namely certificates, competencies, and badges.

First, we are going to provide an overview of skills and incentives in Moodle Workplace, which includes an overview of the typical processes that occur once certain goals have been achieved. We are also going to differentiate between the covered tools in terms of related activities for formative and summative assessments.

The focus of this chapter is on **certificates** since they are unique to Moodle Workplace. You will learn how to manage certification templates and how to construct them using static, dynamic, and validation elements. We will also look at the different means of issuing certificates to users, namely via dynamic rules, manually, or using the new Course certificate activity.

Next, we'll briefly introduce **competencies**, which describe the learner's proficiency or level of understanding in specific subject-related skills. After a brief overview, you will learn how to manage and issue competencies.

Finally, we will cover the basics of **badges**, which are a good way of celebrating achievement and showing learning progress. After a short overview, you will learn how to manage and issue badges.

In this chapter, you will become familiar with the following tools to help you facilitate skills acquisition and to model different types of incentives:

- Introducing Moodle skills and incentives
- Exploring the certificates tool
- Exploring competencies
- Exploring badges

Let's get started!

Introducing Moodle skills and incentives

Skills and incentives are at the heart of each human resource strategy, and since Moodle Workplace is a strategic building block of a modern learning environment, we feel that the two concepts deserve a dedicated chapter.

> **Important note**
>
> A **skill** is the ability to perform a certain action to solve a given problem. Skills are represented in Moodle as competencies.
>
> An **incentive** is a motivator to acquire a skill. Incentives are represented in Moodle as grades, feedback, badges, and – new in Moodle Workplace – certificates.

Moodle's initial target audiences were educational institutions, such as schools, colleges, and universities, as well as other training and learning organizations. In addition to learning per se, assessment is a critical requirement in educational settings, and Moodle offers a wide range of tools to facilitate both formative as well as summative assessment. In fact, most assessment activities cover the full spectrum, from formal to informal assessment.

A good example of this is the Quiz activity, where the author or trainer can choose when and if hints, feedback, and correct answers are shown to learners. The various review options control when information is displayed to the user (during the attempt, immediately after the event, later, while the quiz is open, and after the quiz is closed) and what type of information is shown; for instance, correct/incorrect marks or textual feedback.

In most workplace settings, the emphasis shifts for compulsory learning from exams to compliance or onboarding training, and for optional learning from monitoring progress to skill acquisition. However, the underlying principle of intrinsic and extrinsic motivation remains the same, and thus the full range of available Moodle tools can potentially be applied to workplace environments. Examples of how to track progress include the Quiz activity, which was mentioned in the previous paragraph, SCORM modules for performance checks, and submitting Assignments from trainees, either in individual or group mode. **SCORM** stands for **Shareable Content Object Reference Model** and is the de facto standard for interchangeable learning content.

We are not going to cover any standard Moodle course activities since they are beyond the scope of this book. The same holds for grades, outcomes, and scales; you can find excellent documentation on all these topics at docs.moodle.org/en/Grades. Instead, we are going to focus on three key tools that are continually being used in workplace settings, as depicted in the following diagram:

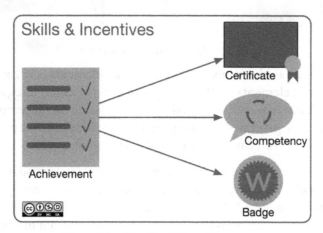

Figure 7.1 – Moodle skills and incentives

The left-hand side of the preceding diagram covers **achievements** in the form of completions at different levels, such as activity, course, program, or certification. Various components support a range of award mechanisms; for instance, issuing a **badge** when completing a course, attaching a **competency** once a certain number of points have been achieved in a quiz, or awarding a **certificate** via dynamic rules after successfully completing a program.

The focus of this chapter is on Moodle Workplace certificates, while the other described components – completions, competencies, and badges – will only be covered briefly since they are part of the standard Moodle experience. To get started, we'll explore the powerful certificates tool and its associated course certificate activity.

Exploring the certificates tool

Certificates are a great incentive for both formal and informal training. Moodle Workplace allows you to design engaging certificates and then award them to users in different ways. Both aspects will be dealt with in great detail so that you can fully support different motivation strategies in your organization.

Moodle Workplace comes with a built-in certificate generator that lets you design templates so that you can issue diplomas or certificates of participation. The basic workflow for this is shown in the following diagram:

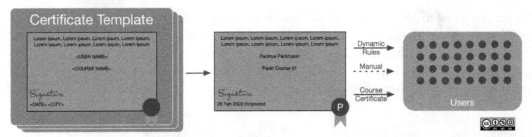

Figure 7.2 – Basic certificate workflow

Certificate templates act as blueprints and contain **static elements** (such as company name or logo), **dynamic elements** (such as username or certification title), and **verification elements** (such as code or digital signature). Based on the template, individual **certificates** are generated and assigned to users. This can take place automatically via dynamic rules, manually, or via the course certificate activity.

The certificate tool has been contributed to the public plugin database so that it can be used in standard Moodle. This tool, called the Workplace certificate manager, can be downloaded from `moodle.org/plugins/tool_certificate`. Its main difference compared to the Workplace version is the lack of capabilities relevant to workplace tenants.

OK; that's enough of the abstract concepts. Let's get started with managing certificates before we look at the various ways of how to issue documents to learners.

Managing certificates

Before we get started, let's have a look at what a Moodle Workplace certificate (template) may look like once it has been designed. We are going to use this specimen as our working sample for the remainder of this section:

Figure 7.3 – Sample certificate template

You can manage certificate templates via **Site administration | Certificates | Manage certificate templates** or directly via the **Certificates** icon in the **Workplace** launcher, as shown here:

Figure 7.4 – Certificate templates launcher

You will see a list of certificate templates. In our demo instance, we have already created four certificate templates. On the right of each item, you will see several actions, some of which are the usual Workplace icons (**Edit**, **Details**, **Preview**, **Duplicate**, and **Delete**), while others are specific to certificates (**Certificates issued** and **Issue certificates**). We will discuss these in detail in due course:

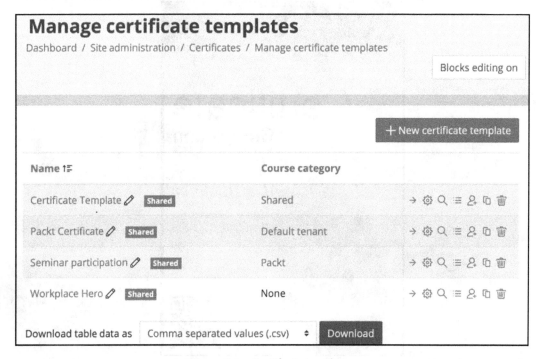

Figure 7.5 – Certificate templates

To create a new certificate template, select the **+ New certificate template** button; you will then be greeted with a pop-up screen and a range of settings, as shown in the following screenshot:

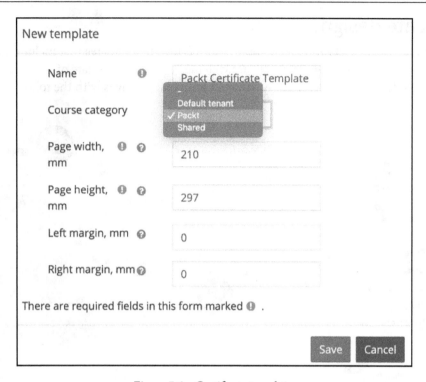

Figure 7.6 – Certificate templates

The following are mostly self-explanatory settings that must be configured:

- **Name**: This doesn't have to be unique, but it is recommended not to use the same name more than once.

- **Course category**: The certificate is available in the tenant that uses the selected course category, as defined in the tenant settings (see *Chapter 4, Tenants, Organizations, and Teams*, for details). When no course category is selected, the certificate is shared across all tenants.

- **Page width** and **Page height**: The default values depend on your server locale. In our example, we have swapped the width and height values since we want to create a certificate in A4 portrait format rather than landscape format. For reference, the dimensions of A4 are 297 mm x 210 mm; the ones for letter size are 279 mm x 216 mm, respectively.

- **Left margin** and **Right margin**: These are for the edge width on the left and right in mm. The default is 0.

As soon as you save the certificate template, you will be directed to Moodle Workplace's powerful certificate designer, which we are going to work with next.

Certificate designer

The certificate designer lets you create multi-page certificate templates that include static elements, such as text or images, and dynamic elements, such as the date of issue, the username, and the course title. Initially, you will see a blank canvas with the following user interface:

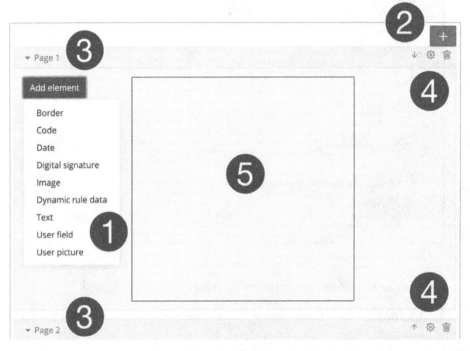

Figure 7.7 – Certificate designer I

The following controls are available in the certificate designer:

1. **Adding elements** to the certificate template. These will be covered in great detail in the subsequent pages.

2. **Adding a new page**. You will have to set the page height and width, as well as the page margins. The default values are the ones for the current page.

3. **Expand** and **collapse** the current page.

4. **Page actions**, which includes **Move up** and **down** (only multi-page certificates), **Settings** (dimensions of the page), and **Delete** (only multi-page certificates).

5. Certificate **canvas**, which fully supports dragging and dropping elements.

Once some elements have been added to a template, each item will be listed on the left, as shown in the following example screenshot:

Figure 7.8 – Certificate designer II

The order of these items can be rearranged via the standard **Move** icon, though this has no relevance to the layout of the certificate template itself. Each item can be renamed via the **Inline Editing** option besides the element name or by simply clicking the label. The **Settings** symbol opens the parameters pop-up window for each item, while the **Delete** icon removes the entry.

Now, let's go through the different elements that can be added to a certificate template. For didactical reasons, we aren't going to cover the elements in the same order as they're shown in the pull-down menu; instead, we are going to group them into the following three categories:

- Static elements
- Dynamic elements
- Validation elements

Let's start by adding some static elements to our certificate template.

Adding static elements

Static elements are fixed for every certificate that will be issued from the certificate template. They will be identical on every certificate that will be generated. The three static elements that are available are **Border**, **Image**, and **Text**.

Static element – Border

The first element we are going to add is a **Border** element. Each item has an **Element name**, and this will be used to identify this element when you're editing a certificate. Note that this will not be displayed on the certificate. **Type** is displayed for information only and cannot be changed. These two fields exist for every certificate template element, no matter what type.

The **Width** element of the border is specified in mm. The default is 1 mm – we have changed it to 4 mm here. The default **Colour** is black (#000000), which we modified to Workplace blue (#215972):

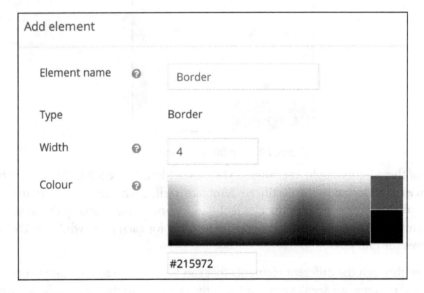

Figure 7.9 – Certificate element – Border

As soon as you save the element, it will be automatically placed on the certificate template.

> **Important note**
> To modify the element values, simply click the element on the canvas.

The border is the only element that cannot be moved around on the canvas. This is different for all other items, such as images, which we are going to cover next.

Static element – Image

The second element we are going to add to our certificate is of the **Image** type. You will need to upload an image that has been prepared elsewhere. Here, we will use our header image, which you already saw in the sample certificate earlier on. The image file types that are supported are GIF, JPG, JPEG, PNG, SVG, and SVGZ. The configuration options for the image elements are shown in the following screenshot:

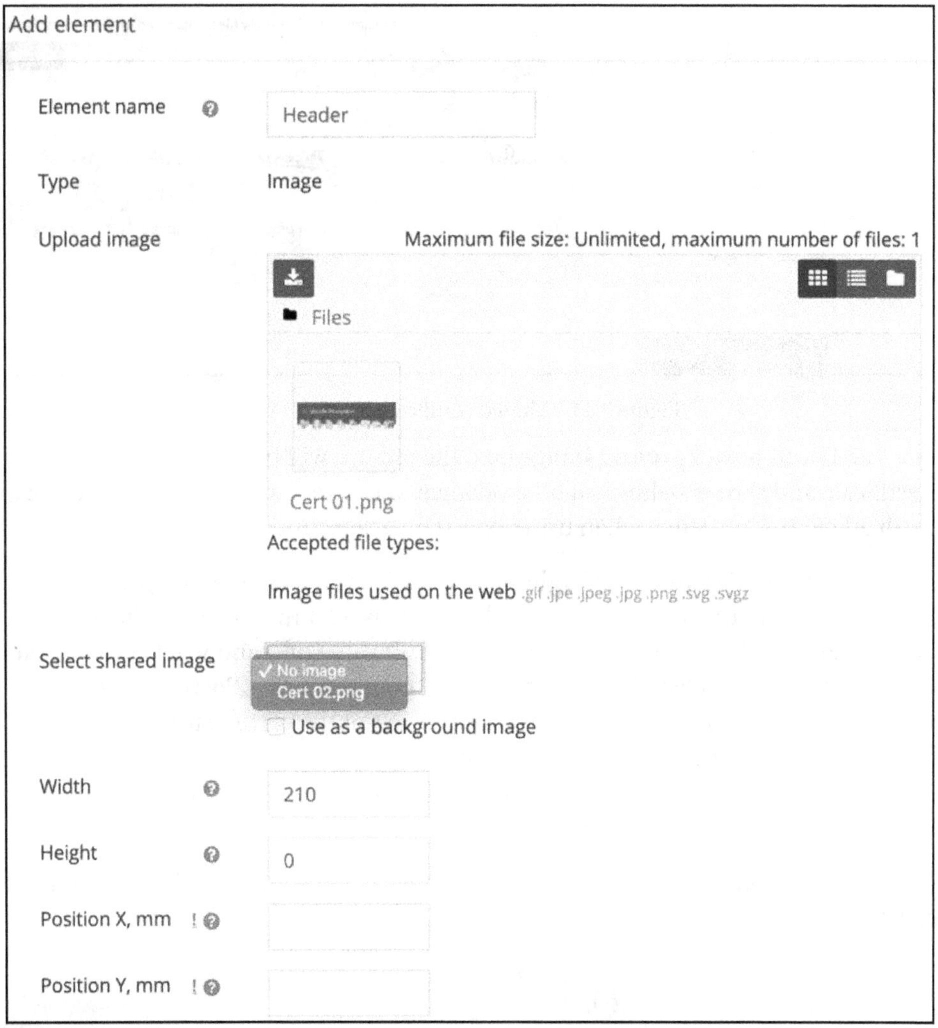

Figure 7.10 – Certificate element – Image

Alternatively, you can select a **shared image**. Shared images are managed centrally and act as simple repositories for assets that will be used on multiple certificates; for instance, your company logo or the signatures of certificate signees. You can manage shared images in **Site administration | Certificates | Certificate images**, as shown in the following screenshot:

Figure 7.11 – Shared certificate images

If you tick the **Use as a background image** box, the picture will be stretched across the entire certificate and shown behind all other elements. It is recommended that you use an image with added transparency when using one as a background.

The next two settings – **Width** and **Height** – are useful if you wish to scale your image to a particular size. In our case, we specified the width as 210 mm to cover the full width of the page. The height will remain at the default value of 0 and will be calculated automatically. When you select **Show more…**, two more settings – **Position X** and **Position Y** – will be shown, with the apex at the top-left of the certificate template. Usually, you position your image by dragging and dropping it onto the canvas; however, sometimes, it is useful to position elements manually, especially when you need to align multiple items horizontally or vertically.

Now that we have added the border and the header, we'll add some text elements to the certificate template.

Static element – Text

The last static element type is **Text,** which is effectively a label that can be placed freely on the canvas. In addition to the text to be displayed, you can configure the **Font, Size** (in **pt**), and **Colour** elements. You also have three **Text alignment** options, namely **Left, Centre,** and **Right.** Right alignment of the text means that the element coordinates' **Position X** and **Position Y** will refer to the top-right corner of the textbox; in center alignment, they will refer to the top middle, and in left alignment, they will refer to the top-left corner, respectively. The **Width** setting specifies the size of the textbox; if it's left at the default value of 0, there will be no width constraint; that is, the text can run over the margins of the page. All these settings are shown in the following screenshot:

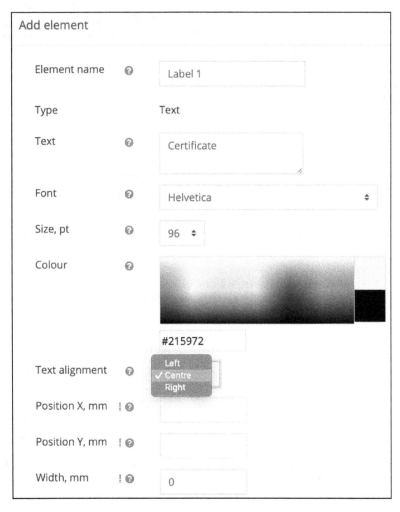

Figure 7.12 – Certificate element – Text

Here, we have added three more **Text** elements to the certificate template. By now, the certificate, with all our added static items, should look something like this:

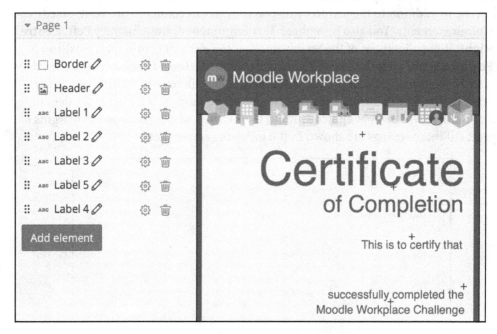

Figure 7.13 – Sample certificate after adding some static elements

Now that we have added all the required static elements, namely **Border**, **Image**, and **Text**, let's look at the different dynamic elements that can be placed on a certificate template.

Adding dynamic elements

Dynamic elements are going to be replaced with specific data for every certificate that will be issued from the certificate template. Thus, each dynamic element acts as a mini placeholder on the certificate template. Typical dynamic values include the name of the receiver, the title of a program, or simply the date when the certificate will be issued. The four dynamic elements that are available are **Date**, **Dynamic rule data**, **User field**, and **User picture**.

Dynamic element – Date

As the name suggests, the **Date** element adds a date field to the certificate template. This can either be the **Issued date** field (when the PDF will be generated) or the **Expiry date** field (when the validity of the certificate ends). You can also choose from one of the seven available **Date format** options. Please note that the **Date format** options will be adjusted according to the active language pack while you're editing the certificate template. In the following screenshot, you can see the values for English and Spanish, respectively:

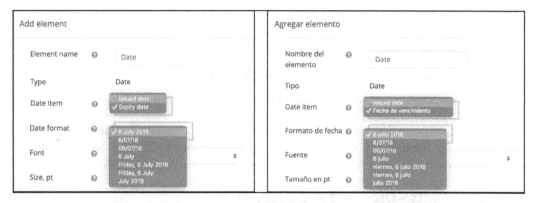

Figure 7.14 – Certificate element – Date (English and Spanish)

While there is no limit to the number of date elements you can put on a certificate template, usually, one item is placed on the document. The same cannot be said for our next dynamic element: rule data.

Dynamic element – Dynamic rule data

There are three ways certificates can be issued: manually, in courses (both to be discussed later in this chapter), and automatically via dynamic rules, which we covered in *Chapter 5, Automation and Dynamic Rules*. The **Dynamic rule data** element type supports this automatic issuing process by providing a number of fields, as shown in the following screenshot:

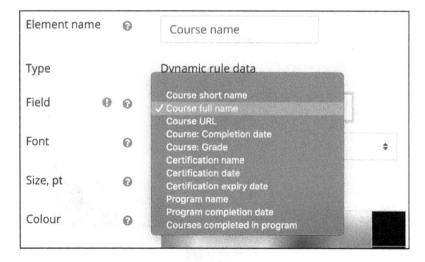

Figure 7.15 – Certificate element – Dynamic rule data

Currently, there are three types of fields that are on offer:

- **Certifications**: Name, date, and expiry date
- **Courses**: Short name, full name, URL, completion date, and grade
- **Programs**: Name, completion date, and courses completed in the program

In our example, we have selected Course full name, which will be displayed on the PDF once it has been generated. If you want to select multiple related fields – for instance, all three certification fields – you will need to add a separate element for each field.

Dynamic elements – User field and User picture

The final two related dynamic elements are of the **User field** and **User picture** types. The former displays textual information on the certificate, while the latter adds the image of the user to the template.

The **User field** type supports all plain text fields (that is, no rich text/HTML text fields) in the user profile. This also includes custom profile fields (here, CPD_Points represents a continuing professional development score and DOB), as displayed in the following screenshot:

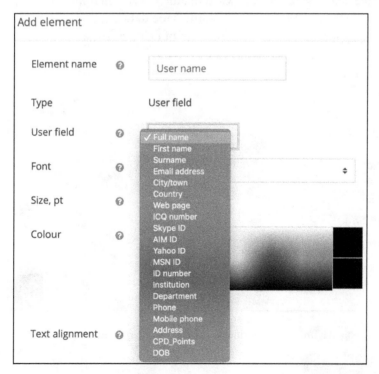

Figure 7.16 – Certificate element: User field

For our certificate, we have added the full name of the user, which is almost always part of a personalized certificate. As we did previously, you will need to add a separate element for each field.

The **User picture** element only contains the four location settings we have already come across: **Weight**, **Height**, **Position X**, and **Position Y**. User pictures are handled in the same way as elements of the **Image** type; the only difference is that the picture cannot be selected since it has already been set in the user profile.

This concludes this subsection on dynamic certificate elements, where we covered Date, Dynamic rule data, User field, and User picture. Next up is validation elements.

Adding validation elements

Certificates are regularly issued in settings where their validity is critical. Examples include diplomas, compliance documents, and qualification credentials. To ensure that the certificates have been generated by the Moodle Workplace system, two validation mechanisms are offered:

- Every certificate that is issued contains a unique **code**, which is made up of 10 digits plus two uppercase letters; for instance, 0123456789AB. The last two letters are the initials of the user.

- **Digital signatures** can be added to a certificate (template). These are based on self-signed CRT certificates that follow the X.509 standard.

Both types can be added as elements to a certificate template. We will be dealing with this in this following two subsections.

Validation element – Code

As we mentioned previously, every generated certificate has a unique code that is recorded in the Moodle Workplace database. This **Code** can be displayed on the certificate in four different formats, as demonstrated in the following screenshot:

Figure 7.17 – Certificate element – Code

The **Display** options are as follows:

- **Code only (default)**: The code is displayed as plain text.
- **Code with link**: The code links to the verification page (more on this shortly).
- **Verification URL**: Only the link to the verification page will be displayed, but it won't be linkable. This option should be used on printed certificates where it is not possible to click the link.
- **QR Code**: A QR code is displayed that redirects the user to the verification page.

To verify the validity of the certificate (code), Moodle Workplace offers a dedicated form that can be reached via one of the four described display options. It is also possible to enter codes manually via **Site administration | Certificates | Verify certificates**, as shown in the following screenshot:

Figure 7.18 – Certificate validation

Once you select **Verify**, information regarding the certificate's metadata is displayed. You also have the option to access the PDF version of the document by selecting the **View certificate** link at the bottom.

The code element is a secure option that's used to minimize the fraudulent generation of certificates. However, it is insufficient for certain organizations or qualifications where a higher degree of security is required. This has been addressed by digital signatures, which we are going to look at next.

Validation element – Digital signature

The second validation element that can be added to certificate templates is a **digital signature**. When a certificate is issued (see the next subsection), a PDF document is generated. Files in PDF format can be signed with a self-signed certificate in order to prevent forgery and falsification of certificates. To simplify this mechanism, a dedicated element has been created, which you can add like any other element.

It is common to sign an image in a document using a logo, a signature, or a seal, although it is possible to create signed PDFs with no in-document visualization. We are going to attach the digital signature to an image. Since the image parameters are identical to the **Image** element we covered earlier, we are going to focus on the digital signature parts, as shown in the following overlapping screenshots:

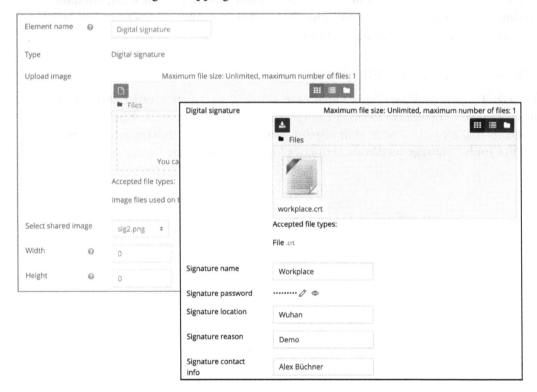

Figure 7.19 – Certificate element – Digital signature

The only compulsory field is the digital signature itself, which is a CRT file. You will either have to use an existing CRT file from your organization or generate a self-signed certificate. Follow these three steps via the Linux command line:

```
openssl req -x509 -nodes -days 365000 -newkey rsa:1024 -keyout
workplace.crt -out workplace.crt
```

```
openssl pkcs12 -export -in workplace.crt -out workplace.p12
```

```
openssl pkcs12 -in workplace.p12 -out workplace.crt -nodes
```

The first command creates a self-signed signature that's valid for 10 years (365,000 days) and is RSA-encrypted with 1,024 bytes. It contains both the private key and the certificate part. The second step is to export the CRT file in P12 format before converting it into a PEM file. You will need to provide the CRT file – here, **workplace.crt** – to the digital signature on your certificate, which is using the standard key part to tag the certificate as being valid and verifiable. Internally, the PDF generator uses functionality available in the TCPDF library.

The other fields (**Signature name**, **Signature password**, **Signature location**, **Signature reason**, and **Signature contact info**) provide information about the CRT file. While they are all optional, it is recommended to provide these.

Managing certificate element plugins

By default, all available certificate plugins are shown in alphabetical order in the certificate designer menu. If you wish to either change the order of the elements or hide any elements that are not in use in your organization, go to **Site administration | Plugins | Admin tools | Manage certificate element plugins** and configure the list as required:

Manage certificate element plugins

Name	Version	Hide/show	Order
Border	2020092400	👁	↓
Code	2020092400	👁	↑ ↓
Date	2020092400	👁	↑ ↓
Digital signature	2020092400	👁	↑ ↓
Image	2020092400	👁	↑ ↓
Dynamic rule data	2020092400	👁	↑ ↓
Text	2020092400	👁	↑ ↓
User field	2020092400	👁	↑ ↓
User picture	2020092400	👁	↑

Figure 7.20 – Managing certificate element plugins

It is also possible for a developer to create new certificate element plugins. Once this add-on has been installed, it will also appear in this list and will be treated like a core element.

This concludes this section on static, dynamic, and validation elements that can be placed on certificates. Hopefully, you have been able to create an engaging certificate template, either by following our design, which we used as an example, or by coming up with your own visual. Now that we have created our first certificate template, let's learn how generated certificates are issued in Moodle Workplace.

Issuing certificates

The key objective of certificates is that they are awarded to users once they have successfully completed a certain task or solved a given problem; for instance, they've completed a course, achieved a competency, or attended a webinar. There are three ways certificates can be awarded in Moodle Workplace:

- Automatically via dynamic rules
- Manually
- Course certificate activity

We will cover all three modes of issue during the following three subsections, starting with dynamic rules.

Issuing certificates via dynamic rules

Certificates can be **issued automatically** via dynamic rules (see *Chapter 5, Automation and Dynamic rules*). A simple but representative example is shown in the following set of screenshots, where the condition states that if the Moodle Workplace Challenge course has been completed, the certificate we created in this section will be issued and a notification will be sent to the user:

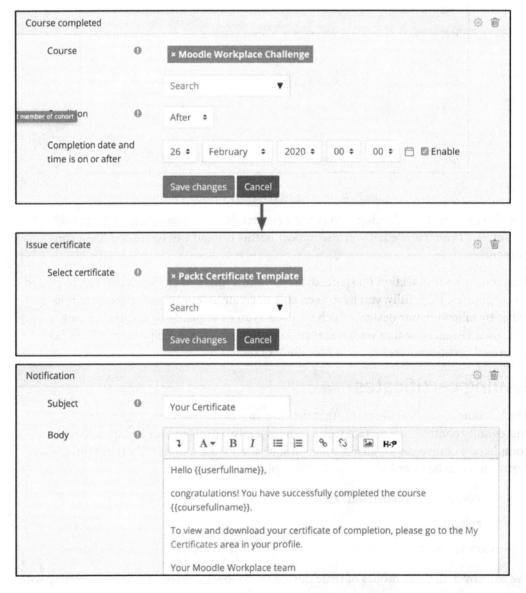

Figure 7.21 – Dynamic rule to automatically issue certificates

In the notification, you might have spotted the reference to the **My certificates** section in the user profile. A generic link to this area is `<URL>/admin/tool/certificate/ my_certificates.php`. This is where all the certificates of a user are listed, including a PDF view of them and a download option.

Issuing certificates manually

There are scenarios where a certificate has to be **issued manually**; for example, if the number of recipients is too low to justify a dynamic rule or if recognized prior learning of individual users leads to issuing a certificate. To manually issue a certificate, you have to select the **Issue new certificate from this template** icon to the right of the certificate template. This will open a pop-up form where you have to choose at least one user and, optionally, specify an expiry date. In the following screenshot, two users have been selected:

Figure 7.22 – Manually issuing certificates

For every issued certificate, no matter how it has been generated, metadata will be stored in the underlying Moodle database. To view this data, select the **Certificates issued** icon beside the respective certificate template. This will show the following data:

- **Full name**: First and last name of the user.

- **Awarded on**: Date and time when the certificate was awarded.

- **Expires on**: Expiry date and time when the validity ends.

- **Code**: The code of the certificate and a link to the verification page.

- **Preview**: The generated PDF file will be displayed.

- **Regenerate issue file**: The PDF file will be regenerated on the fly and re-issued to the user. However, the award date and time will remain unchanged.

- **Delete**: Used to revoke the certificate.

A sample list of issued certificates is shown in the following report. There is currently no way to distinguish between which certificates have been issued via dynamic rules and which ones have been issued manually:

Packt Certificate				
First name / Surname	Awarded on ↓F	Expires on	Code	
Amanda Weaver	Tuesday, 27 October 2020, 11:31 AM	Saturday, 26 February 2022, 12:00 AM	8963635121AW	
Liberty Cooke	Tuesday, 27 October 2020, 7:34 AM	Saturday, 26 February 2022, 12:00 AM	6448576901LC	
Justine Cantrell	Tuesday, 27 October 2020, 7:34 AM	Saturday, 26 February 2022, 12:00 AM	5702952855JC	
Stone Barlow	Tuesday, 27 October 2020, 7:33 AM	Saturday, 26 February 2022, 12:00 AM	94412270625B	
Rhea Baxter	Monday, 26 October 2020, 8:06 PM	Saturday, 26 February 2022, 12:00 AM	2769317486RB	

Download table data as   Comma separated values (.csv) ⊕   Download

Figure 7.23 – List of issued certificates

This report can be reproduced using the **Certificates issues** data source. A second data source related to certificates is called **Certificate templates**. It contains data fields for the templates on your system. Data sources will be discussed in more detail in *Chapter 8, Generating Custom Reports*.

Issuing certificates via the Course certificate activity

Moodle Workplace has introduced a new course activity that lets you issue certificates from within courses:

Figure 7.24 – Course certificate activity

Like the Workplace Certificate Manager add-on we mentioned previously, the course activity has also been contributed to the public Moodle plugin database. To make use of this activity in a standard Moodle system, you will need to install **mod_coursecertificate** from `moodle.org/plugins/mod_coursecertificate`.

Once the **Course certificate** activity has been selected from the activity chooser, the following configuration options become available:

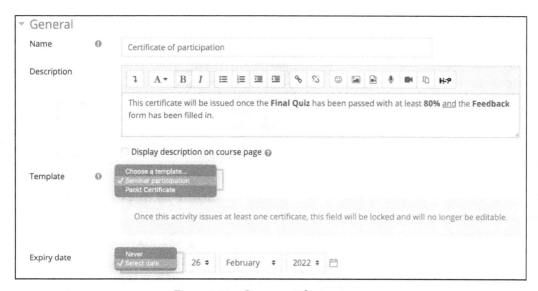

Figure 7.25 – Course certificate settings

There are only two certificate-specific settings:

- **Template**: Select one of the certificate templates that you created earlier. As the note on the screen indicates, this field will be locked once a certificate has been issued via this activity.

- **Expiry date**: This is an optional setting that indicates when the validity of the issued certificate runs out.

The Course certification activity is mostly used in combination with other activities. In the following example, the certificate will only be available to learners when the final quiz has been passed and the feedback questionnaire has been filled in. These are configured in the standard **Restrict access** section of the Course certificate activity:

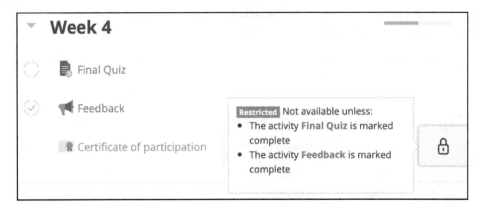

Figure 7.26 – Restrict access clauses

There are two ways learners can be issued with their certificate once they have access to the activity:

- When **automatic sending** is **enabled**, the certificate will be issued automatically once users have access to it. All learners will receive a PDF copy of the certificate as soon as they meet the activity's access restrictions.

- When **automatic sending** is **disabled**, learners can manually issue the certificate themselves. Learners won't automatically receive a PDF copy of the certificate; instead, they will need to click on the activity link displayed on the course page to receive the certificate once they have met this activity's access restrictions.

As a trainer (or any user with the **mod/coursecertificate:viewreport** capability), you can toggle between the two certificate sending modes when selecting the Course certificate activity. Here, you can also view a list of course participants who have already been issued with a certificate. This displays the familiar columns **Email address**, **Status**, **Expiry date**, **Date issued**, and **Code**, as well as the **Preview** and **Delete** actions:

Figure 7.27 – Course certificate report

Certificates issued at the course level will be treated exactly the same as certificates issued via dynamic rules or manually. They will appear in the user's **My certificates** profile section and also show up in any custom reports.

This concludes this comprehensive section on certificates, the first type of incentive in Moodle Workplace. Here, we covered creating certificate templates with static, dynamic, and validation elements, as well as issuing them via dynamic rules, manually, or inside courses. Next, we will look at the competencies you can use to model the skill sets of your staff.

Exploring competencies

Competencies describe the learner's proficiency or level of understanding in certain subject-related skills. Moodle has a powerful competency management system that fully supports modeling and awarding competencies. In this section, we will cover the basics of competency management. The main components and issuing mechanisms of competencies have been depicted in the following diagram:

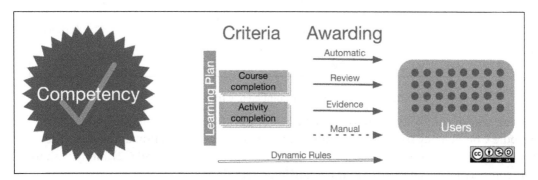

Figure 7.28 – Moodle competencies

A **competency** has certain properties, such as a name, scale (for instance, not competent, competent with supervision, and competent), a competency framework it belongs to, and a parent to model competency hierarchies. A competency is usually tied to course and/or activity completions. Competencies can be part of a **Learning Plan** (template) so that they can be assigned to users or cohorts. Moodle supports different awarding mechanisms, namely **Automatic** upon completion, following a **review** process after providing additional **Evidence**, or **Manual**. Alternatively, competencies can be awarded via dynamic rules where competencies can be configured via the rule action.

Detailed information on competencies can be found at `docs.moodle.org/en/Competencies`. We will now focus on the main mechanisms of how to manage and award competencies in a workplace setting. Modern talent management is aligned with skills and competency mapping. This is the focus of the next section.

Managing competencies

Speaking a foreign language is a universal skill that is desirable in most – and essential in some – jobs. We are going to use the **Common European Framework of Reference for Languages** (**CEFR**) as a competency framework since it is used across Europe and, increasingly, in other countries for measuring the language skill sets of a learner.

First, you need to create a competency framework at **Site administration | Competencies | Competency frameworks**, as shown in the following screenshot:

Competency frameworks

| Add new competency framework | Competency frameworks repository |

List of competency frameworks

Name	Competencies	Category	Actions
CEFR (2016)	0	System	Edit

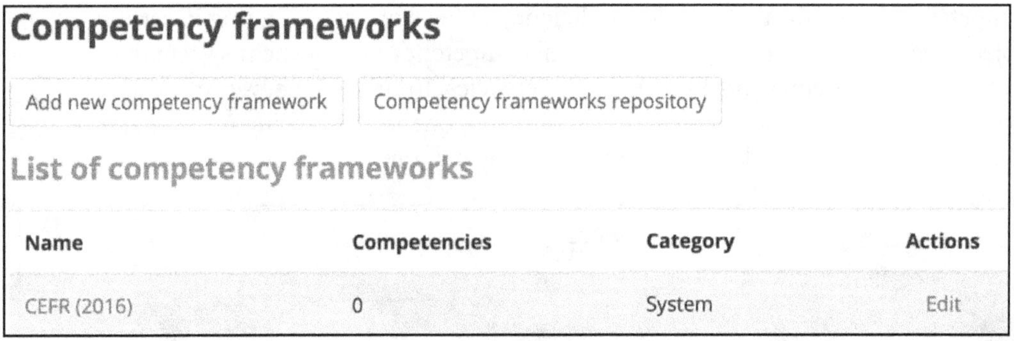

Figure 7.29 – Moodle competency frameworks

For the sake of simplicity, we have imported the **CEFR** framework from the public Moodle Competency framework's repository (via the respective button at the top). The result of the framework and its competencies (**A1**, **A2**, **B1**, **B2**, **C1**, and **C2**), along with its sub-competencies, can be seen in the following screenshot:

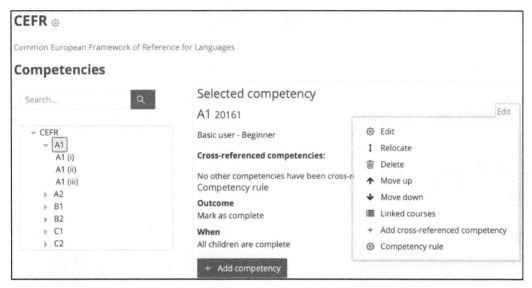

Figure 7.30 – CEFR competency framework

Once a competency framework is in place, there are different ways to award competencies to learners, all of which will be introduced briefly in the next subsection.

Awarding competencies

Once competencies have been modeled in a competency framework, the next step is to configure how to award competencies to users once they are proficient in the skill to be acquired.

There are three options regarding how to award a competency to learners. Two are available in standard Moodle, while the other is (currently) only available in Moodle Workplace:

- Via course and activity completion, where proficiency is achieved by completing certain tasks

- Via learning plans, to ensure that groups of users achieve competency; for instance, all data protection officers

- Via dynamic rules, to award competency based on flexible criteria, such as cohort membership

Let's start with course and activity completion.

Course and activity competencies

Awarding a competency can be tied to the successful completion of an activity or a course. You need to be inside a course and select the **Competencies** option in the drawer menu on the left so that you can add **course competencies**. In the following screenshot, we have added all the sub-competencies of competency A1 to the course. One out of four of the competencies has already been achieved, as indicated by the progress bar at the top:

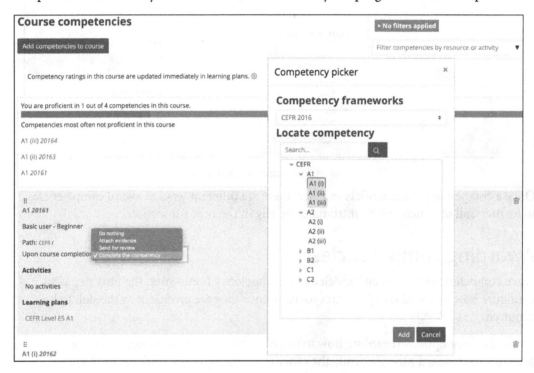

Figure 7.31 – Course competencies

Similar to course competencies, you can also specify **activity competencies**, for instance, when a test has been completed with at least 80% success. Within the settings of an activity, you can find the **Competencies** section, where at least one competency has to be selected, alongside an action that is triggered upon the activity's completion (**Do nothing**, **Attach evidence**, **Send for review**, or **Complete the competency**):

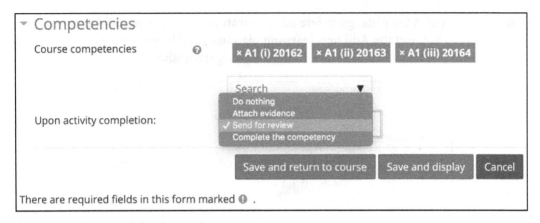

Figure 7.32 – Activity competencies

The most straightforward option is competency **completion**, which concludes the user's process of achieving the competency. Attaching **evidence** allows users to submit a testimony of training that's been received outside of Moodle; for instance, a link to a public webinar or a certificate of participation to an external seminar. The last option is for the learner to request a **review** by the instructor. This leads nicely to learning plans, which support an even more sophisticated multi-stage review process.

Competencies and learning plans

Learning plans are a means of ensuring that all of your learners have targeted learning based on their goals and training needs, and that it has been delivered in a structured way based on learning plan templates, which themselves are based on competencies. Based on the learning plan template, you can create learning plans, either manually for individual users or automatically via cohorts.

> **Important note**
> A learning plan template defines a set of competencies that's assigned to users.

To add a learning plan template, go to **Site administration | Competencies | Learning plan templates** and select the **Add new learning plan template** button. We have already created a number of templates, as shown in the following screenshot:

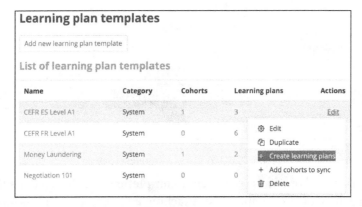

Figure 7.33 – Learning plan template I

When you select a learning plan template, you will see the already familiar competency view and also have the option to add more competencies via the **Add competencies to learning plan template** button:

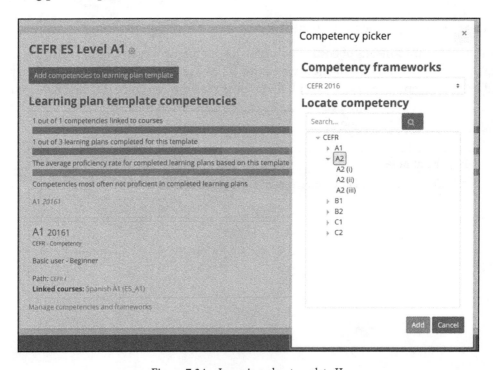

Figure 7.34 – Learning plan template II

Once a learning plan template has been finalized, you can create individual learning plans one by one via the **Create learning plans** option in the **Edit** menu, or automatically via **Add cohorts to sync**. Users can view their learning plans via the **Learning plans** link in their respective user profiles, where they also have the option to provide evidence of prior learning; for instance, documentation of previous activities.

Competencies and dynamic rules

We covered awarding competencies via **dynamic rules** in *Chapter 5*, *Automation and Dynamic Rules*. **Award competency** is an action in the **General** category where you need to select a competency. To award multiple competencies, you have to set up multiple actions. As we described previously, the Moodle competency mechanism mainly focuses on the successful completion of courses and activities. To support other constructs, such as certifications, programs, or cohort membership, you will need to make use of dynamic rules.

This concludes our quick rundown of Moodle's powerful and flexible implementation of competencies, which included modeling competency frameworks and awarding certificates via activity and course completion via learning plans and dynamic rules. We have used CEFR to run through the basics of competencies. Another good example of core competencies and work-based skill and behavior structuring is the ICE competency framework (`www.theice.com/publicdocs/ICE_Competency_Framework.pdf`). Next up is the third incentive type: badges.

Exploring badges

Badges are a good way of celebrating achievement and showing learning progress. Moodle supports the management of badges, as well as different ways to award badges. Both mechanisms will be dealt with in this section. Moodle badges are fully compatible with Open Badges and can be published in any Open Badges-compatible backpack.

Badges are awarded based on a variety of chosen criteria and will be displayed on a user's profile. The main components and issuing mechanisms of badges are depicted in the following diagram:

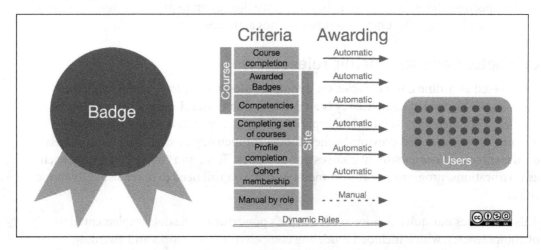

Figure 7.35 – Moodle badges

A badge has certain properties, such as a name, expiry date, and issuer. Additionally, badges have one or many **criteria** that have to be fulfilled to trigger it being awarded. Some criteria only exist at the **course level**, while others exist at the **site level**. The **awarding** process itself is usually automatic, with the exception of manual assignment. Alternatively, badges can be awarded via dynamic rules, where badges can be configured via the rule action.

Detailed information on badges can be found at docs.moodle.org/en/Badges. We are now going to focus on the main mechanisms of how to manage and award badges in a typical workplace setting.

Managing badges

Once you or some creative whiz kid in your marketing department has created the badges to be awarded to your learners, you will need to add and manage these in your learning management system. In Moodle, there are two types of badges:

- **Course badges** are assigned at the course level and are related to the activities and completions that take place inside a course.

- **Site badges** are assigned site-wide and are related to site-wide achievements, such as completing a program or certification.

Awarding a **course badge** can be tied to the successful completion of an activity or other achievements. You need to be inside a course and select the **Badges** option from the drawer menu on the left, where you can add badges via the **Add new badge** button. In the following screenshot, we have already added two badges with different awarding criteria for our Spanish courses:

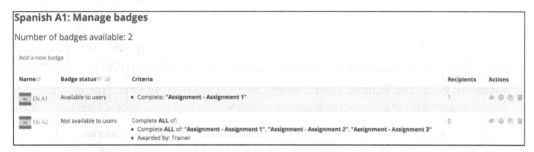

Figure 7.36 – Course badges

Site badges are managed under **Site administration | Badges | Manage Badges**. How we handle them is identical to course badges but with a single exception: there are two types of award **badge criteria**, as shown in the following screenshot comparison:

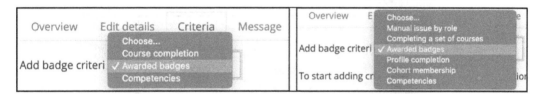

Figure 7.37 – Course badge criteria versus site badge criteria

The following badge criteria are available:

- **Course completion** (course): User has completed the current course.

- **Awarded badges** (both): User has been awarded the selected badge(s).

- **Competencies** (both): User has been awarded the selected competencies.

- **Manual issue by role** (site): To be awarded manually by users who have a particular role within the site or a course.

- **Completing set of courses** (site): User has completed the selected course(s).

- **Profile completion** (site): User has completed the selected user profile field(s).

- **Cohort membership** (site): User is a member of the selected cohort(s).

These criteria lead us nicely to the next subsection, which deals with awarding badges.

Awarding badges

As with competencies, there are three options regarding how to award a badge to a learner. Two are available in standard Moodle, while the other is (currently) only available in Moodle Workplace:

- **Automatic**: All of the preceding criteria, except **Manual issue by role**, trigger awarding a badge to the users who have successfully fulfilled the respective criteria.

- **Manual**: When the **Manual issue by role** criterion has been selected (site badges only), a user with the correct permissions can award a badge to another user.

- Via **dynamic rules**: We already covered awarding badges via **dynamic rules** in *Chapter 5, Automation and Dynamic Rules*. **Award badge** is an action in the **General** category. Here, you need to select a badge.

Users can view their awarded badges in the **Badges** section of their user profile. A sample view is shown here, which contains three different badges. When you select a badge, details such as the issuer appear:

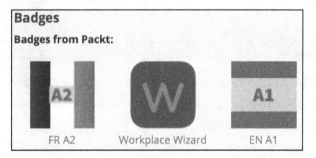

Figure 7.38 – Badges in the user profile

This completes our brief introduction to badges. Here, we covered the management and awarding mechanisms available in Moodle. This also completes our look at the trio of skills and incentives that we aimed to cover in this chapter.

Summary

In this chapter, you learned how to manage and award different types of incentives in Moodle Workplace, namely certificates, competencies, and badges.

First, we provided an overview of the skills and incentives that are available in Moodle Workplace, which included an overview of the typical processes that occur once specific goals have been achieved. Next, you learned how to manage certification templates and how to construct them using a range of static, dynamic, and validation elements. We then looked at different means to issue certificates to users, namely via dynamic rules, manually, and using the course certificate activity.

Second, we briefly introduced competencies, which dealt with managing competency frameworks and competencies per se. We then covered three awarding options, namely via course and activity completion, via learning plans, and via dynamic rules.

Third, we covered the basics of course and site-wide badges. After a short overview, you learned how to manage badges and different award criteria. We then covered three awarding options, namely automatic, manual, and via dynamic rules.

Skills and incentives cover a broad spectrum of topics, ranging from formal assessments and exams, to summative evaluations and CPD points, all the way to various types of gamification. Depending on the type of setting and learning goal, a combination of different assessment tools, progress tracking mechanisms, and incentives must be applied.

We briefly mentioned two report sources – **Certificate templates** and **Certificate issues** – that can be used to create custom reports containing data regarding certificates and certificate templates. The powerful report generator is the topic of the next chapter.

8
Generating Custom Reports

Moodle Workplace provides a custom report builder that allows administrators to create custom site-wide reports that are then distributed to users, such as managers and trainers, so that they can review and manage employee training programs.

The report builder sources data from many features in Moodle Workplace to provide reports on areas such as training completion, certification statuses, and seminar session attendance. In this chapter, you will learn how to create these reports and make them available to different users in your organization.

First, you will become familiar with the built-in reporting tool and how data is processed in both system reports and custom reports. Then, you will deal with the data and record sources that are supported and learn how to utilize these in your own reports.

Second, you will learn how to build reports with various customization options, such as conditions, filters, aggregation, groupings, and sorting. You will then learn about using the scheduling mechanism to automatically distribute reports to your users and how to configure audiences to grant access to reports.

Finally, you will become familiar with Moodle Workplace's data store, an alternative to saving records permanently beyond their lifetime in courses.

So, by the end of this chapter, you will know how to manage reports and how to make these reports available to different audiences in your organization. This chapter comprises four main parts:

- Exploring the reporting tool
- Selecting data and recording sources
- Building reports
- Exploring the Workplace data store

Exploring the reporting tool

You might not have realized it, but you have already been using reports in the last four chapters! How? Well, Moodle has done something very smart: it uses internal reports for key features in Moodle Workplace. For example, the list of active programs is a report. Active or archived certifications? Another two reports. The overview of all job assignments? You guessed it, yet another report. Every time you see a table list view in any of the Moodle Workplace tools, it is highly likely to be a built-in system report.

Moodle Workplace distinguishes between two types of reports:

- **System reports**: Embedded, pre-defined reports that are part of Moodle Workplace. System reports cannot be modified or removed since various Workplace features rely on them.
- **Custom reports**: User-generated reports made available to other users.

This chapter exclusively deals with custom reports, so let's see how reporting works in Moodle Workplace. The following diagram illustrates the high-level elements of the reporting workflow:

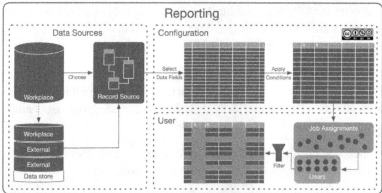

Figure 8.1 – Reporting workflows

Moodle Workplace supports two types of reporting data sources: a **Workplace database** and a so-called **Workplace data store**. The database is where all Workplace data is stored, excluding files. The data store is an alternative, xAPI-compatible data source that keeps track of permanent records in Workplace as well as external sources.

The most flexible reporting tool would let you select individual fields from every entity in the underlying database. However, this would require users to be familiar with the entire database model, which contains well over 100 tables and even more relationships between them. Instead, Workplace offers a range of **record sources** to simplify the usage of the report builder. A record source contains a pre-defined set of fields that are available when building a report.

Based on the selected record source, a certain amount of data will be available, which can be reduced by the following mechanisms. Configuring **data fields** lets the report creator decide which columns are being made available—for example, employee name, course name, and completion status. Applying **conditions** lets the report creator decide which rows will be made available—for instance, all records from the manufacturing division. **Access** to reports is granted via job assignments—for example, all department managers.

The viewer of the report then has the ability to reduce the amount of data further via filters. A **filter**, which has to be configured by the report creator, allows the selection of one or more criteria—for instance, by organization.

Important Note
A report isn't static; it is an interactive view of the data.

The next section is dedicated to each building block of the reporting workflow. Let's get started with the first (and main) part of the diagram: data and record sources.

Selecting data and record sources

In this section, we will deal with the input options for the report builder—you will learn what they are and when to use each option. Moodle Workplace supports two types of **data sources**: the Workplace database and the Workplace data store.

The **Workplace database** is the underlying database where Moodle Workplace stores its data. Courses, users, job assignments, programs, and other data—such as information about learning resources added by authors, forum posts contributed to by learners, and system settings configured by the administrator—are mostly stored in the Workplace database.

The **Workplace data store** contains historical information and snapshots of past events, such as course completion. We will dedicate an entire section to the data store at the end of this chapter.

The decision of what data source is used in a report is specified in the **report source**. A report source defines the primary type of data that will be used in a report. The set of available report sources includes data such as user profile information, course completion, certification statuses, and seminar session details. Additional report sources can be created by Moodle developers programmatically.

Let's have a look at the report sources available in Moodle Workplace. You access the management of programs via **Site administration | Reports | Manage custom reports** or directly via the **Report builder** icon in the Workplace launcher:

Figure 8.2 – The Report builder icon in the Workplace launcher

You will see a list of available reports—actually, what you will see is a report. A report of reports! In our example instance used throughout, we have already created a number of reports, as shown:

Report name	Plugin	Created	Last modified	Modified by
Certificates issued	Report builder	3/11/20	3/11/20	Alex Büchner
Course catalogue	Report builder	3/11/20	3/11/20	Alex Büchner
Course completion	Report builder	3/11/20	3/11/20	Alex Büchner
Course resets	Workplace	3/11/20	3/11/20	Alex Büchner
Program completion	Program	22/10/20	3/11/20	Alex Büchner
Seminars	Appointment	2/11/20	2/11/20	Alex Büchner
Users	Report builder	3/11/20	3/11/20	Alex Büchner

Figure 8.3 – A report of reports

The self-explanatory fields shown in the report table are **Report name**, **Plugin**, **Created**, **Last modified**, and **Modified by**. The standard actions/icons available are edit content, edit details, preview, and delete. There is a single filter available on the right that lets you limit the number of reports shown by selecting a report source.

> **Important Note**
>
> Each report has **one** report source.
>
> The selected report source cannot be changed once a report has been created. To use a different report source, a new report must be created.

To create a new report, select the **+ New report** button on the **Reports** page. You will then be greeted with a pop-up screen, as shown:

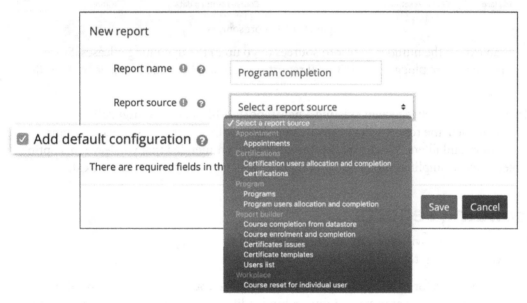

Figure 8.4 – Report details

A report contains the following two compulsory settings: **Report name** (displayed whenever the report is being made available to users) and **Report source** (defines where the data for the report will come from). The following report sources are currently available in Moodle Workplace:

Report Plugin	Report Source	Description
Appointment	Appointments	Seminars, sessions and participants
Certifications	Certification users allocation and completion	Certification details including users' progress information
	Certifications	Certification details
Program	Programs	Program details
	Programs users allocation and completion	Program details including users' progress information
Report Builder	Course completion from datastore	Data in Workplace data store
	Course enrolment and completion	Course details, user enrolments, and course completion
	Certificate templates	Available certificate templates
	Certificate issues	Issued certificates to users
	Users list	Users and their job assignments
Workplace	Course reset for individual users	Course resetting data during recertification

Figure 8.5 – Report sources

You can expect the number of record sources to go up in the upcoming releases. Since report sources are pluggable, additional report sources will be made available by Moodle developers, too.

There is one last setting when creating a new report: **Add default configuration**. When enabled, the report will already be populated with several pre-defined columns, conditions, and filters. When you get started, it is recommended that you leave this option ticked since it simplifies the building of reports, which we are going to cover next.

Building reports

In this section, we will deal with all the various facilities the report builder has on offer. You will learn what these are and how to apply them in real-world scenarios.

The report generator allows you to build and customize your own reports with a drag-and-drop option, instant preview, inline column editing, groupings, and aggregation. The following annotated screenshot shows the key elements of the Workplace report generator:

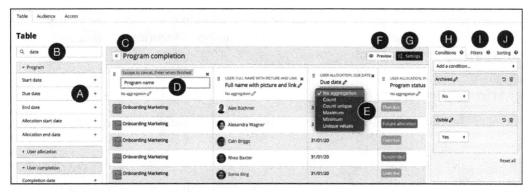

Figure 8.6 – Report generator key elements

The following actions are available in the report generator:

- **A – The data field panel**: List of data fields, grouped by entities
- **B – The data field panel search**: Live search for fields (not for entities)
- **C – The data field panel toggle**: The showing and hiding toggle of the data field panel
- **D – The preview panel**: Inline editing of column names and headings
- **E – The preview panel selection**: Selection of the field aggregation method
- **F – The preview panel toggle**: The **Preview** toggle
- **G – The settings panel toggle**: The open and close toggle of the **Settings** panel
- **H – The settings panel tab**: The **Conditions** tab
- **I – The settings panel tab**: The **Filters** tab
- **J – The settings panel tab**: The **Sorting** tab

Underneath the preview table, you might have spotted the **Current query** option. Once expanded, this shows the underlying SQL query that is generated based on the configuration of your report. For the database boffins among you, it might be helpful to map the report elements to their SQL counterparts:

- Selected data fields: **SELECT … FROM …**
- Conditions: **WHERE**
- Aggregation: **GROUP BY**
- Sorting: **ORDER BY**

Now that you have had a first glimpse of the report creation interface, let's take a closer look at the various elements, which can be grouped into two categories: configuring fields (columns) and configuring settings (rows).

Configuring fields

In this sub-section, we will deal with all available options to customize the columns in a report.

In the left-hand side panel of the Moodle Workplace report generator, you will see all available fields for the selected report source, which have been grouped into entities. Each entity can be expanded or collapsed for better usability. You can also search for field entries to limit the number of displayed items. These items have been labeled **A** and **B** in the previous screenshot.

To add columns to the report, click on the selected field in the list on the left. The column will be added automatically as the rightmost column in the table. You can then rearrange the column order via the standard **Move** handle. To remove a column, click on the standard delete icon.

There are three fields types available that can be added as columns to a report:

- **Text fields**: For example, surname, department, or course name
- **Image fields**: For example, program icon or user picture
- **Actions**: For example, sending a message to a user or viewing a progress report

Most text fields reflect a value from the underlying Workplace database. However, some text fields are preprocessed by the report generator to support additional functionality:

- **Hyperlinked text fields**: Mainly to direct viewers directly to entries—for example, to a user profile or a course.
- **Highlighted text fields**: To visualize a status. You have already come across these status fields in programs and certifications.
- **Calculated text fields**: To provide a numeric value—for instance, the number of courses in a program or the course progress for each user as a percentage.
- **Grouped text fields**: To provide multiple data points as a single cell—for example, the courses in a set of a program. The values are available one per line or comma-separated.

Custom fields, such as custom user profile fields or custom course fields, are fully supported by the report generator. They will appear in the list of available fields, such as any built-in variable. In the following screenshot, you can view a sample report (accessed via the **Preview** button) using the **Course enrolment and completion** report source containing two built-in fields (**Course name** and **Username**) plus a custom course field called **Duration**:

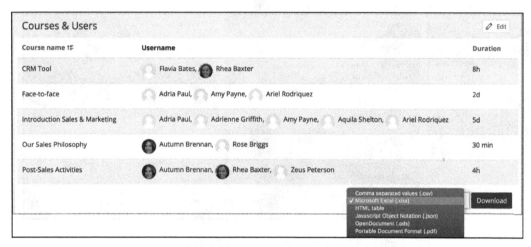

Figure 8.7 – Sample report preview

Viewers also have the option to download the table data in various formats, namely CSV, XLSX, HTML, JSON, ODS, and PDF. You can reduce or rearrange the options in that list in **Site administration | Plugins | Data formats | Manage data formats**. The XLSX format is useful if you wish to visualize data using Excel's charting tools.

You might wonder how you can display multiple usernames in a single cell. Well, you achieve this by using the aggregation operation, which is dealt with in the next sub-section.

Understanding aggregation and grouping

The Moodle Workplace report generator supports the **aggregation** and **grouping** operations at a column level. Depending on the data field selected, different methods are at your disposal, which are shown here:

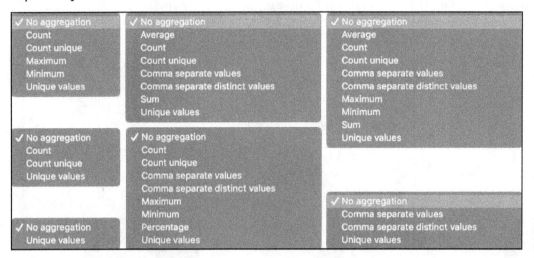

Figure 8.8 – Report generator aggregation methods

There is no system behind what methods are available for which field type. For each data field, a set of possible aggregation methods is offered by Moodle Workplace. The exception is the last entry in the previous list—**Unique values**—which technically isn't an aggregation method but a **grouping** operation.

> **Important Note**
>
> Data is grouped by the **Unique values** aggregation method.

A more detailed view is shown in the following table, which provides descriptions for each aggregation method and the SQL function used internally:

Aggregation Method	Description	SQL Function
Average	Average of all (numeric) values	AVG()
Count	Number of values in column	COUNT()
Count unique	Number of unique values in column	COUNT DISTINCT()
Comma separate values	List of data points, separated by comma	GROUP_CONCAT()
Comma separate distinct values	List of unique data points, separated by comma	GROUP_CONCAT(DISTINCT)
Maximum	Biggest (numeric) value in column	MAX()
Minimum	Smallest (numeric) value in column	MIN()
Percentage	Ratio of (numeric) values in percent	AVG()
Sum	Sum of all (numeric) values in column	SUM()
Unique values	Grouping operator	GROUP BY

Figure 8.9 – Report generator aggregation methods

An aggregate function calculates on a set of values and returns a single value. For example, **Average** takes a list of values and returns—you guessed it—the average. Because an aggregate function operates on a set of values, it is often used in combination with the grouping operator. The **Unique values** method divides the result set into groups of value, and the aggregate function returns a single value for each group. Have a look at the following report, which contains two fields: **Department** and **Certified** (from the **Certifications** record source):

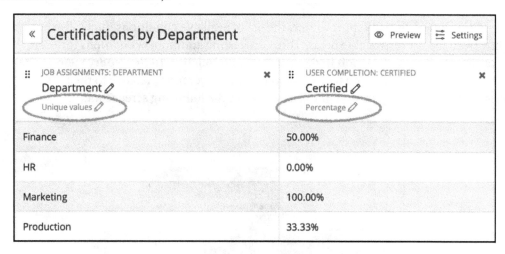

Figure 8.10 – Sample report using grouping and aggregation

The data has been grouped (**Unique values**) by **Department** and a percentage is calculated over all **Certified** values (**1** is certified, **0** is not certified). That way, the report shows the certification level for each department. This combination is commonly used for data represented in graphs, where the grouped values represent the x axis and the aggregated values represent the y axis.

Now that we have exhausted all the options for customizing columns in a report, let's look at how to configure the second dimension in a table: rows.

Configuring settings

In this sub-section, we will deal with all the available options for customizing or limiting the rows in a report. This is done via the **Settings** panel on the right-hand side. Make sure you toggle the **Settings** icon to access the **Conditions, Filters,** and **Sorting** tabs. These configuration options will be described in the following three sub-sections.

Conditions

Conditions let you limit the number of data that is being presented to the report viewer.

> **Important Note**
>
> Conditions are a pre-defined set of criteria that are always applied when viewing a report. Conditions cannot be changed in viewing mode.

Depending on the selected report source, the list of available conditions might differ slightly from the list of available fields. Three interesting additional conditions for users are **Has job in position**, **Has job in department**, and **Relation to the report viewer**. The latter condition specifies which users should be listed in a report, relative to the person who is viewing it; the application of this is shown in the following screenshot:

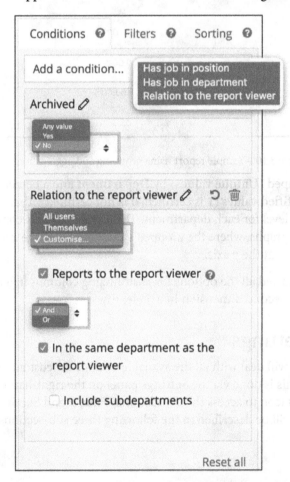

Figure 8.11 – Report generator conditions

The first condition specifies that archived programs will be excluded from the data presented to the viewer. The second condition is more sophisticated: the user entry listed in the data record has to report to the report viewer and has to be in the same department as the report viewer. The beauty of this feature is that you can create and maintain a single report that shows different results to different users, depending on their department and managerial duties. The **Customise...** option provides the following two user relations:

- **Reports to the report viewer**: For users with a managerial position, this option will include users who report directly to the user viewing the report.

- **In the same department as the report viewer**: Includes users who are members of the same department (optionally including sub-departments) as the user viewing the report.

If both of these options are selected, it is possible to combine them with the AND and OR Boolean operators to further refine the report content.

There is also a further relation called **Themselves**, which will limit the report to information relating to the report viewer.

Both relations take effect according to the user who is viewing the report, meaning it will return different results according to the report viewer and/or their own position within the organization.

Filters

The second mechanism for limiting the number of displayed records is filters. However, it is up to the report viewer to apply these.

> **Important Note**
> Filters are a pre-defined set of criteria that are not applied automatically but are available for report viewers.

The following two screenshots show the configuration of filters (left) and what the first two entries look like from a user's perspective when viewing the report (right):

Figure 8.12 – Report generator filters

You can add as many filters as you wish. Furthermore, the list of filters is not limited to the fields shown in the report. If you recall the report showing certification completion rates by department, you might add a filter to narrow the search down to individual positions, even though they are not shown in the report.

Sorting

The last of the three settings deals with the order in which the data is presented.

> **Important Note**
> Sorting defines the initial order that fields are being sorted in.

In the following screenshot, the data is ordered by **Full name** (in ascending order), **Program status** (in descending order), **Due date** (in ascending order), and **Completion date** (in ascending order):

Figure 8.13 – Report generator sorting

If we take another sneak peek at the underlying SQL query, the sorting is performed by the following ORDER BY clause:

```
ORDER BY
    c0_fullnamewithpicturelink ASC,
    c2_programid DESC, c2_certificationid DESC,
    c1_duedate ASC, c1_duedatelocked ASC,
    c3_completeddate ASC
```

When in viewing mode, the preceding order will initially be applied. Once a user has clicked on a column name, the data will be sorted by this field. When the same column is clicked again, the sort order will be reversed.

Limiting the number of custom reports

Your site administrator can restrict the number of custom reports that can be created per site and tenant, respectively, by adding the following settings to the config. php configuration file located in the main directory of your Moodle system ($CFG->dirroot), as shown:

```
$CFG->tool_reportbuilder_limitsenabled = true;
$CFG->tool_reportbuilder_sitelimit = <VALUE>;
$CFG->tool_reportbuilder_tenantlimit = <VALUE>;
```

Omitting the $CFG->tool_reportbuilder_limitsenabled configuration or setting it to false indicates that no limit should be applied to the number of custom reports that can be created. Enabling limits and setting the values to 0 will disable the creation of custom reports. Note that the tenant limit cannot exceed the site limit.

Now that we have completed the configuration of a report, the next step is to look at when the data is delivered to users.

Scheduling reports

By default, all reports are available as **pull reports**; that is, users have to proactively select and view a report. This section provides instructions on how to configure the automatic delivery of reports via the report scheduler, also known as **push reports**. Having users log in to see a report is less effective than having the report land directly in their email inbox.

To access the scheduler, select the **Schedules** tab of a report. You have probably already guessed it: the list of schedules is yet another system report with a pre-defined filter, as shown:

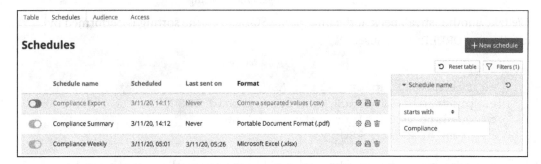

Figure 8.14 – Report scheduler

A schedule contains the following three elements, which we are going to cover in this section:

- Basic information (what and when)
- Recipients (who)
- Custom message

To create a new report schedule, select the **+ New Schedule** button at the top right. You will then be presented with a pop-up window with the three sections mentioned in the preceding list.

Basic information

This part of the screen contains information about the schedule, including what report to send, in which format the report should be sent, and the timing settings, as shown:

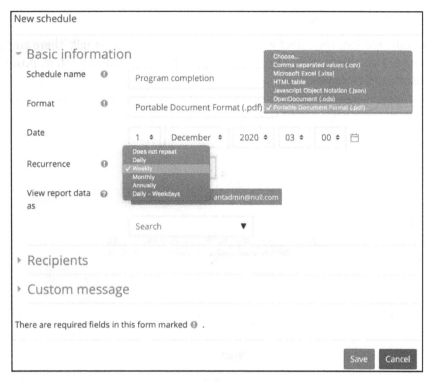

Figure 8.15 – Report scheduler—basic information

Schedule name is only used in the list of schedules. The **Format** dropdown lets you pick the file format of the report. The options are **CSV**, **XLSX**, **HTML**, **JSON**, **ODF**, and **PDF**. You can reduce or rearrange the options in that list in **Site administration | Plugins | Data formats | Manage data formats**.

The **Date** setting specifies when the report is to be sent for the first time. The **Recurrence** option lets you specify whether the report should be sent once (**Does not repeat**) or frequently. The repeating options are **Daily**, **Weekly**, **Monthly**, **Annually**, and **Daily – Weekdays**. The Moodle **cron** process triggers the execution of the report being sent.

The last setting in this section is **View report data as**. If a user is selected, the attached report data will be included as if viewed by this masquerading user; that is, all recipients will receive the same report. If left empty, the recipient of the report will be used; depending on the way the report has been configured, individual reports will be sent out. How do you specify who the recipients are? That is covered in the **Audience** part of the schedule, which will be covered in the *Audience and access* section later.

Recipients

In the **Recipients** section, you select who will receive the report by email. There are four settings available (which can be used in any combination)—by department, by position, individual users, and externals:

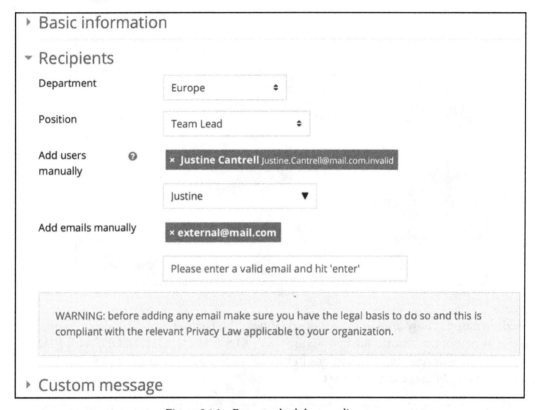

Figure 8.16 – Report scheduler—audience

You can choose **Department** and **Position**, respectively. Unfortunately, at the time of writing, there is no option to include sub-departments or sub-positions. You can also add users manually; these are users from the current tenant.

In addition to internal users, there is an option to include external users via the **Add emails manually** setting. When you add recipients manually, make sure you read the displayed warning message, which reads **before adding any email make sure you have the legal basis to do so and this is compliant with the relevant Privacy Law applicable to your organization**.

Now that we have specified who is going to receive the report, we will need to configure the accompanying message that will be sent out.

Custom message

The third and final part of a reporting schedule contains the custom message, which includes the two standard elements of any email message: **Subject** and **Message**. Currently, no placeholders are supported, so you will have to tailor the message text accordingly:

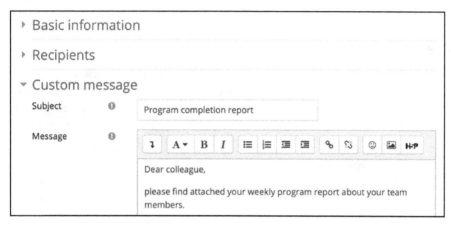

Figure 8.17 – Report scheduler—custom message

Make sure you save the schedule. To test what the message looks like, you should add yourself to the receiving audience and then use the **Send** action in the list of schedules.

You can create as many schedules for each report as required. You can further enable and disable each schedule using the toggle in the first column of the list of schedules.

To access the schedules of all reports, select the **Schedules** tab in the main **Report builder** menu. The list of schedules you see here is effectively the same as before but with the following differences:

- An additional column to list the report name
- An additional filter to filter by **Report name**

You can also create schedules from here using the same **+ New schedule** button. The pop-up screen is the same as before but with one additional field where you need to select the report that the schedule is for. The selected record cannot be changed once a schedule has been created. To use a different report, a new schedule must be created. If a report is deleted, any schedules that make use of this report will also be deleted.

So far, we have covered what data a report contains (data and record sources, column fields, conditions, filters, aggregation, and groupings) and when the data is delivered to users. Next, let's look at who is allowed to view reports by restricting access to specific audiences.

Granting access to reports

By default, all users with permission to view `tool/reportbuilder:read` or manage the `tool/reportbuilder:edit` report can view all the custom reports defined in their tenant. Additionally, it is possible to specify the individual jobs that will be granted access to the reports. We are going to cover this in the next sub-section before adding links to reports to the main menu.

Audience and access

To specify which users should be able to access a report, select the **Audience** tab when editing the report. You can add as many job assignments to set the audience for the report as necessary via the **Add job** button. You then need to select the required position and department, as in the following screenshot:

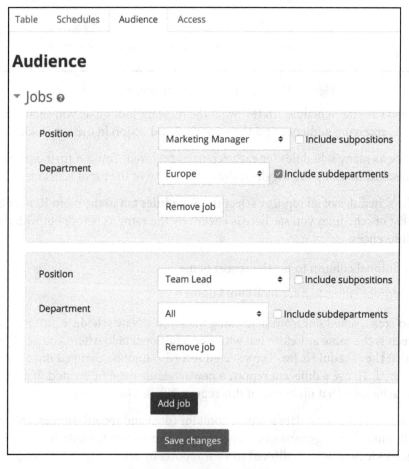

Figure 8.18 – Report audience

In our example, all the marketing managers in Europe and all the sub-departments will be allowed to view the report, as well as all the team leads, regardless of their department.

To confirm which users have access to the report, switch to the **Access** tab at the top. You will then be presented with a table showing the full names of users, including a user picture, their position, and the department. A sample list of users is shown here:

| Table | Schedules | Audience | Access |

Access

Full name	Position	Department
Amanda Weaver	Marketing Assistant	Central Europe
Anton Richter	VP Marketing	Europe
Latifah Hood	Pre-Sales Assistant	UK & Ireland
Rhea Baxter	Pre-Sales Assistant	UK & Ireland
Charissa Baldwin	Marketing Manager	UK & Ireland

Figure 8.19 – Report access

You probably guessed that the list showing the users who are allowed to access the report is yet another system report.

In addition to granting user access to reports, it is also possible to specify which users should be listed in any given report. We already dealt with this in the *Configuring settings* sub-section when we introduced the **Relation to the report viewer** condition.

Now that we know how to grant access to the report, let's look at a neat way of how users can quickly and intuitively navigate to their reports.

Adding reports to the custom menu

Users who have been granted access can open a report via the **Report builder** icon in the Workplace launcher. A potentially attractive alternative is to add a link to the report on the main menu. That way, it appears to the user that the report is part of the learning management system.

> **Important Note**
> By using custom menus and reporting, you can extend the functionality of
> Moodle Workplace without using a single line of code!

To add a report to the main menu, you need to run through the following steps:

1. Select **Report builder** in the Workplace launcher to get to the table of reports.

2. Click on the preview icon (the magnifying glass) beside the report you wish to add
   to the main menu.

3. Copy the URL of the report to the clipboard.

4. Go to **Site administration | Appearance | Theme settings**.

5. Scroll down to **Custom menu items** and add a menu item name and the copied
   URL to the list, separated with | (a pipe symbol).

   The new menu item will appear in the menu for all users.

The following screenshot shows a sample entry and the resulting custom menu, including
a sub-menu as well as a menu separator:

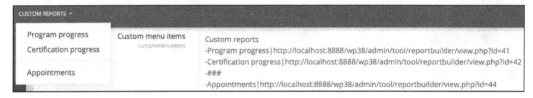

Figure 8.20 – Adding a report as a custom menu item

For more details on how to customize Moodle's menu, check out the help page in the
Moodle documentation at `docs.moodle.org/en/Theme_settings#Custom_`
`menu_items`.

This concludes the main section of this chapter on reporting. Finally, let's take a closer
look at the Workplace data store, which we briefly mentioned earlier.

Exploring the Workplace data store

The Workplace data store is a **permanent record store** used to keep track of course
completions. Additionally, the data store supports course completions that were carried
out outside Workplace but have to be tracked in Workplace.

Initially, you need to enable the data store at **Site administration | Reports | Data store settings**. On the same screen, you can also specify which user and course fields can be stored in the data store:

Data store settings

Enable data store tool_datastore | enabled	☑ Default: No Allow start tracking the user actions in the data store tables
Fields of user entity to store tool_datastore | fieldsuser	username,idnumber,firstname,lastnam Default: username,idnumber,firstname,lastname,email Enter field names separated with a comma (,).
Fields of course entity to store tool_datastore | fieldscourse	category,fullname,shortname,idnumbe Default: category,fullname,shortname,idnumber,summary,summaryformat,format Enter field names separated with a comma (,).
	Save changes

Figure 8.21 – Data store settings

Once the data store has been enabled, the course completion data will be stored permanently, alongside specified user data. This information also supersedes course resets or user deletions. Additionally, it is possible to populate the data store with external data via the course completion CSV upload.

Any user who has the `tool/datastore:uploadcoursecompletion` capability can upload course completion data, which will be stored in the data store for users who belong to the same tenant as themselves. The CSV file import has been extended with two new fields to support the course completion data:

- `coursecompleted`: The short name of the course that has been completed. The course has to exist before the upload is started.

- `coursecompleteddate`: The date that the course was completed on. You need to use the `YYYY-MM-DD` ISO standard format, which will then be localized during the upload process. If this variable is omitted, the date of the day you are filling it out will be used.

Both variables have to have a numeric postfix to support multiple courses. The following is a sample CSV file that uploads three course completions for two users:

```
username,coursecompleted1,coursecompleteddate1
user1,crsNegotiations,2020-02-26
user1,crsMoneyLaundering,2020-01-01
user2,crsNegotiations
```

Once you have created your CSV file, go to **Users | Accounts | Upload users** in the **Site administration** section and follow the upload process using your CSV file.

As soon as records are stored in the data store, use the **Course completion from datastore** report source to create reports. When and why would you make use of the data store and its reporting facility? There are two scenarios where using the data store would be useful:

- When you have to incorporate the **historical data** of your learners in Workplace, you can add these records using the course completion upload facility.

- For **auditing** or other legislative exercises, data often has to be kept for longer than it is stored in the learning management system or after staff have left the company.

At the time of writing, the data store is in its infancy and it is expected that more xAPI-compatible operations will be made available in future releases.

Summary

In this chapter, you learned how to manage reports and how to grant access to different audiences in your organization.

We first dealt with the inner workings of the report builder and how data is processed. We then looked at different data and record sources, which you used to create new custom reports.

To customize reports, you applied conditions, filters, aggregation, groupings, and sorting. While these already provide a comprehensive and flexible set of operations, there is a crucial feature missing that would make the report builder even more useful—the ability to display aggregation and grouped data in a separate footer row (for example, to provide the sum of all attendees below a table). Currently, two separate reports are needed to provide this data, which is not ideal.

Once our reports were created and configured, we looked at different ways of how to schedule reports to be sent automatically to users and how to grant access to the reports. We concluded this chapter by using the built-in Workplace data store to handle permanent data that might exceed the lifetime of your courses or staff.

One last point—don't build reports unless they will be used. Just giving information to people doesn't work, unless there is an agreed expectation of action on the data within a report. It is too easy to assume someone will act upon a report, but if there isn't a process and agreement for them to act, the report has little value and potentially frustrates everyone involved.

With the skills you have acquired, you are now able to provide your colleagues with valuable data about their personal training progress and managers with data about their teams' learning development.

One report source we briefly mentioned but didn't go into great detail about is called **Appointments**, which deals with face-to-face training. In-person activities or classroom-based training will be the subject of the next chapter on seminar management.

9
Seminar Management

Face-to-face training is still a key component in most organizations' staff development strategies. This can either be purely in classroom-based setups—for instance, in the form of seminars and one-on-one training sessions—in blended settings where in-person activities are accompanied by online learning, or synchronous virtual sessions, such as webinars. In this chapter, we will look at Moodle Workplace's appointment facility to organize and manage face-to-face training activities, also known as seminar management.

First, you will learn about Workplace's unique approach to seminars, which is based on the **Appointment booking** activity, comprising appointments and sessions.

Second, we will be dealing with the **management of appointments**, where you will be adding appointment bookings, appointments, and sessions. You will further manage the appointment workflow, which covers steps such as signing up to and canceling an appointment, handling waitlists, taking attendance, and customizing notifications.

Third, we will be looking at **reporting on appointments**, where you will put the skills acquired in the previous chapter into action by creating reports on face-to-face training.

So, by the end of this chapter, you will know how to organize and manage classroom-based and one-to-one training for your organization. This chapter comprises the following three main sections:

- Understanding Workplace's approach to seminars
- Managing appointments
- Reporting on appointments

Understanding Workplace's approach to seminars

So far, all the Moodle Workplace-specific features have been modeled using dedicated tools, such as multi-tenancy, certification, and reporting. The approach Moodle has taken with seminars is slightly different—an activity called **Appointment booking** has been adopted, which supports face-to-face learning. The following diagram attempts to visualize the structure of appointment bookings and how they are embedded in courses:

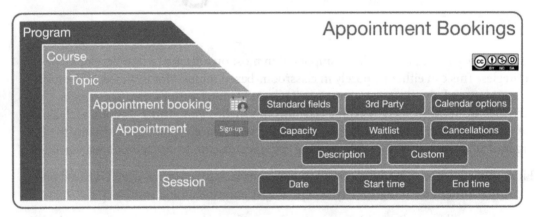

Figure 9.1 – Appointment bookings in Moodle Workplace

As we saw in *Chapter 3, Moodle Courses, Users, and Roles*, **courses** are organized into **topics**. Courses can also be part of **programs** or certifications, which we covered in *Chapter 6, Onboarding and Compliance*. **Appointment booking** is a module that is placed within a course like any other Moodle activity or resource.

> **Important Note**
> An appointment booking comprises one or many appointments, and each appointment consists of one or many sessions.

An **appointment booking** contains all the standard fields and settings, such as the name, description, access restrictions, activity completion criteria, tags, and so on. However, there are two appointment booking-specific features—namely, the handling of **third parties** to support external trainers and **calendar options**, where calendar display settings can be configured.

The **appointment** itself contains a range of settings to configure each face-to-face meeting:

- **Capacity**: The maximum number of participants
- **Waitlist**: The handling of participants on standby
- **Cancellations**: Support for self-withdrawals
- **Description**: Information and appointment details
- **Custom**: User-defined fields, such as location or cost
- **Attendance**: The users signed up to the appointment and their attendance status

> **Important Note**
> Sign-up always takes place at the appointment level.

A **session** comprises a date, a start time, and an end time. Moodle sometimes refers to these as appointment sessions; in this book, we will stick to the term session to avoid confusion.

Details of all three levels—appointment booking, appointments, and sessions—will be dealt with in the latter half of the chapter.

What is the advantage of modeling seminars as part of courses, instead of having a dedicated seminar tool? The main benefit of a course activity is the ability to easily model and implement **blended learning** setups. Let's have a look at a basic example seminar course in the following diagram:

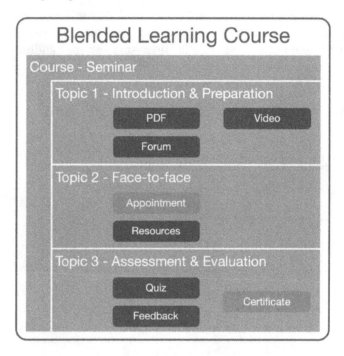

Figure 9.2 – A sample blended learning course

The course has been split into three topics:

- **Introduction and preparation**: This includes some up-front reading material as PDFs as well as an introductory video. This section also contains a forum where all participants are asked to introduce themselves.

- **Face to face**: The actual appointment booking activity plus resources made available by the coach.

- **Assessment and evaluation**: After the face-to-face appointment, participants need to take a quiz and are asked to provide feedback. Once this has been completed, a certificate of participation will be issued (either via dynamic rules or via the new **Certificate** activity).

OK, enough of the theory. Let's get started with the aforementioned **Appointment booking** activity and how to set up your first in-house seminar, which is the first step of managing appointments.

Managing appointments

In this section, we will introduce the **Appointment booking** activity and look at its various options to model seminars and person-to-person training in your organization. This will comprise the following sub-sections:

- Adding appointment bookings

- Adding appointments and sessions

- Managing the appointment workflow (signing up, canceling, waitlists, and attendance)

- Customizing notifications

Let's start by creating our first appointment booking.

Adding appointment bookings

To add an appointment booking, you need to be in editing mode within a course. For demonstration purposes, we are going to use the standard Workplace list course format; if you have applied another course format or theme to your site, some visual elements may differ from the ones shown here. Select **Add an activity or resource** and then pick the **Appointment booking** activity from the activity chooser:

Figure 9.3 – Adding an Appointment booking activity

Once the activity has been added, you will be presented with the settings screen of the appointment booking, as in the following screenshot. We are only focusing on the parameters unique to the **Appointment booking** activity; that is, we are not dealing with common settings such as restricting access, tags, or competencies:

Figure 9.4 – The Appointment booking activity settings

Once you have provided the standard fields, including a name and an optional description, you can include details for **Third-party email address(es)**, with each email address separated by a comma. You will need to add these if you wish to notify external people who are not on your Moodle Workplace system about the appointment—for instance, external instructors. Typically, notifications are sent out when a user signs up to a seminar or cancels their participation. If **Notify third-party about wait-listed sessions** is ticked, the specified third parties will also be sent a message when a learner signs up to a waitlisted appointment. If the **Allow cancelling default** option remains selected, the default setting when creating new appointments will be to allow sign-up cancelations.

The dates and times of sessions will be added automatically to a user's standard Moodle calendar. The **Calendar display settings** option lets you select which event type will be used for calendar entries. The three choices are as follows:

- **None**: The session details will be displayed as user events on the attendees' calendars, provided the **Show on user's calendar** option remains selected.

- **Course**: The session details will be presented as a course event on the course calendar, as well as on the site calendar. They will be visible to all users who are enrolled on the course.

- **Site**: The session details will be shown as global events on the site calendar and will be visible to all users.

By default, the **Name** field of the activity will be used as the calendar entry. You can override this via the **Short name** setting, which will be applied as the session description instead.

Now that we have created and configured the **Appointment booking** activity, the next step is to add appointments and sessions.

Adding appointments and sessions

At the beginning of this chapter, we described the structure of an appointment booking, which consists of appointments, which themselves comprise sessions. On our example site, we offer manual handling training every first Wednesday of the month. In the following screenshot, you can see five entries; the first two have already taken place, and the last one is fully booked:

Figure 9.5 – Appointments and sessions

Each row represents an appointment. The first two columns display session-related information—namely, the date and time. An appointment can comprise either one or multiple sessions. For each appointment, the **Capacity** limit is displayed (this takes the format of the number of users signed up/the total number of seats), as well the **Status** field (displaying either **Open, Finished,** or **Full**). If the status is set to **Open**, users can sign up to the appointment via the **Book** button; if the status is set to **Full**, a waitlist can be joined if it has been enabled. Both processes are described in more detail later on in this chapter. Selecting the **Details** button will show the same data in a pop-up window, plus information on the appointment's description and any custom fields, should they exist. In our example **Details** window, shown in the following screenshot, there are two custom fields—namely, **Cost** and **Discount**:

Figure 9.6 – Appointment details

Now, we are going to add additional appointments to our **Appointment booking** activity. There are two variants, which we are going to cover in the subsequent sub-sections:

- Adding a single appointment

- Adding multiple appointments

OK, let's start with single appointments as they also form the basis for adding multiple appointments afterward.

Adding a single appointment

To add a single appointment, select **Appointment** from the **Add** menu at the top right. You will see a pop-up screen, where the first section deals with sessions. A session is created automatically with the following default values:

- **Date**: Today's date
- **Start time**: The next full hour
- **End time**: 1 hour after the start time

You will need to adjust these three values to the date and times of your actual session. In the following screenshot, we have already created a second session:

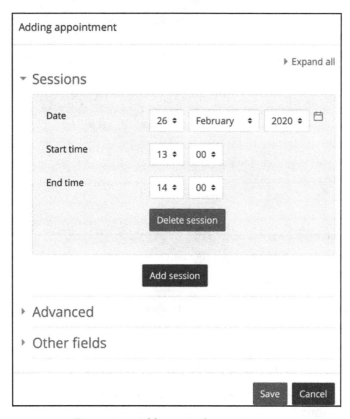

Figure 9.7 – Adding a single appointment

If your appointment contains multiple sessions—for instance, on consecutive days or one in the morning and one in the afternoon—you need to add more sessions via the **Add session** button. Be aware that there are no consistency checks for overlapping sessions. You have to ensure that the times that are set are correct to avoid inconsistencies.

It is also possible to create an appointment with no session (you need to remove the initially created session via the **Delete session** button). Any users signing up for this appointment will be put on the waiting list, which we will deal with shortly. Session-less appointments are a good way to mimic an interested-in feature; once there is sufficient interest, the session information can be added to the appointment.

The second part of the appointment's settings screen is labeled **Advanced**, shown in the following screenshot:

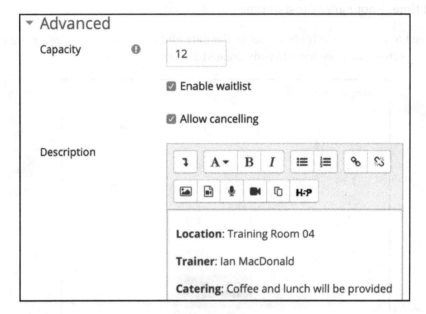

Figure 9.8 – Appointment settings

The **Advanced** section contains the following appointment parameters:

- **Capacity**: The maximum number of participants who can sign up for the appointment.

- **Enable waitlist**: If ticked, sign-up will remain open once the capacity limit has been exceeded. Potential participants will be put on a waiting list.

- **Allow cancelling**: If enabled, users can withdraw after they have signed up. The first user on the waiting list will automatically be given the available seat.

- **Description**: Add free-text details about the appointment. In our training example, we have provided information about the location, the trainer, and catering arrangements.

The last part of the appointment settings covers **Custom fields**. Here, you can specify any parameters that are relevant for your context—for example, seminar fees, such as the cost and discount, as shown:

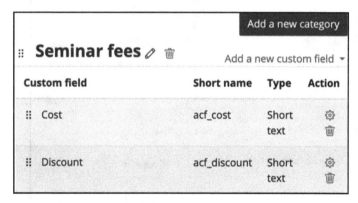

Figure 9.9 – Appointment custom fields I

To manage user-defined appointment fields, you can either go to **Site administration | Plugins | Activity modules | Appointment custom fields** or select the **Manage custom fields** link underneath the **Description** text box. Appointment custom fields work in precisely the same as any other custom fields in Moodle—for instance, as they do for courses (for more details, see the Moodle docs at docs.moodle.org/en/Course_settings#Course_custom_fields). In our example, you can see the **Cost** and **Discount** fields grouped in a section labeled **Seminar fees**:

Seminar fees 🖉 🗑			Add a new category
		Add a new custom field ▾
Custom field	**Short name**	**Type**	**Action**
⠿ Cost	acf_cost	Short text	⚙ 🗑
⠿ Discount	acf_discount	Short text	⚙ 🗑

Figure 9.10 – Appointment custom fields II

So far, we have added single appointments, which is sufficient when organizing an event with a small number of sessions. If you run a seminar twice or more frequently, you can use the standard **Duplicate** functionality in the settings menu of each appointment. In addition to this cloning functionality, Moodle Workplace also offers a shortcut to add multiple appointments, which we will cover in the subsequent sub-section.

Adding multiple appointments

The primary use case for adding multiple appointments is to set up recurring one-on-one sessions with all your team members. For example, if you lead a team of six and you wish to have individual review meetings spread across a day, you could tediously create six separate appointments manually, as described previously, or you can make use of **Timeframes**, as in the following screenshot:

Figure 9.11 – Adding multiple appointments

A timeframe is effectively a one-off template specifying how appointments are created automatically. In our example, we have created two timeframes—one for the morning and one for the afternoon—with three appointments each. In the specified **Date** field, you need to provide a start time and an end time. Within this timeframe, the **Automatic split** and **Break time** values are distributed equally. This mechanism is shown in the following diagram:

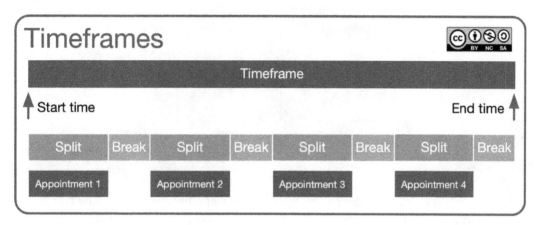

Figure 9.12 – Appointment timeframes

The start time and end time specify the beginning and the end of the timeframe.

> **Important Note**
> Each split defines the duration of each appointment within the timeframe. The break is the pause between splits.

If the split is set to 0, a single appointment will be created, covering the full timeframe. If the break is set to 0, appointments will be created back to back. It is not possible to have appointments with multiple times/dates when adding multiple appointments.

If a split-break combo doesn't exactly fit in the timeframe, Workplace lets the last appointment run over, as long as it commences within the timeframe. For example, if you have a timeframe from 10:00 to 11:00 with an automatic split of 15 minutes and a break time of 10 minutes, the first appointment will be from 10:00 to 10:15, the second slot from 10:25 to 10:40, and the last one from 10:50 to 11:05.

Now that we have created appointments and sessions, the next step is to manage the appointment workflow, which we will deal with in the next sub-section.

Managing the appointment workflow

Once an appointment is available for a course, potential attendees can view details and initiate the appointment workflow outlined in the following flowchart:

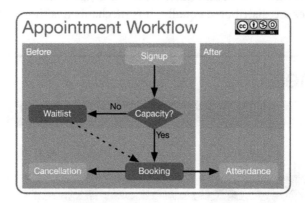

Figure 9.13 – Appointment workflow

If there is spare capacity, users can either **sign up** for the appointment or be signed up by somebody with appropriate permissions—for instance, a manager. If the **capacity** limit has been reached and the **waitlist** has been enabled, users will be added to the back of the queue; otherwise, the **booking** will be successful. Once a participant's seat is **canceled**, the first user on the waitlist will be moved to the list of attendees. After the event has passed, the trainer can take the **attendance** of all participants. Each of these steps will be described in the following four sub-sections:

- Signing up for an appointment
- Canceling an appointment
- Handling waitlists
- Taking attendance

We are going to start with the first step in the overall process—signing up for an appointment.

Signing up for an appointment

There are two ways that users can become attendees for an appointment:

- Signing up via the booking option
- Being signed up by somebody else

We are going to cover both options in the following section.

Signing up via the booking option

Signing up to an appointment takes place within a course. This might seem counter-intuitive since often, signing up for a seminar takes place within a course catalog or similar. Moodle Workplace takes an alternative approach to also facilitate person-to-person meetings.

> **Important Note**
> A user has to be enrolled in a course to be able to sign up for an appointment.

When learners access the course, they will see the number of available seats for all appointments and each appointment activity. Accessing the appointment activity displays the list of available appointments and the **Book** button to sign up. After the user has signed up for an appointment, the status will change from **Open** to **Booked**, and the course page will now show the date of the next session, rather than the number of available seats. If the date is not set, the user will just see the **Booked** status. This sign-up process is shown in the following cascade of screenshots:

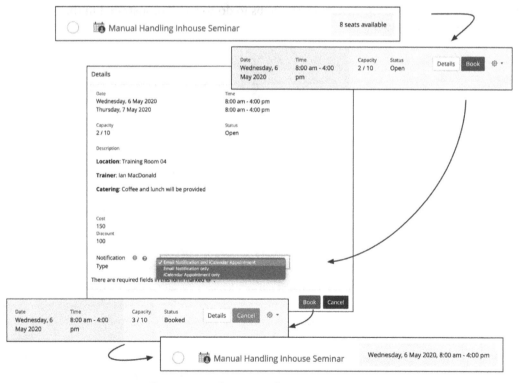

Figure 9.14 – Signing up for an appointment

The booking form is identical to the **Details** screen we saw earlier, with an additional **Notification Type** selection that allows the user to select how they would like to be notified about their booking. The options are as follows:

- **Email Notification and iCalendar Appointment**: Sends the appointment information via email and sends an iCalendar invitation

- **Email Notification only**: Sends the appointment information via email

- **iCalendar Appointment only**: Sends an iCalendar invitation

Notifications will be covered later in this section when we deal with messaging customization.

Signing up other users

In addition to the described self-sign-up process, Moodle Workplace also supports a workflow where a user with the correct permissions can sign other users up for a seminar. A typical example where this takes place is when a manager books a team member onto a session, or a seminar administrator books an appointment on behalf of a customer who signed up via email. The steps to do so are demonstrated in the following series of screenshots:

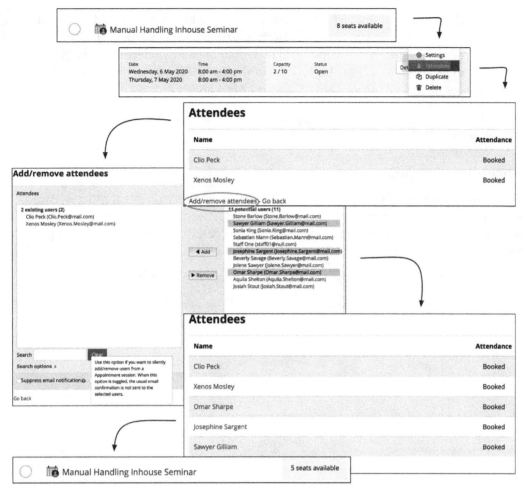

Figure 9.15 – Signing up attendees

As before, the appointment activity displays the number of available spaces for all appointments. To sign up users, you will need to select the **Attendees** option from the menu to the right-hand side of the appointment. This will direct you to a screen that displays the list of all the participants already signed up—in our case, two—and an option at the bottom labeled **Add/remove attendees**.

Once you select this link, you will see the standard Moodle user-selection screen. All users of the current tenant are available for selection, not just users who are already enrolled in the course. Any selected users will be enrolled in the course automatically before they are signed up for the appointment.

There is an option at the bottom left called **Suppress email notifications**, which should be enabled if you wish to add or remove participants from an appointment silently. If this option is toggled, no email confirmation will be sent to the newly selected users. Once you have added users and you navigate back, you can see that the list of participants has been amended accordingly and the number of seats has been updated.

Now that we have signed up users to appointments, let's see how to reverse this process and look at cancelations.

Canceling an appointment

Canceling appointments is a standard feature of any seminar management process. As soon as a user has (been) signed up for an appointment, the booking can be canceled if cancelations are permitted in the advanced settings, as described earlier. The two-step process to do this is shown in the following screenshots:

Figure 9.16 – Canceling attendance

When the **Cancel** button has been hit, the participant can provide an optional **Reason for cancellation** message and then click on **Confirm cancellation**. The user will then be removed from the list of attendees. If a waitlist is in place, the next user will take the freed-up spot; the handling of waitlists is described in the next sub-section.

To cancel other users, you need to follow this same process, but instead of adding users to the list of participants, you need to select participants and remove them from the list.

Currently, there is no way to see all the users who have canceled their attendance. However, this feature is currently on the roadmap and is likely to arrive shortly in Moodle Workplace.

Handling waitlists

A waitlist is a queue of users who wish to sign up for an appointment, where its capacity limit has already been reached. If the waitlist facility has been enabled at the appointment level, potential attendees can add themselves to the waiting list via the **Join waitlist** button. This option is only available when the appointment status is **Full**:

Date	Time	Capacity	Status			
Wednesday, 6 May 2020	8:00 am - 4:00 pm	10 / 10	Full	Details	Join waitlist	⚙ ▾
Thursday, 7 May 2020	8:00 am - 4:00 pm					

Figure 9.17 – Joining a waitlist

Interestingly, when a user signs up other users via the mechanism described previously, it is possible to overbook an appointment; the capacity might then show as **12/10**. This might be necessary when a compulsory training session has to be completed by a specific number of staff, exceeding the usual capacity, or when a senior manager has to be squeezed in at the last minute.

> **Important Note**
> The waitlist operates on a first-in, first-out basis.

The first person who joins the waitlist will be at the top of the queue. Once a place becomes available, this first user will be moved to the list of attendees and all users on the waitlist move up a spot. This mechanism is depicted in the following diagram:

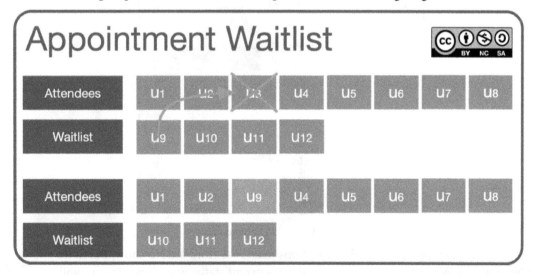

Figure 9.18 – Waitlist handling

Initially, the list of attendees contains eight users, which is the maximum capacity that has been set for the appointment. Four more users are on the waitlist, with user **u9** in the top spot. If user **u3** cancels the appointment, user **u9** will take the free spot, and the waitlist will only contain three remaining users.

This concludes our look at the part of the attendance workflow before the in-person meeting takes place. Next up is taking attendance, which takes place during or after the actual event.

Taking attendance

Once a session has started, the trainer of the course has permission to take attendance. First, go to the **Attendees** option in the menu to the right of the appointment. If the status of the appointment has changed to **Finished**, a new option called **Take attendance** will appear at the bottom left of the screen. Once you select this, you will be shown the list of all the signed-up users, as well as options to specify the attendance status, as in the following screenshot:

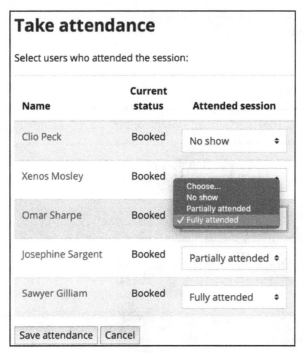

Figure 9.19 – Taking attendance

The three self-explanatory attendance options to choose from are **No show**, **Partially attended**, and **Fully attended**. Once saved, the current status of each participant will change to the selected value.

At the time of writing, the attendance status is for informational use only. What is missing is an activity completion criterion that makes use of the status, which would allow us to specify whether an appointment has to be fully attended to complete a course. This feature is expected to be implemented very shortly.

Phew, that was a very vast section with a lot of intertwined processes. To recap, we have dealt with the various workflows that are currently supported by Moodle Workplace's **Appointment booking** activity, which were divided into the setup (managing appointments, sessions, and date/time slots) and the participants (sign-up, waitlist, cancelation, and attendance taking). The last element of the **Appointment booking** facility that we will cover is customizing notifications.

Customizing notifications

A feature that has been mentioned a few times in this chapter is sending out notifications to participants and external users. You have the option to customize the content of these messages via the **Customised notifications** activity option:

Customised notifications

▸ Confirmation message ❷

▾ Reminder message ❷

Subject	Appointment booking reminder: [appointmentname], [starttime]-[fini
Message	This is a reminder that you are booked on the following appointment: Participant: [firstname] [lastname] Appointment: [appointmentname] Date(s): [alldates] Location: [session:location] Venue: [session:venue] Room: [session:room] ***Please arrive ten minutes before the appointment starts*** To re-schedule or cancel your booking
Days before message is sent ❷	1 ⬍

▸ Wait-listed message ❷

▸ Cancellation message ❷

Save changes   Cancel

Figure 9.20 – Customizing notifications

There are four messages that can be configured:

- **Confirmation message**: Sent out when signing up for the appointment takes place.

- **Reminder message**: Sent out a number of days prior to the session start date. The number of days is defined in the **Days before message is sent** setting.

- **Wait-listed message**: Sent out when a user is added to the waitlist.

- **Cancellation message**: Sent out when a user's participation is canceled.

Each message contains a subject (notification title) and the message itself (notification body), which has to be in plaintext—that is, HTML text is currently not supported. Placeholders are a flexible means to customize each message. The following placeholders are available for all four message subjects and bodies:

Message placeholder	Description
[alldates]	Dates and times of all sessions, for instance 6 May 2020, 8:00 am to 4:00 pm 7 May 2020, 8:00 am to 4:00 pm
[appointmentname]	Name of the appointment activity
[attendeeslink]	Link to the list of all attendees
[details]	Description of appointment activity
[finishtime]	End time of last session
[firstname]	Recipient's first name
[lastname]	Recipient's surname
[reminderperiod]	Number of days before the event when a reminder message will be sent out.
[sessiondate]	Date of first session
[starttime]	Start time of first session

Figure 9.21 – Message placeholders

Appointment messaging can be configured from **Site administration | Plugins | Activity modules | Appointment**. There are a number of parameters that have an impact on how appointment messages are sent out. These are listed in the following table:

Appointment setting	Description
Sender address	Email address of the sender of all appointment messages. Make sure this is accepted by your mail server.
Manager email	These three settings are currently not in use. Prepare for manager approval in the next release!
One message per day	If enabled, multiple confirmation emails are sent for multi-date events. If there is more than one appointment on a single day then each session will generate an email. One session spanning over multiple days will generate only one email.
Disable iCalendar cancellations	If ticked, no iCal attachment will be sent when the participation of appointment is cancelled.

Figure 9.22 – Global appointment settings

Please bear in mind that these work in tandem with the standard messaging settings in Moodle core. This completes the section on appointment activity. To complete this chapter, let's have a look at the **Appointments** report source provided by Workplace's report builder, which takes into account any user- and appointment-related data that we have dealt with so far in this chapter.

Reporting on appointments

In the previous chapter, you learned how to generate custom reports using the built-in report generator. One report source that we only mentioned briefly but didn't go into great detail about is **Appointments**, which deals with the face-to-face training covered in this chapter. The **Appointments** report source is unique in that it provides data from an activity, rather than users and courses.

First of all, you need to create a report using the **Appointments** report source. It is best to add the default configuration, as in the following screenshot:

Figure 9.23 – Creating an appointment report

In addition to the fields we find in most report sources (such as relating to the course, course enrollment, course completion, and job assignments), the attendance report source provides fields on all three appointment levels (**Appointment activity**, **Appointment**, and **Appointment sessions**), as well as on **Attendees**, as shown in the following field selectors:

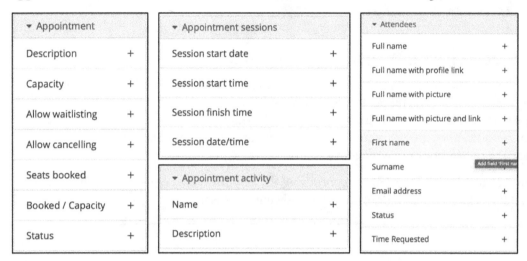

Figure 9.24 – The Appointments report source fields

The interesting aspect of the attendance report source is the fact that the data from course activities can be consolidated in a single report, which allows the creation of seminar status reports. The key elements of the report source are the following three data fields to be used in conditions and filters, respectively:

- **Capacity** (appointment): The number of users registered versus the total seats available

- **Session availability** (appointment): **Full**, **Empty**, or **Partially full**

- **Status** (participant): **User Cancelled**, **Waitlisted**, **Booked**, **No show**, **Partially attended**, or **Fully attended**

The following example report shows the name of the seminar (the course name could have been displayed, too), the date and time of all the sessions, the **Booked / Capacity** pair, and the session's status:

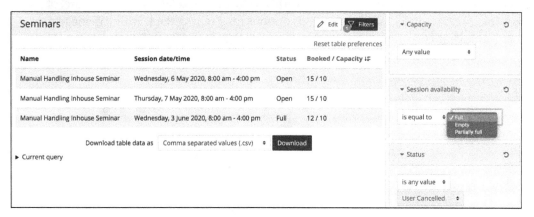

Seminars					Edit Filters
					Reset table preferences
Name	**Date / Time**		**Booked / Capacity**		**Status**
Manual Handling Inhouse Seminar	Wednesday, 6 May 2020, 8:00 am - 4:00 pm		15 / 10		Open
Manual Handling Inhouse Seminar	Thursday, 7 May 2020, 8:00 am - 4:00 pm		15 / 10		Open
Manual Handling Inhouse Seminar	Wednesday, 3 June 2020, 8:00 am - 4:00 pm		12 / 10		Full
Manual Handling Inhouse Seminar	Monday, 4 May 2020, 8:00 am - 12:00 pm		2 / 10		Open
Manual Handling Inhouse Seminar	Tuesday, 5 May 2020, 1:00 pm - 4:00 pm		2 / 10		Open
Manual Handling Inhouse Seminar	Thursday, 5 March 2020, 9:00 am - 4:00 pm		1 / 10		Finished
Monthly review	Friday, 17 April 2020, 10:45 am - 11:15 am		0 / 10		Open
Monthly review	Friday, 17 April 2020, 10:00 am - 10:30 am		0 / 10		Open
Monthly review	Sunday, 12 April 2020, 10:00 am - 11:00 am		0 / 10		Finished
Manual Handling Inhouse Seminar	Wednesday, 26 February 2020, 1:00 pm - 2:00 pm		0 / 10		Finished

1 2 3 4 5 6 7 8 9 10 ... 20 »

Figure 9.25 – Sample appointment report I

Using the aforementioned filters, the same report can easily be modified to provide information on all the **Full** sessions or any sessions with a waitlist:

Seminars					▾ Capacity
					Any value
Name	**Session date/time**	**Status**	**Booked / Capacity**		
Manual Handling Inhouse Seminar	Wednesday, 6 May 2020, 8:00 am - 4:00 pm	Open	15 / 10		▾ Session availability
Manual Handling Inhouse Seminar	Thursday, 7 May 2020, 8:00 am - 4:00 pm	Open	15 / 10		is equal to ✓ Full / Empty / Partially full
Manual Handling Inhouse Seminar	Wednesday, 3 June 2020, 8:00 am - 4:00 pm	Full	12 / 10		

Download table data as Comma separated values (.csv) Download

▸ Current query

▾ Status

is any value
User Cancelled

Figure 9.26 – Sample appointment report II

The list of fields available for the report itself and for use as conditions and filters will be extended in future versions. For instance, once we have the option to directly link to an appointment activity, it will be possible to mimic a basic seminar catalog. Until then, we will have to make do with the elements available in the attendance report source.

Summary

In this chapter, you have learned how to organize and manage seminars and other face-to-face training using Moodle Workplace's attendance activity. These can also be applied for blended settings as well as pure online setups, such as webinars.

First, we dealt with Workplace's unique approach to classroom-based settings, which is based on the **Appointment booking** activity, comprising appointments and sessions.

Next, we dealt with the **management of appointments**, where we added appointment bookings, appointments, and sessions. We then looked at different aspects of the appointment workflow, namely signing up to and canceling an appointment, handling waitlists, taking attendance, and customizing notifications.

Lastly, we covered the **reporting of appointments**, where some sample reports on classroom-based training were created.

If face-to-face training is a crucial component of your organization's staff development strategy, you should now be familiar with the tools available in Moodle Workplace to set up and manage the required workflows. The **Appointment booking** activity is certainly a first step in the right direction toward full-blown seminar management. Expected enhancements in future releases will close the gap to implement more aspects of classroom-based and blended setups.

This concludes the last chapter that deals with a Moodle Workplace-specific feature, of this book. Next, we will look at the various options for aligning the learning management system with your corporate identity and corporate design.

10
Mobile Learning

In most organizations, mobile learning is becoming the norm for e-learning and forms a crucial part of the learning and development strategy. Mobile learning gives your team more flexibility whenever and wherever learning takes place; it offers self-directed and independent learning, supports on-the-job training, boosts micro-learning, and engages with the millennials in your team. Mobiles are typically used for consumption and communication, rather than authoring and administration.

Moodle has released an app for iOS and Android that allows users to interact with a Moodle Workplace system. The app is best suited for learners and supports key functionality for participants to access course content, receive notifications, upload data, monitor progress, and interact with other users. The Workplace app is an alternative to accessing Moodle via a web browser on a mobile device (smartphone or tablet) and has the advantage of being specifically designed for mobile usage, both online and offline.

Firstly, you will learn about any preparatory steps that your learners should take to start using the Workplace app. We will distinguish between accessing Moodle Workplace from mobile browsers and through the app, which is the focus of this chapter. We will then go through the centrally managed settings to enable the app and configure different authentication types. We will also briefly look at installing the app on mobile devices.

Secondly, we will briefly explore the Moodle Workplace app, which is based on its Moodle counterpart. As always, we will focus on Workplace-specific features, namely programs and certifications, appointment bookings, and the Teams dashboard. The latter is only available on the branded app, which we will also briefly introduce.

Lastly, we will look through options of how the Workplace app can be configured to provide your colleagues with a suitable mobile learning experience. This includes mobile features and mobile notifications.

So, by the end of this chapter, you will know how to prepare, configure, and use the Moodle Workplace app. This chapter comprises the following three main sections:

- Preparing to use the Moodle Workplace app
- Exploring the Moodle Workplace app
- Configuring the Moodle Workplace app

Preparing to use the Moodle Workplace app

Before users can learn new content, cooperate with colleagues, or monitor progress from a mobile device, there are several things to consider. First, a decision has to be made on how to access the learning management system, either from a mobile web browser or a dedicated app. The focus of this chapter is on the mobile app, which has to be enabled centrally. Users will have to download and install the app before the first login takes place. All these items will be covered in this section, starting with a short introduction about the two ways to access the Moodle Workplace app from a mobile device.

Accessing Moodle Workplace from mobile devices

Generally, there are two ways that a learner can access Moodle Workplace via a mobile device—directly via a web browser on a cell phone or a tablet, or via Moodle's app for iOS and Android.

The **web browser** view is effectively the same as we have seen throughout the book, only it is optimized via **responsive design** for smaller screen sizes. There are three main arguments relating to using Moodle Workplace via a mobile browser—users have the same functionality available as on a desktop device, the handling is identical, and users won't have to install an extra app onto their mobile device.

The **Moodle Workplace app** provides an alternative view of the same data, and interactions have been optimized for mobile usage. Furthermore, offline usage and synchronization are supported, which is indicated by a little cloud symbol. Another advantage of the mobile app over the browser view is the support of push notifications, which we have all become accustomed to.

The following two screenshots show the difference between the two usage types when accessing the same dashboard:

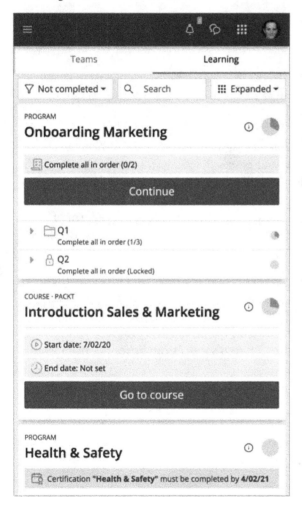

Figure 10.1 – Browser view versus app view

The following diagram shows a simplified process of what happens when Moodle Workplace is accessed from a mobile device (details for the web browser are at the top and for the app are at the bottom):

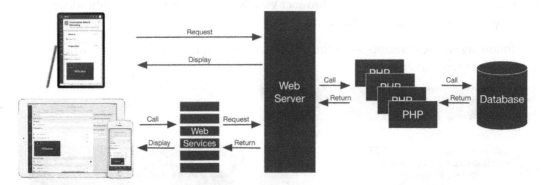

Figure 10.2 – Accessing Moodle Workplace via the browser and app

Let's go through the preceding diagram from left to right and back again. When a user makes requests via the web interface, the browser passes the request to the web server, which calls the PHP module responsible for the call. The PHP module calls the database with an action (a query, update, insert, or delete operation), which returns the requested data. Based on this information, the PHP module returns data (usually in the form of HTML or JavaScript code) to the web server, which passes the information to be displayed back to the user's browser.

When accessing a Moodle Workplace instance via the app, the process is precisely the same, except for the first step, which involves calling web services, which request data from the web server. The same applies to the returning information, which is also passed through web services. Web services are the standard communication protocol between web and mobile applications. More information on web services can be found in *Appendix A, Moodle Workplace Web Services*.

We will be exclusively focusing on the Moodle Workplace app in this chapter. Before your learners can use the app, however, the following prerequisites must be fulfilled:

- App usage must be enabled on your site.
- Users must download and install the app on their mobile device.
- Users must authenticate via the app.

We are going to run through all three steps before exploring the Workplace-specific features of the app itself. Let's start by enabling the app.

Enabling the app

The process of enabling the Moodle app to interact with your Moodle site has been greatly simplified. Go to **Site administration | Mobile app | Mobile settings** and tick the **Enable web services for mobile devices** option, as in the following screenshot:

Mobile settings

Enable web services for mobile devices enablemobilewebservice	☑ Default: No
	Enable mobile service for the official Moodle app or other app requesting it. For more information, read the Moodle documentation
App policy URL tool_mobile | apppolicy	locuments/public/app/app_policy.html | Default: Empty
	The URL of a policy for app users which is listed on the About page in the app. If the field is left empty, the site policy URL will be used instead.
	Save changes

Figure 10.3 – Enabling the Workplace app

That's it. No other steps are required. Well, almost. You should also enable the **Mobile** notification option, which you can find under **Site administration | Messaging | Notification settings**. We are going to cover the settings of the mobile notifications plugin later on in the section on customization.

The second configuration option is **App policy URL**. If set, this page will be listed on the app's about page; if left empty, the main site policy will be used instead.

> **Important Note**
> It is highly recommended that you enable HTTPS with a valid certificate. The Workplace app will always try to use a secured connection first.

Now that the app usage has been enabled, let's look at how your workforce can install the app on their snazzy mobile devices.

Installing the app

Your learners will need to download and install the app from Apple's app store or Google Play. There is no charge for the app. Screenshots of both of these apps on the Apple app store (on a tablet) and Google Play (on a phone) are shown as follows:

Figure 10.4 – The Workplace app for iOS and Android

To install the app, users need to follow the usual steps on their mobile devices (starting with **GET** on iOS and **Install** on Android).

The Moodle Workplace app is based on the official Moodle app. It has the same functionality plus some extra features to cater for programs and teams (branded version only). It is expected that more Workplace-only tools will be supported in future releases of the Workplace app.

> **Important Note**
> The Moodle Workplace app only works with Moodle Workplace. The Moodle app only works with standard Moodle.

Don't be discouraged about any negative reviews since almost all poor feedback comes from users who expected the app to work standalone without access to an existing Moodle Workplace system. This leads nicely to the final enablement step—accessing your Moodle Workplace system via the app and authentication.

Authenticating on the Moodle Workplace app

Once the app has been installed and launched for the first time, each user will have to authenticate with the Workplace instance. Moodle Workplace supports three different login types, which have to be selected by the administrator at **Site administration | Mobile app | Mobile authentication**, as in the following screenshot:

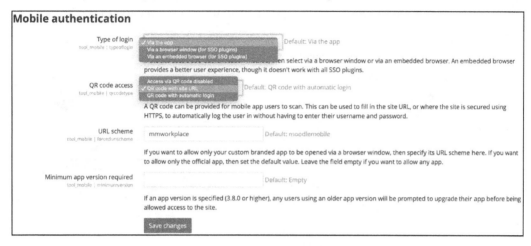

Figure 10.5 – Authentication types

The **Type of login** field provides the following three options:

- **Via the app** (default): This is the default authentication mechanism that applies to all manual accounts.

- **Via a browser window (for SSO plugins)**: If your site uses an SSO authentication method, such as MS-AD, LDAP, or OAuth, this mechanism opens a separate browser window where the login credentials have to be provided.

- **Via an embedded browser (for SSO plugins)**: This is effectively the same as the previous option but provides a better user experience. However, not all authentication plugins will work in an embedded browser—for instance, when JavaScript popups are required.

QR code access is an alternative way to let your users access the site by scanning the matrix barcode. This mode can be configured with a site URL (users will have to enter their credentials) or with automatic login. The latter option may be restricted depending on your app subscription plan.

If your organization uses a custom branded app and **Type of login** is set to one of the two SSO types, then the **URL scheme** option can be set. This will result in only the custom branded app working for the site, whereas the official Moodle Workplace app will not work.

The **Minimum app version required** option can usually be left empty and should only be set if you want or need to force users to update to an up-to-date version of the Moodle Workplace app.

The three different login types will show up for the users differently, as shown in the following sequence of screenshots:

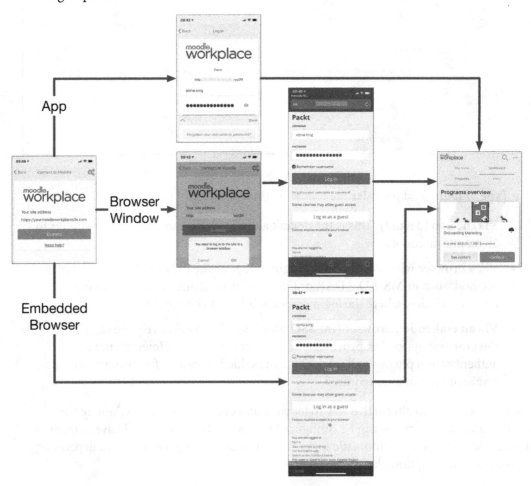

Figure 10.6 – Different login types and authentication

During the initial launch, the URL must be entered; on subsequent launches, this will already be pre-filled. The same applies to the login credentials unless the admin has enforced logout in **Site administration** | **Mobile App** | **Mobile features**.

On the branded app, no URL has to be entered since it is hardcoded into the app. Also, the branding of the app will (obviously) look different from the ones shown in this chapter.

Logging in via the app displays a login window as part of the app. When logging in via a browser, a notification will be displayed telling the user that the default browser on the mobile device will be opened before the redirection takes place. Once the credentials have been entered, Moodle Workplace re-directs the user back to the app. The embedded browser view effectively looks the same, but no external browser will be opened.

This concludes the section on the preparatory steps that have to be taken before the Moodle Workplace app can be used. We first discussed two options on how to access your Workplace system from a mobile device, before focusing on the mobile app for iOS and Android. Next, we enabled the app and configured authentication. We also briefly covered the installation of the app on users' devices. Now that this has been done, your learners are ready to use the Workplace app, which we are going to explore in the following section.

Exploring the Moodle Workplace app

The Moodle Workplace app is based on the standard Moodle app and comes with some extra features to cater to the Workplace-specific functionalities, as well as another color scheme. The objective of this section is to list the key features of the Moodle app, before covering the features that are unique to the Moodle Workplace app in more detail.

This section comprises the following two sections:

- The standard Moodle app
- The Moodle Workplace app features

The standard Moodle app

While the standard Moodle app only supports a sub-set of learner-centric features, it has the advantage of being specifically designed for mobile usage and also supports offline content. The Workplace app is based on the Moodle app and contains all its functionality, as well as some Workplace-specific elements. Here is a short list of highlights of the features provided by the Moodle app (derived from `docs.moodle.org/en/Moodle_app`):

- Access the course dashboard.

- Browse the content of courses, both online and offline.

- Connect with course participants and quickly find and contact other people on courses.

- Receive instant notifications of messages and other events, such as being allocated to an onboarding program or being awarded a badge.

- Upload images, audio, video, and other files from mobile devices.

- Track progress by checking the course completion progress.

- Browse learning plans and competencies.

- Complete activities anywhere and at any time and attempt quizzes, post in forums, play SCORM packages, or edit wiki pages.

A full list of the Moodle app's features and links to other Moodle app-related pages can be found on the Moodle docs at `docs.moodle.org/en/Moodle_app_features`. Now that we have briefly covered the Moodle app, let's have a closer look at the Workplace-specific features.

The Moodle Workplace app features

This app has been designed with learners and managers in mind; that is, it is neither intended nor possible to create or modify courses, set up or configure workflows, or carry out administrative tasks. A vast majority of Moodle Workplace-specific features, such as managing tenants, setting up job positions based on organizations and positions, or creating dynamic rules, fall in the latter two categories. So, what are Workplace-specific features that are relevant to learners and managers on a mobile app? The following table lists the key features and how the Moodle Workplace app supports them:

Feature	App Support
Programs	Dashboard and details
Certifications	Via programs
Certificates	Custom link in menu
Reports	Custom link in menu
Appointment bookings	External link in course
Teams	Dashboard (Branded app only)

Figure 10.7 – Workplace-specific learner features

In the remainder of this section, we will briefly present the following features directly supported in the app:

- Programs and certifications
- Appointment bookings
- The Teams dashboard

The Workplace features that are currently only supported via custom menu items will be dealt with in the next section, where we will cover the customization of the app. Let's get started with programs and certifications.

Programs and certifications

Programs allow you to establish learning pathways for your employees by adding a combination of courses or a hierarchical sequence of courses. From a learner perspective, programs contain several courses that have to be completed. The app provides insight into programs via the **Programs** view of the dashboard. The first screenshot in the following figure shows an example of a dashboard tile, indicating the program's name, due date, and completion progress. The download icon indicates that the program's content is available offline:

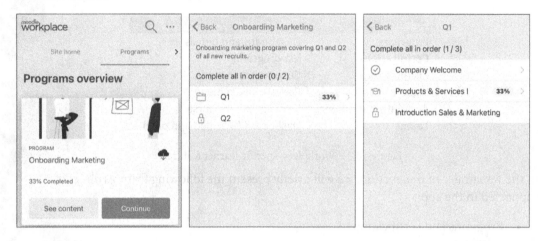

Figure 10.8 – Programs in the app

If you select the **See content** button, you will navigate to the first level of the program. Here, there are two sets, called **Q1** and **Q2**. When you choose an available level, you will be directed to a level further down; in our case, the one that contains the courses. Once you select a course, you will be at the familiar course-level view.

Certifications are based on programs, as we learned in *Chapter 6, Onboarding and Compliance*. Right now, certifications are not explicitly supported by the app; that is, meta-information about issuing and expiry are not displayed. Instead, programs that are contained in certifications are presented and handled as described previously.

Depending on the program's status, the following will be displayed on the right button on the program tile:

- **Open** or **Overdue**: The **Continue** button jumps straight to the last course that the user has been working on. If the program hasn't been started, the button is labeled **Start** and will jump to the first course in the program.

- **Completed**: This button will be inactive and will be labeled **Completed** next to a checkbox.

- **Future allocation** or **Suspended**: The program will be hidden from the app dashboard.

Within a course, all standard Moodle activities are fully supported, both for viewing as well as contributing activities. The only Workplace-specific activity is **Appointment booking**, which we are going to deal with next.

Appointment booking

The standard behavior of the Moodle app is to open the default web browser when a third-party or unsupported plugin is selected in a course. All core Moodle activity and resource types are fully supported in the Moodle app, both online and offline. The same holds for Moodle Workplace, with one exception—the **Appointment booking** activity, containing data on seminars. At the time of writing (version 3.9.2), appointment bookings can only be viewed in the web browser, as shown in the following screenshot:

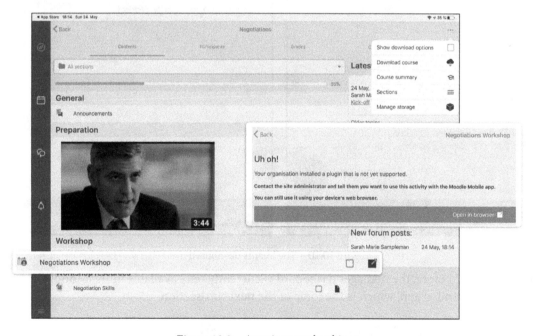

Figure 10.9 – Appointment bookings

It is expected that the **Appointment bookings** plugin will be supported in the mobile app in an upcoming release. The same holds for the **Course certificate** activity, which is currently not supported natively. However, the associated notifications are fully mobile-aware; that is, when a certificate is issued, the user will be notified accordingly.

The Teams dashboard

The Teams dashboard is central for managers to monitor the progress of their subordinates. The branded Moodle Workplace app supports a dedicated dashboard that contains all their team members, as well as information about active, overdue, and completed programs and certifications. An example of the Teams dashboard can be seen in the following screenshot:

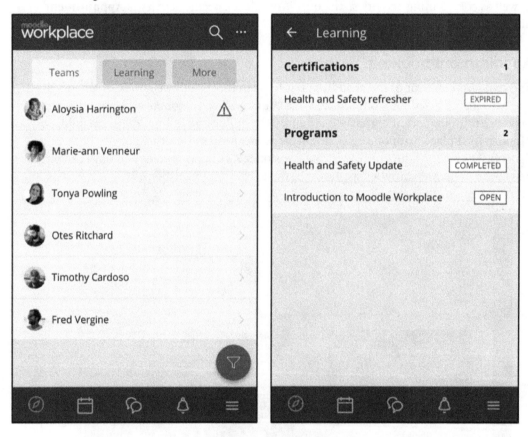

Figure 10.10 – The Teams dashboard

As mentioned before, the manager dashboard is currently only available in the Moodle Workplace branded app, which is the topic of the next sub-section.

The Moodle Workplace branded app

Moodle offers an attractive service, called the Moodle Workplace branded app. As the name suggests, its main aim is to provide you with an app where the look and feel are in line with your corporate brand, which we will look at in *Chapter 11, Corporate Identity*. However, on top of supporting your brand itself, the branded Moodle Workplace app comes with several additional advantages:

- A separate entry in the Apple and Google Play app stores.

- The URL is already fixed in the app, so there is no need for your users to add the web address.

- Separate hosting space in Moodle's GDPR-compliant push notifications infrastructure.

- Tracks mobile engagement analytics to better understand behaviors and improve your mobile-friendly learning experience. It also gets insights into how your learners use your app with personalized access to mobile engagement data.

- Supports the Teams tab as mentioned previously.

Bear in mind that the branded Moodle Workplace app is a subscription service provided by Moodle. For more details, contact your local Premium Moodle Partner or check out more details at `moodle.com/app`.

This concludes the section on the standard features of the Moodle Workplace app. Next up are options to centrally customize the app from within your Workplace instance.

Configuring the Moodle Workplace app

The beauty of the Moodle Workplace app is that it can be customized "from the outside"— that is, by configuration only. In this chapter, you will learn how to tailor the app to your learners' needs. The two main areas of customization are as follows:

- Mobile features

- Mobile notifications

It is also possible to extend the functionality of the mobile app via development. However, that is beyond the scope of this book since programming skills are needed. More details can be found at `docs.moodle.org/dev/Mobile_support_for_plugins`. Let's get started with the mobile app features.

Mobile features

The Moodle app lets you customize some features that can also be harnessed in Moodle Workplace. You will find the two relevant settings under **Site administration | Mobile app | Mobile features**, as in the following screenshot:

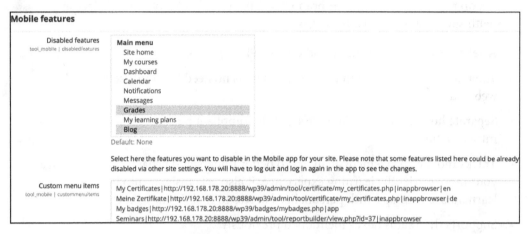

Figure 10.11 – Mobile features

The **Disabled features** list lets you remove features from the mobile app. In most commercial setups, some standard Moodle tools are not used since they are targeted at educational institutions. Typical features that are disabled are grades, blogs, and notes. It is recommended that you remove any features that are not being used to reduce the app's complexity and, therefore, improve your learners' learning experience.

The opposite of removing features is adding additional items to the app's main menu. These items have to be specified with **Custom menu items**. The format of each entry is as follows (all entries have to be separated by the pipe symbol):

```
item text|link|opening method|[language code]
```

`item text` is the label that will appear in the app. The `link` field sets the URL that the user will be directed to. The app supports four different opening methods:

- `app`: For linking to items supported by the app. For instance, on our site, the link to **My badges** is supported since badges can also be accessed via the user's profile.

- `inappbrowser`: For opening the link in a browser without leaving the app.

- `browser`: For opening the link in the device default browser outside the app.

- `embedded`: For displaying the link in an iframe in a new page on the app (no scrolling possible).

The following is a screenshot from the Workplace app, where grades, the site blog, and tags have been removed and the three custom menu items have been added. The before and after screenshots demonstrate the impact on a user's menu on the app:

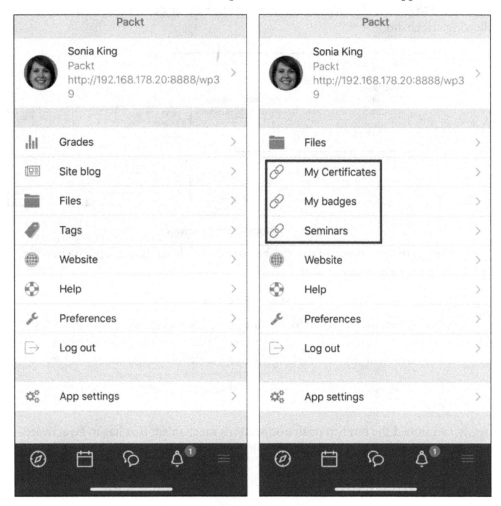

Figure 10.12 – Mobile custom menus

The optional `language` parameter displays the item to users of the specified language only. In our sample, the link to my certificates has also been provided in German.

The **Custom language strings** setting provides a further language-related configuration option. Since the Workplace app is based on the Moodle app, some terminology is aimed at educational establishments, which isn't suitable for a commercial setting. For instance, you might want to change the term `student` to `learner` or `course` to `module`, as in the following screenshot:

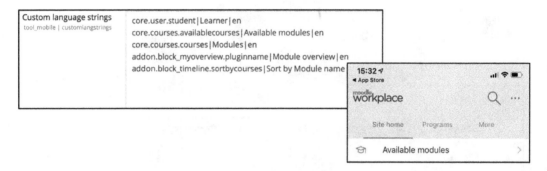

Figure 10.13 – Custom language strings

Words and phrases displayed in the app can be customized by adding a separate line for each entry using the following notation:

```
string identifier|custom string|language code
```

The full list of string identifiers can be found under the *Custom language strings* section at `docs.moodle.org/en/Moodle_app_guide_for_admins`. The `custom string` is the replacement text for the language set via the **language code**.

Make sure you sync the app to apply the configured changes (**Menu | App settings | Synchronization**).

We already mentioned the built-in push notifications mechanism that has to be activated, which we will cover in the next sub-section.

Mobile notifications

The Moodle Workplace app supports push notifications for different mobile platforms. We already enabled mobile notifications from **Site administration | Messaging | Notification settings** when we activated the app in the first section. To configure the mobile notifications, navigate to the form shown in the following screenshot by going to **Site administration | Messaging | Mobile**:

Mobile

Airnotifier URL airnotifieruri	https://messages.moodle.net	Default: https://messages.moodle.net

The server url to connect to to send push notifications.

Airnotifier port airnotifierport	443	Default: 443

The port to use when connecting to the airnotifier server.

Mobile app name airnotifiermobileappname	com.moodle.workplace	Default: com.moodle.moodlemobile

The Mobile app unique identifier (usually something like com.moodle.moodlemobile).

Airnotifier app name airnotifierappname	commoodleworkplace	Default: commoodlemoodlemobile

The app name identifier in Airnotifier.

Airnotifier access key airnotifieraccesskey	████████████████	Default: Empty

The access key to use when connecting to the airnotifier server.

Request access key

Save changes

Figure 10.14 – Mobile messaging settings

The default values connect to the public Moodle messaging server. All you need to do is click on **Request an access key** (the link at the bottom). This requires your site to be registered with moodle.org (via **Site administration | Registration**).

The following is a schematic overview of how push notifications work. **Apple Push Notification Service (APNS)** and Google Cloud Messaging are the respective gateways for relaying push notifications on iOS and Android devices:

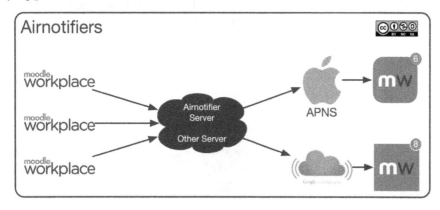

Figure 10.15 – AirNotifier

Moodle's messaging server is a public AirNotifier system and, therefore, carries a (small) degree of risk. For some privacy-conscious organizations, this approach will not be acceptable, so it is possible to set up your own notification infrastructure, which involves setting up a local Airnotifier server. You will find instructions on how to do this and links to related resources at `docs.moodle.org/en/Moodle_app_notifications`.

This concludes the section on customizing the Moodle Workplace app, which dealt with various mobile features and setting up mobile notifications.

Summary

In this chapter, you learned how to prepare, use, and configure the Moodle Workplace app.

Firstly, we dealt with any preparatory steps to take before your learners can commence using the Workplace app. We showed the pros and cons of accessing Moodle Workplace from mobile browsers and through the app, which was the focus of this chapter. We then went through centrally managed settings to enable the app and configured different authentication types.

Secondly, we briefly explored the Moodle Workplace app, which is based on its Moodle counterpart. We focused on the Workplace-specific features, namely programs and certifications, appointment bookings, and the Teams dashboard. We briefly introduced the branded Workplace app service offered by Moodle.

Lastly, we look through options on how the Workplace app can be customized, which included the configuration of mobile features and mobile notifications.

You might have spotted one administrative area of the mobile app administration section we left out, namely **Mobile appearance**, which deals with the look and feel of the app. How to bring Moodle Workplace visually in line with your corporate design, both in a web browser and on the app, is the topic of the next chapter.

11
Corporate Identity

Corporate identity is how an organization presents itself to the public, typically represented by pre-defined visualizations, known as branding.

Moodle Workplace provides a modern interface, ensuring an engaging user experience. The applied responsive technology guarantees that this is the case on various devices across an array of popular platforms. Most companies want to bring their applications' visual styles in line with the corporate branding guidelines of the organization. This chapter shows you how to adjust Moodle Workplace to create a learning environment where the look and feel will be familiar to your learners.

First, we will provide a brief overview of Moodle designs, covering **appearance** configuration options and **themes**. The former deals with settings that impact user experience elements such as navigation or menus, while the latter looks at Moodle's (S)CSS-based skinning mechanism.

Second, you will learn how to brand tenants, which includes basic appearance settings, such as colors and logos, as well as more advanced settings, where samples of CSS snippets will be provided.

Third, we will be styling the mobile app, which we covered in great detail in the previous chapter. Moodle Workplace provides a beautiful mechanism to perform this level of customization remotely. We will also present the branded Moodle app, a commercial alternative provided by Moodle HQ.

So, by the end of this chapter, you will know how to customize your Moodle Workplace instance in order to provide your staff with a fully branded learning experience. The chapter comprises the following three main sections:

- Moodle design overview

- Branding tenants

- Branding the mobile app

Important Note

Theme creation is not covered in this book as it is usually the task of a designer with good CSS skills. *Moodle Theme Development* by *Silvina Paola Hillar, Packt Publishing* is a very good book to familiarize yourself with the basics of Moodle's themes and designs.

Moodle design overview

We will first provide you with an overview of generic design options in Moodle environments. There are numerous ways to customize the appearance of your Moodle site so that it blends in with your company's corporate brand. These boil down to two categories:

- **Appearance configuration options**: There are a plethora of settings in standard Moodle that impact the learner's user experience—for instance, items to be displayed in the user menu or content being shown on the dashboard. The majority of these settings can be found under the **Appearance** tab of the **Site administration** menu. In this chapter, we will only focus on Workplace-specific appearance configuration options.

- **Themes and related settings**: **Moodle themes** provide a skin to completely change the look and feel of your site. The same mechanism, of course, also applies to Moodle Workplace. The main difference is that standard Moodle ships with two themes—**Boost** and **Classic**—whereas Moodle Workplace comes with an additional theme, aptly named **Workplace**.

  You should either customize the default Workplace theme to reflect your organizational branding guidelines or develop a new theme tailored to your requirements. We will only focus on the former, while the latter should be performed by an experienced Moodle designer or a Premium Moodle Partner. To learn more about theme basics, go to `docs.moodle.org/dev/Themes_ overview`, where you will find a very well-documented and detailed help section.

> **Important Note**
> Do **not** use a standard Moodle theme in Moodle Workplace. They will display certain elements incorrectly and potentially break your system.

Moodle uses **Cascading Style Sheets** (**CSS**) to describe the presentation of each element that is displayed. CSS is used to define different aspects of the HTML presentation, including colors, fonts, layouts, and so on. At the heart of CSS are so-called styles; Moodle consistently uses plain English for the naming of styles. For the Workplace login elements that are displayed in the following screenshot, four sample styles have been labeled:

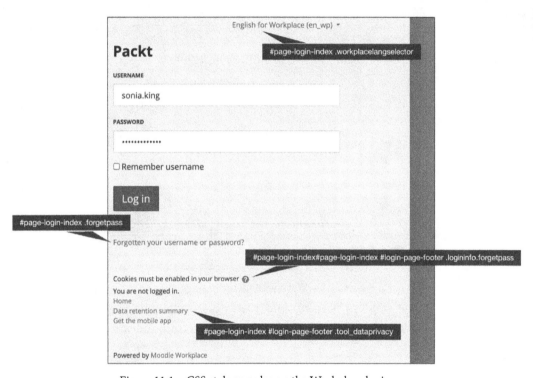

Figure 11.1 – CSS style samples on the Workplace login page

The class selectors, such as `.forgetpass` or `.tool_dataprivacy`, and the ID selectors (for instance, `#page-login-index` or `#login-page-footer`) are best identified using the **Inspect** mechanism built into every modern desktop web browser. We will be using some of these classes later in the chapter.

In more recent versions, Moodle has started supporting **SCSS** (known as **Sassy CSS**), which is a superset of CSS providing additional features such as variables and nesting. SCSS is a preprocessor language that is converted to CSS before it is applied to any site. For the sake of simplicity, we are going to stick to CSS throughout this chapter.

If you already have any SCCS code or libraries, feel free to use these for your visual customizations. Any code you wish to inject side-wide should be applied directly in the Workplace theme at **Site administration | Appearance | Themes | Workplace**. Here, you will find two settings that let you override the initial SCCS variables and add new SCCS to themes without modifying any code in the backend: **Raw initial SCCS** (code injected before any other code) and **Raw SCCS** (injected at the end of the style sheet). In the following example, I have added some variables to add some weight to all fonts throughout the site:

Workplace

Workplace launcher as modal theme_workplace | wpmenumodal	☐ Default: No Show the Workplace launcher in a popup instead of a dropdown menu
Raw initial SCCS theme_workplace | scsspre	/* Add some weight to fonts to assist my old peepers */ $font-weight-light: 500 !default; $font-weight-normal: 600 !default; $font-weight-bold: 700 !default;
	Default: Empty In this field you can provide initialising SCSS code, it will be injected before everything else. Most of the time you will use this setting to define variables.
Raw SCSS theme_workplace | scss	
	Default: Empty Use this field to provide SCSS or CSS code which will be injected at the end of the style sheet.
	Save changes

Figure 11.2 – Workplace theme settings

Now that you are familiar with the Moodle theme basics, we will be configuring appearance options at the tenant level, before applying CSS to some advanced settings to brand our tenants.

Branding tenants

Moodle Workplace supports tenants for separate users, courses, and other data, as well as workflows. These features were discussed in detail in *Chapter 4, Tenants, Organizations, and Teams*. Branding can also be applied to individual tenants, which is the topic of this section.

Navigate to **Site administration | Users | Manage tenants** or go directly to **Tenants** via the Workplace launcher. Then, choose the tenant to be branded and select the **Appearance** tab. You will see the three main categories, **Images**, **Colours**, and **Advanced**, which we will deal with in this section. The objective is to Packt-ize our site in terms of its look and feel.

Basic appearance settings

The first set of settings in the **Appearance** tab deals with images displayed on your site. The following four images should be uploaded:

- **Header logo**: The company logo to be displayed in the navigation bar.
- **Login logo**: The organization logo displayed above the username and password fields on the login screen. This is often the same as the header logo.
- **Login background image**: The picture to be displayed on the login screen. We will take a closer look at the login screen(s) later in this section.
- **Favicon**: The icon associated with this site is usually shown in the browser's address bar.

Here, we will only show the header logo; the handling of the other three images is exactly the same:

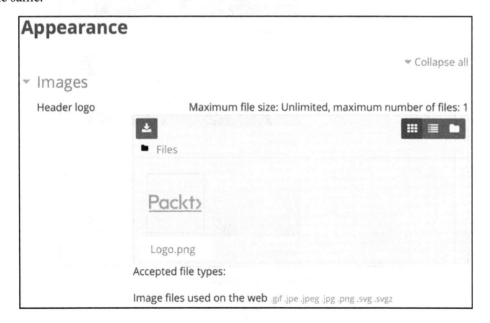

Figure 11.3 – Images

The second part of the **Appearance** section deals with some basic colors used throughout the site. In the following screenshot, we have already applied the RGB values of the Packt color scheme:

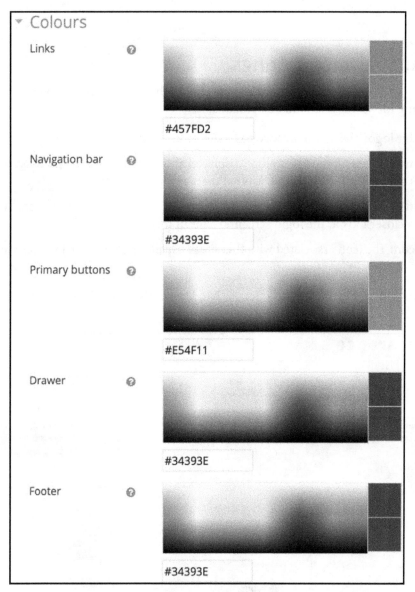

Figure 11.4 – Colours

The five available customization options are as follows:

- **Links**: The color used for links and interactive elements
- **Navigation bar**: The color used for the top navigation bar
- **Primary buttons**: The color of the main action buttons
- **Drawer**: The color used for the navigation drawer background
- **Footer**: The color used for the footer background

It may take several minutes before changes are visible on your site. To expedite this refreshing process, clear your cache by going to **Site administration | Development | Purge caches**.

Advanced appearance settings

There are two settings in the **Advanced** section, namely **Custom SCSS** and **Footer text**. The custom SCSS option lets you effectively modify any visual part of Moodle Workplace. Here, we have hidden any content from the footer, apart from the **Powered by Moodle Workplace** link. We have also added a copyright note in the footer, as displayed at the bottom of the screenshot:

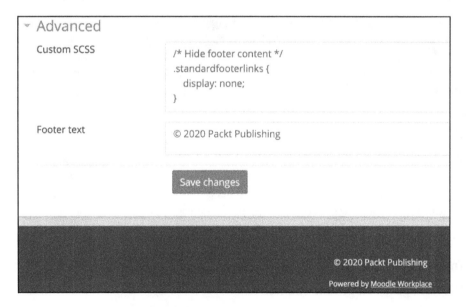

Figure 11.5 – Advanced

There is no limit to what you can add to the custom CSS entry, so here are a few more Workplace-specific snippets that might come in useful (with brief explanations in the comments):

```
/* Change color of drawer button & give it a bit of a curve */
#page-wrapper >.fixed-top >div>.drawer-toggle-button {
    background: #E54F11;
    border-top-right-radius: 1em;
}
/* Change font color in Workplace launcher */
.workplace-menu >div>div>.card-deck>a>span {
    color: #E54F11 !important;
}


/* Change background and text colors of left login panel */
#page-login-index .loginmain {
    background: #34393E !important;
}
.loginmain * {
    color: grey !important;
}
```

The last code snippet changes the background color of the login screen, which is the topic of the following and last sub-section on tenant branding.

Customizing the login screen

If no tenant is specified in the URL, the default settings for tenants (`tenantid=1`) will be applied (for details on this, see *Chapter 4, Tenants, Organizations, and Teams*). This also impacts the login screen the user will see when accessing the site. So far, we have made modifications to the following elements that affect the login page:

- The login logo
- The login background page
- The login page background and font color

Several default items on the login page are not applicable in certain commercial settings; for instance, guest login is activated, and the **Login as a guest** button is shown as a consequence. To remove this option, go to **Site administration | Plugins | Authentication | Manage authentication** and set the **Guest login button** parameter to **Hide**. There is a number of text items and links that you might also want to get rid of (listed from top to bottom):

- **The language selector**:

```
/* Hide login page > Language selector */
#page-login-index .workplacelangselector {
    display: none;
}
```

Hiding the language selector via the **Display language menu** option in **Site administration | Language | Language settings** will not hide this option on the login screen.

- **The link to the "Forgotten username and password" page**:

```
/* Hide login page > Forgotten password */
#page-login-index .forgetpass {
    display: none;
}
```

This should only be hidden if single sign-on options have been activated.

- **The "Cookies must be enabled in your browser" note and information icon**:

```
/* Hide login page > Cookie */
#page-login-index .workplacelogin .mt-5.small {
    display: none;
}
```

Beware that it is not good practice to remove the note about cookies, since this might have to be displayed for regulatory reasons.

- **You are not logged in**:

```
/* Hide login page > Login info */
#page-login-index #login-page-footer .logininfo {
    display: none;
}
```

- **The link to the home page**:

```
/* Hide login page > Home page */
#page-login-index #login-page-footer .homelink {
    display: none;
}
```

- **The link to the data retention summary**:

```
/* Hide login page > Data rentention */
#page-login-index #login-page-footer .tool_dataprivacy {
    display: none;
}
```

Alternatively, untick the **Show data retention summary** setting in **Site administration | Users | Privacy and policies | Privacy settings**. However, this will apply to all tenants.

- **The "Get the mobile app" link**:

```
/* Hide login page > Mobile app*/
#page-login-index #login-page-footer .tool_dataprivacy +
a {
    display: none;
}
```

Once all these settings have been applied, our login page now has a different look compared to its standard Moodle Workplace counterpart. Both versions are shown side by side in the following figure:

Figure 11.6 – The default login screen versus a customized login screen

So far, we have changed some colors and hidden a few elements on the login page. In the current version of Moodle Workplace, it is impossible to add additional tenant-specific HTML code; for instance, providing a different link to separate the help desks for each tenant. To do this, you will have to apply the following trick:

1. Navigate to **Site administration | Appearance | Additional HTML** and create a new class for each tenant in the **Before BODY is closed** setting, such as the aforementioned two different links to two different help desk sites:

```
<!- Tenant-specific code for imPackt tenant -->
<div class="tenant-specific impackt">
<p><a target="_blank" href="https://yoursite/imPackt/
helpdesk.html"> imPackt Contact Help Desk (8am - 5pm) </
a>
</div>


<!- Tenant-specific code for comPackt tenant -->
<div class="tenant-specific compackt">
<p><a target="_blank" href="https://yoursite/comPackt/
helpdesk.html"> comPackt Contact Help Desk (07:00 -
18:00) </a>
</div>
```

The first class defines the text and link for the `imPackt` tenant. The second class looks very similar, but the text and link are different.

2.   Next, hide the just-defined classes globally—that is, on the entire site—no matter what tenant is active. Your **Additional HTML** page should look something like this:

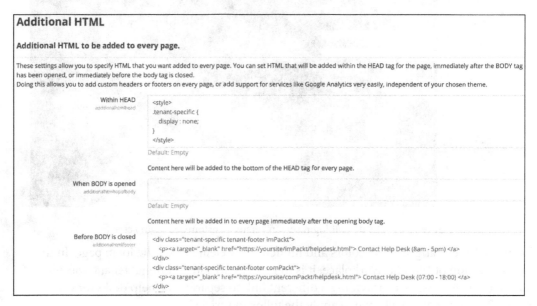

Figure 11.7 – Additional HTML to define tenant-specific links

This mechanism is not limited to simple HTML links in the closing <body> tag but can also be applied to other HTML code for the opening and closing <body> tags.

3.   Go to the tenant-specific settings, select the **Appearance** tab as before, and add the following code to the **Custom SCSS** property in the **Advanced** section:

```
/* Make hidden tenant-specific content visible */
.tenant-specific.impackt {
    display: block
}
```

The preceding snippet displays the content for the `imPackt` tenant; the same applies to the `comPackt` tenant in the following code:

```
/* Make hidden tenant-specific content visible */
.tenant-specific.compackt {
    display: block
}
```

Now, when a user goes to the login page of the `imPackt` or `comPackt` tenants, the following extra information will be displayed, respectively:

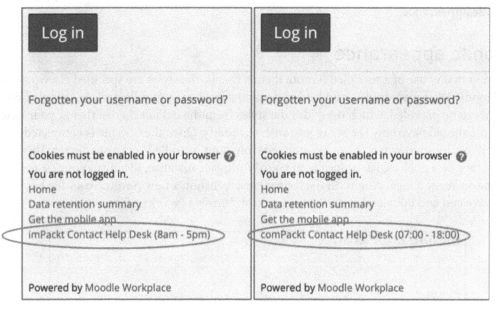

Figure 11.8 – Modified tenant-specific login pages

You can spot the extra links underneath the **Get the mobile app** link. How cool is that?! Technically, there is no limit to how you can modify tenant-specific content throughout the site.

This completes the section on how to apply the basics of branding your site, particularly at the tenant level. Next up is applying branding to the mobile app.

Branding the mobile app

In the previous chapter, we covered the setup, installation, and usage of the Moodle Workplace app. We deliberately left out the branding functionality, which we are going to deal with in this section. We will first cover **remote themes**, which allow the basic branding of the mobile app. Next, we will briefly look at the **branded Moodle Workplace app**, a commercial alternative provided by Moodle HQ. Finally, we will cover the handling of **app banners**, which deal with handling the site when it is accessed from a mobile browser.

To centrally modify the app's look and feel, go to **Site administration | Mobile app | Mobile appearance**.

Mobile appearance

The app makes use of a so-called remote theme; that is, the styles are specified elsewhere—in Moodle Workplace itself—and loaded dynamically to each mobile device. A single CSS file has to be provided, which overrides the styles from the default theme; that is, your new CSS file should have only the styles you wish to modify. Once the CSS file is completed, load it to a location where it can be accessed from your Moodle Workplace server. This can either be a public URL or locally in your Workplace instance, ideally in your custom theme or inside a local plugin. In the following screenshot, a new `packt.css` file has been created and uploaded to `$CFG->wwwroot/theme/workplace`:

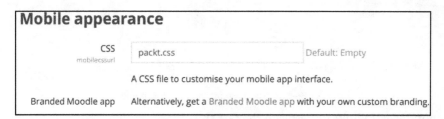

Figure 11.09 – Mobile appearance

For simplicity, we have only changed a single style to modify the app toolbar's background color to reflect the branding of our organization, as follows:

```
/* Change toolbar background color to orange */
.toolbar-background
{
  background: orange;
}
```

How do you know what elements to style in your mobile CSS file? The most convenient approach is to download and install the Moodle Desktop app (`download.moodle.org/desktop`). Once you are logged in to your site, you need to enable the developer tools: (*Ctrl + Shift + I* in Windows and Linux, and *Cmd + Option + I* on macOS). You can now inspect the HTML and identify the styles you wish to change.

> **Important Note**
> To apply the new styles, you need to clear the cache and restart the app.

The result of the modified styles can be seen in the following screenshots, where you can nicely compare the toolbar of the standard app and its customized counterpart:

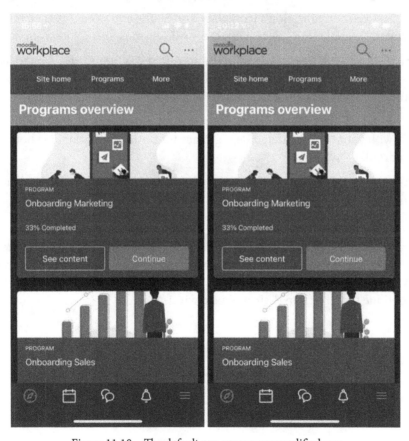

Figure 11.10 – The default app versus our modified app

Like the custom CSS for the browser version of Moodle Workplace, there is virtually no limit to what can be done in the mobile CSS. To tweak your app further, you'd best get an experienced Moodle designer or a Premium Moodle Partner involved.

Branded Moodle Workplace app

Moodle HQ offers a professional service to brand the mobile app on your behalf. You can find more detailed information as well as commercial conditions on the dedicated branded app page: `https://moodle.com/branded-app`.

Why would you want a branded app instead of the remote theme described earlier? Remote theme styles can be tricky to modify. There are lots of CSS rules, and some of them can change between versions. Using your own branded mobile app will have better style integrations because they use Sass variables to change colors and styles.

There is a number of additional advantages when making use of the branded Moodle app compared to a do-it-yourself mobile theme:

- You will get your organization's icon placed on all the app stores. That is, instead of the standard Moodle Workplace icon, users will see the icon of your company.

- A static URL site will be embedded in the app. That way, your users won't have to enter the URL of your Moodle Workplace instance when they use the app for the first time.

- Advanced privacy by providing GDPR-compliant protection for your learners' privacy with your own separate hosting space for push notifications, in both iOS and Android.

- You will get insights into your learners' mobile learning experience via engagement analytics: where and when they access your app, how they interact with notifications, and which courses and resources they spend time on.

In summary, the branded app usually results in a more streamlined onboarding exercise and a better learning experience since your learners get direct and easy access to the content they need. Once your learners download your branded custom app, they simply log in and continue to learn from their mobile device(s).

App banners

App banners let your users know that a dedicated mobile app is available when accessing the site using a mobile browser. In the following figure, you can see two app banners for the Moodle Workplace iOS app—the one on the left is displayed when the app has not yet been installed; the one on the right is displayed when the app has been installed:

Figure 11.11 – App banners in action

App banners are disabled by default. To activate them, you need to tick the **Enable app banners** checkbox. Bear in mind that currently in iOS, app banners are only shown in the Safari web browser. App banners for Android devices are only displayed on the Chrome browser when the app is not installed and when the conditions for its engagement heuristic have been met.

If you are using a branded mobile app, you need to provide the unique identifier for the iOS and Android app; if you are using the Moodle Workplace app, the settings can be left at their defaults, as shown in the following screenshot:

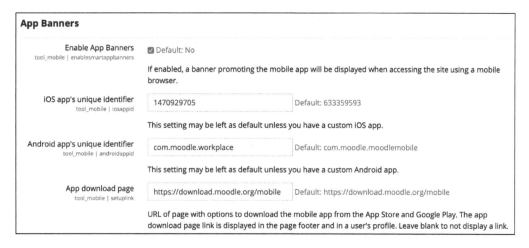

Figure 11.12 – App banners configuration

The last setting in the **App Banners** section is labeled **App download page** and indicates the URL displayed in the page footer and the user's profile. If you have a branded Moodle Workplace app, it is highly recommended to create a dedicated page on your website that provides links to the iOS and Android downloads for your app.

Summary

In this chapter, you learned how to customize your Moodle Workplace system in order to provide your staff with a fully branded learning experience.

First, you acquired some necessary skills on Moodle design, which covered **appearance** configuration options and **themes**. We dealt with settings that impact user experience elements, such as navigation and menus, and looked at some simple CSS-based skinning mechanisms.

Second, you learned how to brand tenants, which included basic appearance settings such as colors and logos, as well as more advanced settings where samples of CSS snippets were provided.

Lastly, you styled the Moodle Workplace mobile app via so-called remote themes. We also presented the branded Moodle app as a commercial alternative. In this context, we also looked at app banners to be displayed when Moodle Workplace is accessed via a mobile web browser as the app is presented on the user's device.

Next up is the final technical chapter, dealing with migrations to facilitate the exchange of different types of data between different Moodle Workplace systems.

12
Migrations

Moving data and elements between tenants and sites is a potentially time-consuming and error-prone task. Moodle Workplace's powerful migration tool expedites and simplifies this process, as we will see in this chapter.

First, we will cover the fundamental concepts of the migration tool. This will provide you with an overview of the different available import and export migrations and also outline the typical migration workflow.

Next, we will deal with the migration tool's intricacies, which covers exporting and importing data. We will also have a closer look at the versatile command-line interface, which is used to automate processes at the system level.

Finally, we will deal with synchronizing HR data and user provisioning, which is critical when configuring your setup in order to synchronize user-related data between your HR system and your learning management system. You will become familiar with the different options available for keeping any user-related data in Moodle Workplace up to date.

By the end of this chapter, you will be familiar with the different ways you can move data and elements between tenants and sites, as well as to and from external systems.

In this chapter, we will cover the following topics:

- Understanding migration
- Working with migration
- Synchronizing HR data

Let's get started!

Understanding Migration

In this section, we are going to cover the fundamental concepts of migration. The migration tool can export various parts of a Moodle Workplace instance and import them into the same or different sites. Currently, the following Moodle Workplace elements are supported:

- Courses and course categories
- Users and cohorts
- Certifications and programs
- Dynamic rules
- Custom reports
- Organization structure (positions, departments, and jobs)
- Entire tenants

Since the migration API is pluggable by design, it is expected that more elements will be supported in future releases of Moodle Workplace. More importantly, it is straightforward to develop **third-party migrations**; for instance, an importer for certificates from an in-house legacy system or an exporter for course completions to the personnel file in your HR system. It would even be feasible to write importers and exporters to and from other learning management systems.

So, what are typical use cases for migrations? There are three levels where you can apply migrations:

- You might want to move or copy data among **tenants**; for instance, the position hierarchy from one subsidiary to another.
- In most professional setups, there is at least a test and a production site. When copying various data between **instances** – for example, once testing of a new feature has been completed – the migration tool offers a fantastic solution.

- Similarly, there are scenarios where data has to be copied between (remote) **sites**; for instance, when you wish to share courses with a partner site or when merging two sites into one.

The following diagram shows a **high-level migration overview**, visualizing the typical workflows of exporting and importing Moodle Workplace data:

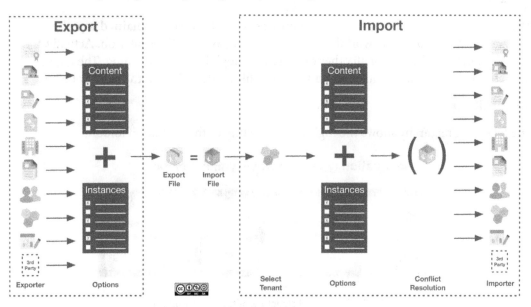

Figure 12.1 – High-level migration overview

The **export process** contains the following key steps:

1. **Selecting the exporter**: Initiating the respective wizard of the selected exporter.
2. **Export options**: This step covers two parts, namely **content** (what data must be exported) and **instances** (which elements should be exported).
3. **Review and exporting**: Executing/scheduling the actual export and creating the export file.

The **import process** contains the following steps:

1. **Selecting a source**: Choosing the import file you will be dealing with.
2. **Selecting a tenant**: Choosing the tenant where the data must be imported to.
3. **Import options**: This step covers two parts, namely **content** (what data must be imported) and **instances** (which elements should be imported).

4. **Conflict resolution**: If the import file contains any inconsistencies for the chosen tenant, manual intervention is required.

5. **Review and importing**: Executing/scheduling the actual import.

We will describe each import and export step in detail for the different migration types in the next section.

The beauty of migration exporters and importers is that they can be **chained together** – that way, import and export workflows can be created, as we will see later on. Actually, the tenant exporter makes use of all other exporters through internal cascading. The high-level structure of the identical export and import files is described in the sidebar below:

SIDEBAR

The following hierarchy shows the high-level structure of the migration folder:

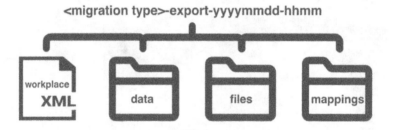

Figure 12.2 – High-level structure of the migration folder

The format of the export filename is `<migration type>-export-yyyymmdd-hhmm`, where `<migration type> ::= certificates | certifications | cohorts | course-categories | courses | custom-reports | dynamic-rules | organisations-structure-frameworks | organisations-structure-jobs | programs | tenants | users`.

A sample folder name is `course-export-20201117-2359`. The four elements in this folder are as follows:

- `workplace.xml`: XML file providing meta-information about the migration file.
- `data`: Folder containing (textual) data in XML format; for example, job assignments.
- `files`: Folder containing (binary) files; for instance, course backups.
- `mappings`: Folder containing associations, such as user IDs and related data.

Knowing the migration file's structure allows the developers of external applications to provide this data so that it can be imported into Moodle Workplace.

END SIDEBAR

Now that you are familiar with the overall migration workflow, let's migrate some data from our Moodle Workplace instance. Our exporters and importers have been implemented as intuitive step by step walkthroughs, all of which we will cover in the following section.

Working with Migration

You can manage your migrations via **Site administration | Migration** or directly via the **Migration** icon in the Workplace launcher. This icon looks as follows:

Figure 12.3 – Migration launcher

You will see a list of **Exports** and, on the second tab, a list of **Imports**, identical in terms of layout and available filters. In our demo instance, we have already created several exports, as can be seen in the following screenshot:

Figure 12.4 – List of exports

The system report contains the following columns:

- **Date** (filter): Date and time the export/import was created. There is a filter to limit the scope of this column.

- **Created by**: User account that initiated the export/import.

- **Exporter/Importer**: Type of exporter/importer.

- **Tenant** (filter): Name of the tenant that the export/import was created for.

- **Size**: Size of the export/import file.

- **Status** (filter): Can be either **Scheduled, In progress, Success**, or **Error**.

- **Actions**: The following actions are available:

  New import from this file (export only): Use the export file as input and start the migration importer.

  Download: Download the export/import file.

  View export/import: Show a status report that includes an error log, if applicable.

  Delete: Remove the export/import file.

We'll look at all the statuses and actions in more detail in the remainder of this section.

Let's get started by exporting some data.

Exporting data

To create a new export, select the standard **+ Export** button on the **Exports** tab. You will then be greeted with the first step of the export process. Select which exporter you want to use from the options displayed, as shown in the following screenshot:

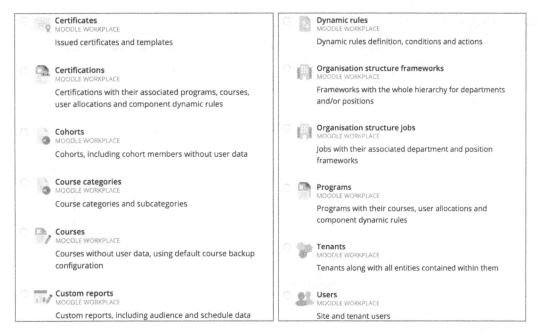

Figure 12.5 – Migration step 1 – exporter selection

Moodle Workplace currently provides 12 exporters; the purpose of each should be self-explanatory. During the second step, you will be able to narrow down your selection and specify which elements you want to export. The exporter options always contain the following two elements:

- **Content**: What attributes and settings may or may not be included in the export file.

- **Instances**: Which elements will be included in the export file.

The content and instances available depend on the chosen exporter, as you will see in the consequent 12 sub-sections – one for each export type.

Exporting certificates

The **Certificates** exporter packages issued certificates and templates. You can see the available options in the following screenshot:

Figure 12.6 – Certificates exporter options – I

The following tables list all the available options for the Certificates exporter, alongside short descriptions of each:

Content	Description
Certificate template details (compulsory)	Includes the certificate template per se, including all pages and elements.
Issued Certificates	Includes information about the certificates issued to users but not the generated PDF files. No user data will be included.

Instances	Description
Select all certificate templates	All certificate templates of the selected tenant will be included.
Select categories and subcategories manually...	When you select categories, all certificate templates within these categories will be included in the exported file.
Select certificate templates manually...	All selected certificate templates will be included in the exported files.

Figure 12.7 – Certificates exporter options – II

Exporting certificates might be required when issued documents have to be transferred to an auditing system or your staff's personnel file. Note that the export file contains information about any issued certificates, but not the PDF certificates per se!

Exporting certifications

The **Certifications** exporter packages certifications with their associated programs, courses, user allocations, and dynamic rules. You can see the available options in the following screenshot:

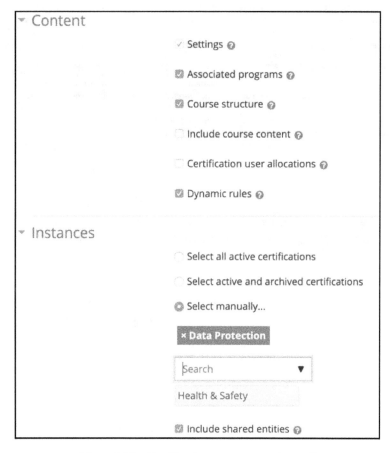

Figure 12.8 – Certifications exporter options – I

The following tables list all the available options for the Certifications exporter, alongside short descriptions of each:

Content	Description
Settings (compulsory)	Properties of exported certifications, such as names, descriptions, dates, tags, and so on.
Associated programs	Properties (names, descriptions, dates, tags, etc.) of any programs the certifications are associated with.
Course structure	See **Course structure** information in **Courses** exporter. The option is only available when **Associated programs** has been selected.
Include course content	See **Include course content** information in **Courses** exporter.
User allocations	Includes user allocations to certifications. No user data per se will be included.
Dynamic rules	All dynamic rule configurations for certifications.

Instances	Description
Select all active certifications	All active certifications in the selected tenant will be included.
Select active and archived certifications	Same as above, but also archived certifications will be included.
Select manually...	Select one or many certifications from the available list.
Include shared entities	Unless individual certifications have been selected, this option will trigger the inclusion of all shared certifications in the selected tenant, any shared programs linked to the certifications, and all courses outside of the tenant course category.

Figure 12.9 – Certifications exporter options – II

Exporting certifications might be useful when you wish to copy a compliance program from one subdivision (tenant) to another subdivision (tenant) within your company.

Exporting cohorts

The **Cohorts** exporter packages cohorts, including its details and members, but without user data. You can see the available options in the following screenshot:

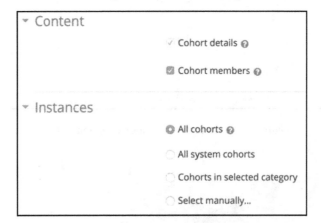

Figure 12.10 – Cohorts exporter options – I

The following tables list all the available options for the Cohorts exporter, alongside short descriptions of each:

Content	Description
Cohort details (compulsory)	Include all cohort details of the selected cohort(s).
Cohort members	Cohort membership will be included in the export file, but actual user details won't be.

Instances	Description
All cohorts	All cohorts of the selected tenant will be included.
All system cohorts	All system cohorts of the selected tenant will be included, that is no cohorts assigned in categories.
All cohorts in selected category	All cohorts will be included which reside inside any of the selected categories and sub-categories.
Select manually...	All selected categories will be included.

Figure 12.11 – Cohorts exporter options – II

Exporting cohorts is particularly useful when used in conjunction with the Users exporter (covered later in this chapter) as you can move groups of users from one tenant to another tenant or site.

Exporting course categories

The **Course categories** exporter packages course categories, including its details, course structures, certificate templates, cohort details, and members from all selected course categories. You can see the available options in the following screenshot:

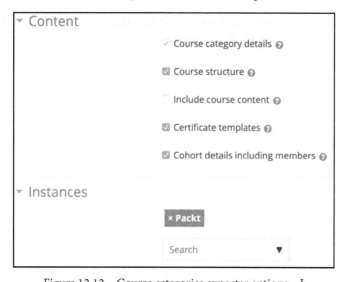

Figure 12.12 – Course categories exporter options – I

The following tables list all available options for the Course categories exporter, alongside short descriptions of each:

Content	Description
Course category details (compulsory)	Include all course category details excluding role assignments and filters.
Course structure	See **Course structure** information in **Courses** exporter.
Include course content	See **Include course content** information in **Courses** exporter. The option is only available when **Course structure** has been selected.
Certificate templates	Include certificate templates, pages, and elements which belong to the categories. Issued certificates are not included in the export file.
Cohort details including members	Include cohort details including membership information but excluding user data.

Instances	Description
	When you select categories, all courses within these categories will be included in the exported file. If you wish to include courses in sub-categories or sub-sub-categories, you need to select these one-by-one.

Figure 12.13 – Course categories exporter options – II

Exporting course categories is particularly useful when used in conjunction with the Courses exporter (covered next) as you can move batches of courses from one tenant or from one site to another.

Exporting courses

The **Courses** exporter packages courses without user data, using the default course backup configuration. You can see the available options in the following screenshot:

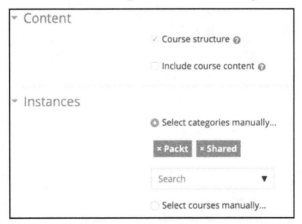

Figure 12.14 – Courses exporter options – I

The following tables list all the available options for the Courses exporter, alongside short descriptions of each:

Content	Description
Course structure	This includes all elements of the selected course(s), except the course content itself. The export will contain the same settings as those set as default when creating a course backup. Note, that no user data will be included.
Include course content	Include all course content, such as activities, resources, filters, calendar events, etc. As for the course structure, the same settings will be applied as those set as default when creating a course backup.

Instances	Description
Select categories manually...	When you select categories, all courses within these categories will be included in the exported file. If you wish to include courses in sub-categories or sub-sub-categories, you need to select these one-by-one.
Select courses manually...	All selected courses will be included in the exported files. Courses from multiple categories can be mixed and matched.

Figure 12.15 – Courses exporter options – II

Course migration is a fantastic feature if you wish to easily move single or multiple courses around your site; that is, among tenants or between sites. While it has been possible to use the backup and restore feature to achieve this, multiple, often time-consuming, manual steps have been required, especially when dealing with a large number of courses. Internally, the migration tool makes use of the course backup and restore features to guarantee compatibility.

By default, only users who have editing rights in the site configuration (usually administrators) have permission to include course content in the migration export. If you wish to allow this feature to be supported for all users who are allowed to perform migrations, go to **Site administration | Migration settings** and tick the option shown in the following screenshot:

Figure 12.16 – Migration settings

It is recommended that you keep this setting unticked, especially when sensitive or valuable content is stored on your site.

Exporting Custom Reports

The **Custom reports** exporter packages Moodle Workplace reports, including audience and schedule data. You can see the available options in the following screenshot:

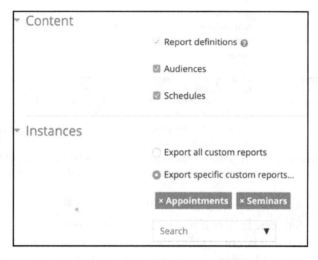

Figure 12.17 – Custom reports exporter options – I

The following tables list all the available options for the Custom reports exporter, alongside a short description of each:

Content	Description
Report definitions (compulsory)	Includes report columns, conditions, filters, and sorting criteria.
Audiences	Includes audiences associated with the report(s).
Schedules	Include schedules associated with the report(s).

Instances	Description
Export all custom reports	All custom reports of the selected tenant will be included.
Export specific custom reports...	All selected reports will be included.

Figure 12.18 – Custom reports exporter options – II

Migrating custom reports is particularly useful when you're exchanging popular reports among tenants or migrating entire tenants.

Exporting Dynamic Rules

The **Dynamic rules** exporter packages Moodle Workplace dynamic rules, including rule definitions, conditions, and actions. Surprisingly, the exporter does not support the selection of individual dynamic rules. You can see the available options in the following screenshot:

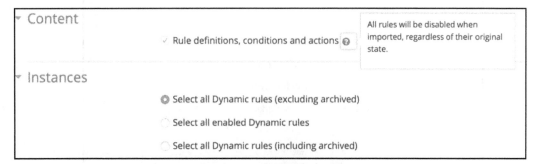

Figure 12.19 – Dynamic rules exporter options – I

The following tables list all the available options for the Dynamic rules exporter, alongside a short description of each:

Content	Description
Rule definitions, conditions and actions (compulsory)	Rules definitions (names and rule action limits) as well as condition and action details will always be included in the exported file.

Instances	Description
Select all Dynamic rules (excluding archived)	All rules – enabled or disabled – will be included, but no archived rules.
Select all enabled Dynamic rules	All enabled rules will be included, but no disabled or archived rules.
Select all Dynamic rules (including archived)	All rules – enabled, disabled, and archived – will be included.

Figure 12.20 – Dynamic rules exporter options – II

The migration of dynamic rules is particularly useful when you're migrating entire tenants. Note that when importing a dynamic rule, it will be disabled, independent of its original state.

Exporting Organization structure frameworks

The **Organization structure frameworks** exporter packages department and/or position frameworks. You can see the available options in the following screenshot:

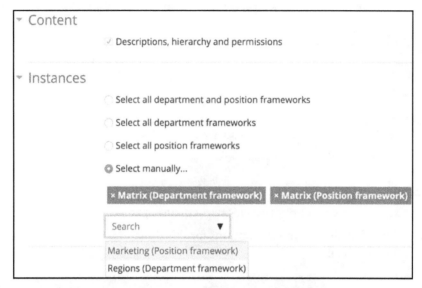

Figure 12.21 – Organization structure frameworks exporter options – I

The following tables list all the available options for the Organization structure frameworks exporter, alongside short descriptions of each:

Content	Description
Descriptions, hierarchies and definitions (compulsory)	For all selected frameworks, properties (name, ID, and description) will be included alongside all positions and departments, hierarchical arrangement, and, in the case of positions, applied permissions (managers and department leads).

Instances	Description
Select all department and position frameworks	All department and position frameworks of the selected tenant will be included in the export file.
Select all department frameworks	All department frameworks of the selected tenant will be included in the export file.
Select all position frameworks	All position frameworks of the selected tenant will be included in the export file.
Select manually...	All selected department and position frameworks will be included in the export file.

Figure 12.22 – Organization structure frameworks exporter options – II

The Organization structure frameworks exporter is potentially very useful when you wish to synchronize data from your HR system with Moodle Workplace. We will be looking at such a scenario in the second part of this chapter.

Exporting Organization Structure Jobs

The **Organisation structure jobs** exporter packages jobs and, optionally, their associated department and position frameworks. You can see the available options in the following screenshot:

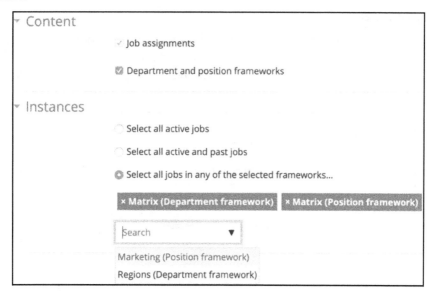

Figure 12.23 – Organization structure jobs exporter options – I

The following tables list all the available options for the Organization structure jobs exporter, alongside short descriptions of each:

Content	Description
Job assignments (compulsory)	This includes all data related to jobs, namely associations to users, positions, and departments as well as start and end dates.
Departments and position frameworks	This is effectively, identical to the data in the organization structure frameworks exporter. If you exclude departments and position frameworks, make sure the target system has the information available to avoid conflicts during the import.

Instances	Description
Select all active jobs	All active job assignments will be included in the exported file, but no past jobs.
Select all active and past jobs	All job assignments – active and past – will be included in the exported file.
Select all jobs in any of the selected frameworks...	You can select individual position and/or department frameworks. Any jobs that hold associations to these selected frameworks will be included in the exported file.

Figure 12.24 – Organization structure jobs exporter options – II

Just like the Organization structure frameworks exporters we covered in the previous sub-section, organization structure jobs exporters are essential when you're dealing with data from your HR system to Moodle Workplace.

Exporting programs

The **Programs** exporter packages programs with their associated courses, user allocations, and dynamic rules. Not surprisingly, the Programs exporter is very similar to its Certifications exporter counterpart. You can see the available options in the following screenshot:

Figure 12.25 – Programs exporter options – I

The following tables list all the available options for the Programs exporter, alongside short descriptions of each:

Content	Description
Settings (compulsory)	Properties of exported programs, such as names, descriptions, dates, tags, and so on.
Course structure	See **Course structure** information in **Courses** exporter.
Include course content	See **Include course content** information in **Courses** exporter.
User allocations	Includes user allocations to the programs. No user data per se will be included.
Dynamic rules	All dynamic rule configurations for selected programs.

Instances	Description
Select all active programs	All active programs in the selected tenant will be included.
Select all active and archived programs	Same as above, but also archived programs will be included.
Select manually...	Select one or many programs from the available list.
Include shared entities	Unless individual programs have been selected, this option will trigger the inclusion of all shared programs in the selected tenant and all courses outside of the tenant course category.

Figure 12.26 – Programs exporter options – II

Exporting programs might be useful when you wish to copy an onboarding program from one subdivision (tenant) to another subdivision (tenant) within your company.

Exporting Tenants

The **Tenants** exporter lets you package up all Moodle Workplace-specific elements in a single export file. You can see the available options in the following screenshot:

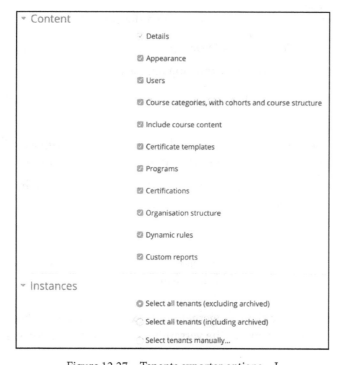

Figure 12.27 – Tenants exporter options – I

The following tables list all the available options for the Tenants exporter, alongside short descriptions of each:

Content	Description
Details (compulsory)	Properties of exported tenants, namely basic tenant information (tenant name, site name, site short name, ID, and login URLs) as well as management data (administrators and associated course category).
Appearance	Exports the look and feel settings of the tenant(s). The three main categories are **Images**, **Colours**, and **Advanced**.
Users	User data of the tenant.
Course categories, with cohorts and course structure	Course categories data of the tenant.
Include course content	Course content of the tenant (only available if course categories have been included).
Certificate templates	Exporting the certificate templated associated with the tenant(s).
Programs	Programs data of the tenant.
Certifications	Certifications data of the tenant.
Organisation structure	Departments, positions, and job assignments of the tenant.
Dynamic rules	Dynamic rule of the tenant.
Custom reports	Exporting the custom reports associated with the tenant(s).

Instances	Description
Select all active tenants (excluding archived)	Self-explanatory
Select all active tenants (including archived)	Self-explanatory
Select tenants manually...	Select one or many tenants from the available list.

Figure 12.28 – Tenants exporter options – II

There are three common use cases for exporting tenants:

- During a merger or acquisition exercise, entire company structures will have to be migrated.

- When splitting a tenant in two, it is usually more efficient to duplicate the tenant (by exporting and importing again) and then remove elements from each tenant.

- When onboarding a new department in a test instance, you might have to migrate the tenant from the test system to the production or live system.

> **Tip**
> It is often more efficient to export a tenant with selected content instead of applying multiple exporters within this tenant.

Internally, the tenant exporter chains together other exporters that have been described in this chapter. This nicely demonstrates the versatility of the migration process.

Exporting Users

The **Users** exporter packages site and tenant users. You can see the available options in the following screenshot:

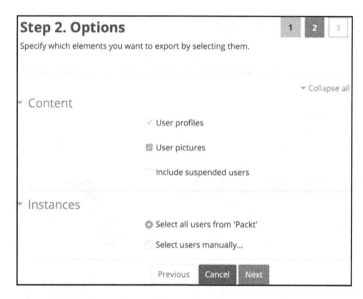

Figure 12.29 – Users exporter options – I

The following tables list all the available options for the Users exporter, alongside short descriptions of each:

Content	Description
User profiles (compulsory)	Include all user data including custom profile fields but excluding user pictures from unsuspended users.
User pictures	Include user profile pictures.
Include suspended users	Include suspended users.

Instances	Description
Select all from <tenant>	All users from the selected tenant.
Select users manually...	Select individual users. If you wish to include site users, you have to perform the export from the default tenant.

Figure 12.30 – Users exporter options – II

Exporting users has been one of the most sought-after features in Moodle Workplace. While it has been possible to download users via the bulk user tool (**Site administration | Users | Accounts | Bulk user actions**), neither Workplace-specific data nor automation is supported. Both shortcomings are essential in commercial setups, as we will see when synchronizing HR data later on.

Phew – that was plenty of export types to go through! Next up is the actual creation of export files based on the selections and options chosen.

Export execution

The final step of any exporter is comprised of reviewing and executing the export process. First, you will be presented with a summary of the selected and unselected options for content and instances. You can check at a glance if everything is correct before proceeding with the final step.

The export can only be started when the resulting file will be non-empty; that is, at least one instance has been selected. For instance, if you choose a course category that does not contain any courses, the **Export** button will remain deactivated. The execution will have to be confirmed, as shown in the following screenshot:

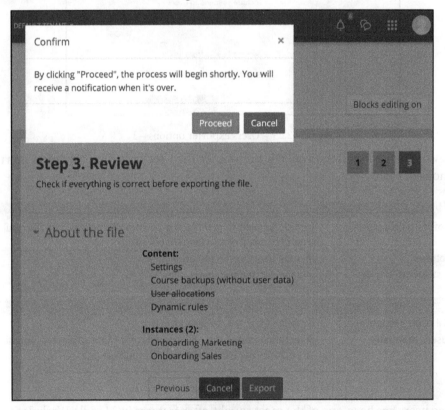

Figure 12.31 – Export review

Once the export has been initiated, its status will be set to **Scheduled**. The export will commence on the next cron execution (see the sidebar in *Chapter 5, Onboarding and Compliance*, for details on Moodle Workplace's cron script).

While the export file is being generated, the status will be changed to **In progress**. This might take some time on larger exports.

When the export file is ready for download or import, the status changes again to **Success**. You will also receive a notification via the usual on-board mechanism, as follows:

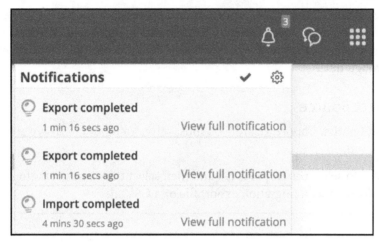

Figure 12.32 – Export notifications

The export process will run in the background. It is safe to continue navigating the site and perform other tasks at this time. What you should avoid is making structural changes to the data you are about to export. For instance, if you are moving courses around during the export process, you might trigger an **Error** status; details will then be shown on the status page:

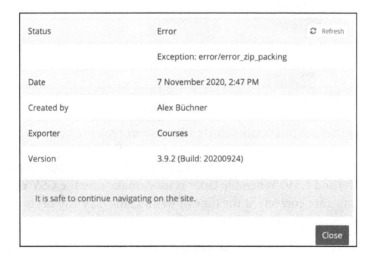

Figure 12.33 – Export status page

Now that you are familiar with migration exports, you will have no problems understanding how to import data since it follows a very similar approach.

Importing data

The import wizard takes a migration export file and processes it according to the type of exporter that has been used. Alternatively, CSV files can be uploaded; however, not all import types are currently supported. The workflow contains multiple steps, all of which we will run through next.

Step 1 – Select Source

To kick off the migration import wizard, you must select an input file. There are two ways this can be achieved.

The first option is to select the **Imports** tab and then select the **+Import** button. You will then need to upload either a migration export file or a CSV file:

Figure 12.34 – Import – Select source

By default, the importer automatically detects what export type has been used before proceeding to step 2. In addition to the **Detect automatically** option, you can also select the file format, where you can choose from **Workplace format** (the one we exported previously) and **CSV**. When the latter is used, make sure the **CSV delimiter** and **Encoding** settings are correct. At the time of writing, the CSV import format only supports departments and positions.

The second option is to select the **New import from this file** icon, next to an exported file on the **Exports** tab. This will take you straight to step 2 using the selected file.

Step 2 – General settings

The second step contains up to three sections, depending on what type of import file you have uploaded. The left-hand side of the following screenshot appears when you're importing a file in Workplace format, while the one on the right-hand side appears when you're importing a file in CSV format:

Figure 12.35 – Import – General settings

The three sections of the **General settings** step are as follows:

- **About this file**: When importing a Workplace file, metadata about its content is shown. When importing a CSV file, a preview of the first three rows is displayed, along with an option to show additional records.

- **Select importer**: This section only displays when you're importing a CSV file. At the time of writing, Moodle Workplace supports a **Departments importer** and a **Positions importer**. The formats of those files will be shown in the next sub-section.

- **Destination**: Here, you select the tenant the file has to be imported to. You can either opt for the current tenant or select a tenant from your site. Note that this section is not available when you wish to import a tenant import file.

Once you have completed any/all of these sections, you will be directed to step 3 of the import process.

Step 3 – Import Options

In the third step, you will have to select content and instances information. The available options depend entirely on the import file type you've chosen and are almost identical to the respective export counterpart. For instance, in the programs importer, the content and **Instances** sections should look familiar since they are very similar to the programs exporter options:

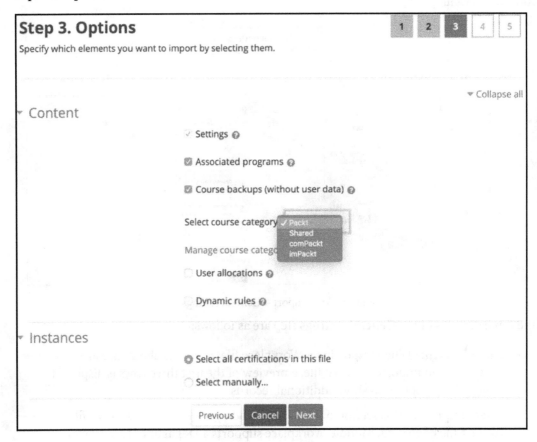

Figure 12.36 – Import – Options (Workplace)

When you import a CSV file, you will see that the content and instances options have been replaced with an alternative screen, as shown here:

Figure 12.37 – Import – Options (CSV)

The following three sections exist when you're importing either departments or positions via CSV files:

- **Position/Department framework**: Either create a new (generic) framework where a name will be provided automatically (`Import <name of import file>`) or select an existing framework.

- **Hierarchy**: Both positions and departments can either be arranged hierarchically or as a list. If your organization structure is hierarchical, you need to provide a position identifier, which will be used to identify the parent.

- **Field mapping**: The import file contains the following, mostly self-explanatory, fields:

`name`: Name of the position or department.

`idnumber`: ID number of the position or department.

`description`: Textual description of the position or department.

`descriptionformat`: The following four format options are available: 1 = Moodle auto format (default), 2 = Plain text format, 3 = HTML format, and 4 = Markdown format.

`parent`: The ID number of the parent. The mapping for this field cannot be the same as the position identifier provided in the hierarchy section.

`manager`: Toggle whether the manager role permissions are all available (1) or not (0). Only available for positions, not for departments.

`departmentlead`: Toggle whether the department lead role permissions are all available (1) or not (0). Only available for positions, not for departments.

The following is an example position import file that excludes the description and description format columns:

```
name;idnumber;parent;manager;departmentlead
CEO;posCEO;;1;0
VP Sales;posVPSales;posCEO;1;0
VP Marketing;posVPMarketing;posCEO;1;0
Marketing Manager;posMarketingMan;posVPMarketing;1;0
Marketing Assistant;posMarketingAss;posMarketingMan;
false;0
Pre-Sales Assistant;posPreSalesAss; posMarketingMan;
false;0
VP Operations;posVPOperations;posCEO;1;1
Project Manager;posProjectManager;posVPOperations;0;1
VP Finance & HR;posFinanceHR; posCEO;1;0
```

When the CSV file does not follow the notation laid out here, you have the option to select columns manually, as shown in the import options screenshot earlier.

If your import file – whether in Workplace or CSV format – contains any data that cannot be imported, the conflict resolution step will be triggered.

Step 4 – Conflict Resolution

If the import file contains any inconsistencies that the migration tool cannot resolve automatically, the conflict resolution screen will be displayed. When would such irregularities occur? The two common scenarios are shown in the following screenshot; that is, a record already exists (for instance, the course name or a position ID) or the associated user accounts do not exist:

Figure 12.38 – Import – Conflicts

This example also demonstrates the two types of resolution mechanisms nicely: either a solution is provided (here, the numeric suffix is added to the course's short name) or the record has to be skipped. You either have to accept this limitation or make sure that the import file is free of any issues.

Step 5 – Review and Import

The final step of any importer is reviewing and executing the import process. First, you will be presented with a summary of the file content to be imported and, if present, how conflicts will be resolved. You can check at a glance if everything is correct before proceeding with the final step. The execution will have to be confirmed, as shown in the following screenshot:

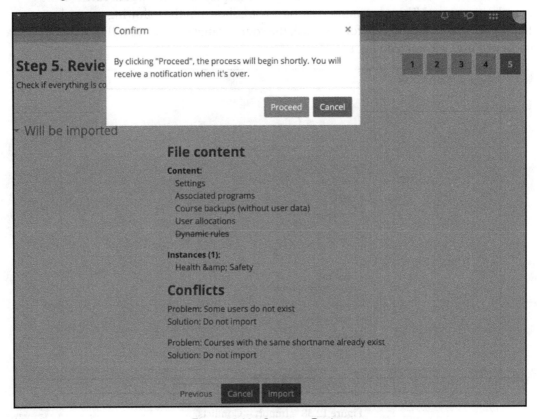

Figure 12.39 – Import – Review

Once the import has been initiated, its status will be set to **Scheduled**. The import will commence on the next cron execution. While the import file is being processed, the status will be changed to **In progress**. This might take some time on larger imports. Once the import file has been process, the status changes to **Success** once more – or, in case of any errors, to **Error**. In both cases, a log will be shown at the bottom of the status screen that contains details about the processed data. This is particularly useful when you're debugging an invalid file. You will also receive a notification via the usual on-board mechanism. The import process will run in the background. It is safe to continue navigating the site and performing other tasks while you do this.

This completes the importer process, along with its various steps and options. Next, we'll have a brief look at how to automate migrations via the versatile command-line interface.

Migrating via the Command-Line Interface

Moodle Workplace provides a powerful **command-line interface** (CLI) for automating integrations. It supports both exports and imports. The following two commands allow you to perform export and import operations via the CLI, respectively:

```
php admin/tool/wp/cli/export.php
php admin/tool/wp/cli/import.php
```

To get a grasp of the flexible shell tool, use the --help parameter, which prints out all the available options, alongside a short description of each parameter. Here, you can see the side-by-side output for the export and import helpers:

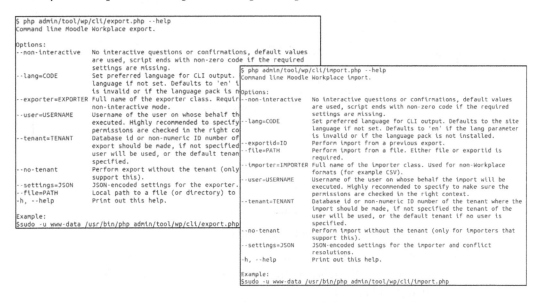

Figure 12.40 – Command-line helpers for Moodle Workplace's export and import options

The two migration CLIs support interactive and non-interactive modes.

During **interactive mode**, you will be asked various questions; such as the program name to be exported, and you have to confirm actions, such as the usage of default values. This is particularly useful during one-off operations and when testing new processes.

As the name suggests, in **non-interactive** mode, no questions are asked, no confirmations are needed, and default values are used. It is intended for usage in scripts to automate regular processes fully.

When run in interactive mode, the CLI's beauty is that the non-interactive counterpart – that is, the valid command – will be displayed. That way, you can create your command step by step and, once completed, use it in your shell scripts. The following shows the interaction with the CLI command in interactive mode, executed as tenantadmin - hence the reduced number of available exporters. The example of the non-interactive counterpart has been highlighted:

```
$ php admin/tool/wp/cli/export.php
Perform export as user [admin]
: packtadmin
Select exporter
  1 Certifications
  2 Custom reports
  3 Dynamic rules
  4 Organisation structure frameworks
  5 Organisation structure jobs
  6 Programs
: 4
................................................................................
Perform export as: packtadmin
Exporter: Organisation structure frameworks (tool_organisation\tool_wp\exporter\orgstructure)
Tenant: Packt
Export settings:
  export_instances=all
  select_frameworks=[]

Available settings:
  -- Content --
  export_content=1             Descriptions, hierarchy and permissions (Locked)
  -- Instances --
  export_instances=all         Select all department and position frameworks
  export_instances=departments Select all department frameworks
  export_instances=positions   Select all position frameworks
  export_instances=selected    Select manually...
  select_frameworks=[...]      Frameworks

Example of performing this export from CLI:
  php admin/tool/wp/cli/export.php --user=packtadmin --exporter="tool_organisation\\tool_wp\\exporter\\orgstructure" --tenant=2 --set
tings="{\"export_instances\":\"all\",\"select_frameworks\":[]}"

Will be exported:
  Packt Departments (Department framework)
  Packt Positions (Position framework)

Continue [Y/n]?
: Y
................................................................................
Starting export...
... export completed with status: Success
Export id: 1
Download at: http://localhost/democli/pluginfile.php/1/tool_wp/export/1/organisation-structure-frameworks-export-20201124-1421.zip
```

Figure 12.41 – CLI's interactive and non-interactive mode

Exporter and importer-specific parameters are currently passed as JSON-encoded strings. If you are not familiar with JSON encoding, then don't worry – plenty of online converters can translate your strings and arrays.

Now that you are familiar with the Moodle Workplace CLI in general, let's look at the two migration tools we'll be using. First up is the migration importer.

CLI migration exporter

The purpose of the CLI migration exporter is to export certain Moodle Workplace elements via the command line (one-off) or shell script (regularly). The syntax of the tool is as follows (key parameters only):

```
export.php --user=<username> --tenant= <tenant ID>
--exporter=<export_tool> --settings=<export_tool_settings>
--file=<file or path>
```

It is recommended to specify a username for the export; some admins prefer setting up a dedicated CLI user to simplify monitoring. If the tenant ID parameter is not specified, the tenant of username will be used or, if no user has been specified, the default tenant. The export_tool parameter specifies the path of the exporter class.

The available values for the settings variable depend on the selected export_tool. As described in the *Exporting data* section, there are settings for content and instances. The following is an example command that can be used to export a specific department from the packt tenant as the admin user and write its content to the packt.zip file (the export_content variable is locked and has only been used for demonstration purposes):

```
sudo -u www-data /usr/bin/php admin/tool/wp/cli/export.php
--user=packtadmin --tenant=packt
--exporter="tool_orgnisation\\tool_wp\\exporter\\orgstructure"
--settings="\export_content\":"\1\","\export_instances\":
"\selected\", "\select_frameworks\":"[PacktDep]}" --file=packt.
zip
```

The best way to construct CLI migration import commands, especially the JSON parts, is to use the tool in interactive mode and provide input to all the requested variables. The corresponding command line will then be displayed by the CLI tool. Expect the number of inline actions to increase in future releases, such as supporting export and cloning operations. Now, let's look at the other side of the CLI migration coin: the CLI migration importer.

CLI Migration Importer

The CLI migration importer works the same as the exporter. The CLI migration importer's purpose is to load a Moodle Workplace migration export via the command line (one-off) or shell script (regularly). The syntax of the tool is as follows (key parameters only):

```
import.php --user=<username> --tenant= <tenant ID>
--exportid=<export ID> | --file=<file >
--settings=<import_tool_settings>
```

The `username` and `tenant` options are identical to the exporter's. When importing an entire tenant, make sure to specify the `--no-tenant` flag. To specify which Moodle Workplace migration export must be used, you need to either specify an `exportid` (a previously generated export) or a `file` (in ZIP format). As we mentioned previously, the available `settings` options depend entirely on the exporter that was used when generating the file. Here is a simple command that imports the department framework to another tenant from the `packt.zip` file we exported a minute ago:

```
sudo -u www-data /usr/bin/php admin/tool/wp/cli/import.php
--user=packtadmin --tenant=compackt --file=packt.zip
```

By default, all content will be imported unless you narrow down the scope by specifying the `settings` variable, for instance, via the `select_framework` setting we already used during the export. The importer CLI also supports the aforementioned interactive mode, which helps identify the correct syntax for the required command.

This concludes this section of working with migration. The two command-line tools we looked at – one for exporting and one for importing – are powerful mechanisms that can potentially automate all 12 migrations we dealt with in this section. Hopefully, you now understand that the exporter and importer are very potent mechanisms, especially when used in conjunction with related facilities. We will demonstrate this in the next section when we look at synchronizing HR data.

Synchronizing HR data

In this section, we are going to put the various migration tools we covered in this chapter into practice. We are going to apply imports and exports to HR data in order to automate typical user provisioning processes.

Enterprise HR systems, whether off-the-shelf or tailor-made, store and maintain critical information about the people making enterprises run. In addition to details about staff, HR systems often also handle data about externals, such as contractors, resellers, suppliers, and other associates. Most people working in an enterprise require regular training and development, which is generally directly related to information that's maintained in the HR system.

HR systems are usually updated daily as people join the organization, change positions, get promoted, retire, leave and return, or change their address or surname, with the latter caused by the blunder commonly known as marriage. The way data is stored in an enterprise's HR system typically depends on how it has been deployed and configured.

Due to this, it is common to synchronize any relevant HR data with the LMS, and Moodle Workplace is no exception. Due to the potentially large number of diverse key data elements that are typically collected and tracked, there is no standardized format for HR data. Instead, each export mechanism supports creating one or many extracted files, which are then processed further. The following diagram shows a typical workflow for such a one-way synchronization process (from the enterprise HR system to Moodle Workplace):

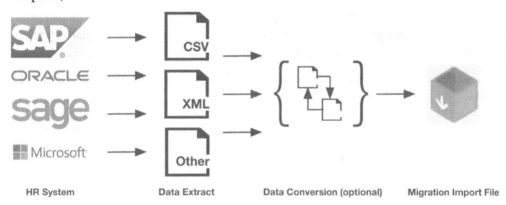

Figure 12.42 – High-level HR data synchronization process

In Moodle Workplace, the minimum amount of data that's transferred is always information about the users themselves and, ideally, supplementary functional and organizational data. Depending on the extracted data format, an optional data conversion step may be required so that you have a file in a compliant Moodle Workplace migration import format. Extracting data from the enterprise HR system and data conversion can be achieved by applying dedicated tools that are not part of Moodle Workplace. The high-level format of the migration import file was briefly described when we looked at the sidebar, earlier in this chapter. For details on the formats each migration type will be in, it will be necessary to get a developer or Premium Moodle Partner involved.

While it would be possible to **manually** import the generated file(s) using the previous section's steps, this approach would not be feasible in a production environment. Instead, full **automation** of the preceding process has to be the goal; this can be achieved via Moodle Workplace's command-line interface, in combination with other Moodle Workplace tools. In the next section, we are going to describe how to provision users and their related information.

Provisioning your users

In the context of learning management systems, user provisioning is the process of creating, managing, and maintaining all required user-related data. Ideally, this process is fully automated, but this depends on where and how your data is stored, as well as the tools provided by the HR system.

In Moodle Workplace, the relevant data that has to be dealt with is stored in tenants, users, departments, positions, and jobs. There might be other data, such as cohorts, groups, and course enrolments, but for now, let's focus on the elements unique to Moodle Workplace. Throughout this book, we have managed all tenant- and organization-related data manually; that is, via the familiar admin interface. While this approach is suitable for demonstration purposes and trivial setups, it is untenable in larger and more complex organizations. Let's change this and look at user provisions in Moodle Workplace by using its powerful CLI and alternative data transfer mechanisms.

A high-level view of user provisioning in Moodle Workplace can be seen in the following diagram:

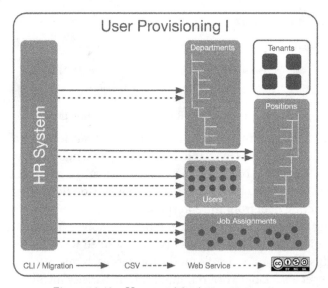

Figure 12.43 – User provisioning components

By taking a closer look at the user provisioning diagram, we can see that there are various components and import processes. We'll look at these in the following sub-sections.

HR system

The HR system is the source of all staff-related data and can also contain information about external users of your **LMS**, such as contractors, suppliers, partners, and so on. This data is usually kept in a commercial HR system, such as SAP HR, Oracle HCM, PeopleSoft HRMS, or Zoho People. Alternatively, the data is stored in several home-grown systems and might even be kept in a pile of Excel spreadsheets. Whatever way your organization's data is managed, it will be the leading system for your user-related data.

Tenants

Tenants themselves should be created manually, which is usually acceptable since the number of tenants rarely exceeds the acceptance threshold when automation is desirable. While it is possible to create a tenant via its import migration tool, it is usually not the approach that's chosen in a user provisioning workflow. There is currently no web service that can be used to create tenants.

Departments

New departments will be brought into existence, existing ones will be split into several standalone departments, and unprofitable entities will have to close down. These types of operations are common after either business restructuring or company acquisition has taken place.

Initially, you need to set up department frameworks. Since this is often a one-off task, their creation is often done manually. However, if there is a high turnover in terms of department frameworks, you can use the Organization structure frameworks migration tool we described in this chapter. To do this, you'll need to create a department framework, which will be used as a template, and generate a migration export. You can then use the migration importer CLI to create new frameworks when needed.

Once the required department frameworks have been created and configured, departments will have to be created. If this is a one-off task since the structure isn't expected to change, importing via CSV files is usually your best bet. If the structure changes regularly, it should be managed via web services. The relevant web services are `tool_organisation_create_departments`, `tool_organisation_department_delete`, and `tool_organisation_department_move`. Workplace-related web services are covered in *Appendix A, Moodle Workplace Web Services*.

Positions

Positions are handled in the same way as departments; that is, position frameworks are either set up manually or via the Organization structure frameworks migration tool and the aforementioned templating mechanism.

Once the required position frameworks have been created and configured, positions will have to be added. Again, if this is a one-off task since the structure isn't expected to change, importing via CSV files is usually your best bet. However, if the structure changes regularly, it should be managed via web services. Positions can be handled via the `tool_organisation_create_positions` (with additional support for managers, department leads, and their permissions), `tool_organisation_position_delete`, and `tool_organisation_position_move` web services. Workplace-related web services are covered thoroughly in *Appendix A, Moodle Workplace Web Services*.

Users

User data is the one that changes the most frequently, which is why Moodle Workplace provides a full set of data transfer options: users can either be handled via the CLI, via CSV file import, or via web services. All variants are standard features of Moodle core. However, the CSV file import has been extended to support tenants and job assignments; the core user web services are currently lacking this feature.

Uploading users in bulk allows you to import multiple accounts from a text file or update accounts that already exist in your system. Before you can upload users, you must generate a text file that conforms to a specific format. Its general format is that of a CSV file. You will find detailed documentation on the text file format and how to upload and update users in batch mode at `docs.moodle.org/en/Upload_users` or in the *User Management* chapter of *Moodle 3 Administration* by Packt Publishing. Once you have created your CSV file, make use of `admin/tool/uploaduser/cli/uploaduser.php`. This tool supports all the available options in the admin interface counterpart, which can be found by going to **Site administration | Users | Accounts | Upload users**. This can be fully integrated into your automation scripts.

The ability to allocate tenants via CSV files has been added to the **Upload users** mechanism in Moodle Workplace. A tenant is matched by its tenant ID number. The following is a sample CSV file that's adding three users to two different tenants (in bold):

```
username,firstname,lastname,email,tenant
cogea,Aileen,Cogé,a.coge@mail.com,imPackt
bittnerh,Helmut,Bittner,h.bittner@mail.com,imPackt
henricku,Ursula,Henrick,u.henrick@mail.com,comPackt
```

The user who uploads the file has to be able to use the **Upload user** tool. If the user also has the `tool/tenant:allocate` capability, they will be able to specify a tenant when uploading users (both when creating new users and updating existing ones). If the user does not have this capability, users can only be created and updated in their own tenant.

Since a user cannot be tenantless, it is impossible to remove tenant allocation. However, you can move a user from one tenant to another by replacing the old tenant in the CSV file with the new value.

Job Assignments

Job assignments also change frequently, and Moodle Workplace honors this by providing the full set of data transfer mechanisms. We already discussed the CLI migration approach earlier.

Interestingly, as of version 3.9.2, Moodle Workplace provides a web service for removing jobs (`tool_organisation_job_delete`), but there isn't a counterpart for creating or modifying job assignments. The expectation is that Moodle will rectify this oversight very shortly.

Let's have a closer look at the new CSV file operations supported in Moodle Workplace. In addition to adding tenants via CSV files, assigning jobs is also supported by Moodle Workplace via the following four new self-explanatory variables:

- `jobdepartment`
- `jobposition`
- `jobstartdate` (optional)
- `jobenddate` (optional)

Each variable has to have a numeric postfix to support multiple job assignments. Just like tenants, departments and positions are matched by their respective ID numbers. For any date field, you must use the **YYYY-MM-DD** ISO standard format, which will then be properly localized during the upload process.

In addition to having permission to upload users, the `tool/organisation:assignjobs` capability is required if you wish to create jobs for users or modify existing ones.

The following is a sample CSV file that's adding two job assignments and changing an existing one (shown in bold). When a user already has a job in a department, as well as a position, the dates will be modified without a new job being created:

```
username,firstname,lastname,email,jobdepartment1,jobposition1,
jobstartdate1,jobenddate1
```

```
cogea,Aileen,Cogé,a.coge@mail.
com,depCentralEurope,posMarketingManager,2020-02-26,
```

```
bittnerh,Helmut,Bittner,h.bittner@mail.
com,depCentralEurope,posMarketingAssistant,,2020-12-31
```

```
henricku,Ursula,Henrick,u.henrick@mail.
com,depUKIRE,posMarketingManager,2020-01-01,
```

This example CSV file demonstrates the importance of providing meaningful ID numbers for departments and positions, respectively. Bear in mind that it is currently not possible to delete job assignments via the **User upload** feature.

Now that we have covered the different ways we can update HR data in Moodle Workplace, let's put all the pieces together in a user provisioning workflow.

Putting together your user provisioning workflow

In an ideal world, Moodle Workplace would provide us with a full range of CSV-/ CLI-based and web service-supported import options so that we can synchronize all organizational data, such as tenants, frameworks, departments, positions, users, and job assignments. The reality, however, is that we currently have to work with a bit of a patchwork to put together a robust and flexible user provisioning workflow, as shown in the following process diagram:

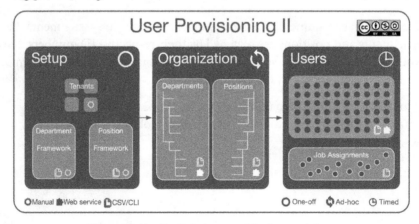

Figure 12.44 – Typical user provisioning workflow

Following on from the components we described in this section, and taking into account the boundaries imposed by Moodle Workplace, a typical user provisioning workflow may look as follows:

1. Carry out the initial setup (one-off):

   a) Create tenant(s): Manual

   b) Create department framework(s): Manual or via CLI (templates)

   c) Create position framework(s): Manual or via CLI (templates)

2. Synchronize organization data with the HR system (ad hoc):

   a) Create departments and positions: Web services or CSV/CLI

   b) Update and delete departments and positions: Web services

3. Manage user data (regularly/timed):

   a) Create, update, and delete users: CLI/CSV or web services. If you're working with web services, at the time of writing, assigning users to tenants can only be done via CSV.

   b) Create and update job assignments: CSV/CLI.

While it is possible to create a solid and scalable user provisioning workflow, the overall setup is far from ideal. Since certain steps can only be carried out via a particular method (that is, manual, web services, CSV files, or migration CLI), a patchwork configuration is necessary to set up the required synchronization process. The expectation is that in the versions that follow, this shortcoming will be rectified by supporting all operations via web services and flat file upload, including full CLI support.

So far, we have focused on transferring data from our enterprise HR system to Moodle Workplace since this is the most common setup. However, the reverse process – from Moodle Workplace back to any of your enterprise systems – also has valid use cases that are not limited to HR; for instance:

- Store successful compliance training completions in an auditing system for external reviews.

- Post course participation information to an accounts system. This will trigger invoices being sent to external participants or internal cost allocation.

- Transfer competencies to your performance management system to plan annual training and development.

- Record course completions in employees' files.

Ideally, an LMS would provide facilities to support the full range of data transfer options: interactive, in batch mode, and in quasi-real time. Let's have a brief look at where Moodle Workplace is at when it comes to these data exporting mechanisms:

- **Interactive data export**: The presented export migrations support the Moodle Workplace-specific tools very well. Specific data, such as program and certification completion, can be reported on using the report builder and then exported in CSV or JSON format. Other data, such as grades, can be exported manually inside the respective tool.

- **Batch data export**: The export migrations can be batched via the CLI mechanism, as described in this chapter. While the report builder contains a scheduler, it currently only supports an email facility; if this were to be extended to exporting to a file on the web server's filesystem, those extracts could then be accessed by an external system.

- **Web service for outgoing data transfer**: Moodle itself provides a large number of web services that support the ability to transfer data to other systems. Moodle Workplace has added more services for this, as we will see in *Appendix A*, *Moodle Workplace Web Services*. If there is any data that has to be extracted where there is no web service available, you can always develop the required service as a custom add-on.

Compared to other learning management systems, Moodle Workplace supports a wide range of options to assist in the integration process for other systems. Given the popularity and open source approach of the software, we can expect that the number of import and export migrations, CLI options, and web services will continue to grow with every upcoming release.

Summary

In this chapter, you learned how to move data and elements between tenants and sites using Moodle Workplace's powerful migration tool.

First, we covered the fundamental concepts of the migration tool. This provided you with an overview of the 12 available import and export migrations. We then outlined a typical migration workflow.

Next, we dealt with the migration tool itself and covered exporting and importing data in great detail. We also had a closer look at the versatile command-line interface, which can be used to automate processes at the system level.

Finally, we dealt with synchronizing HR data and user provisioning. Here, you became familiar with the different options available for keeping any user-related data in Moodle Workplace up to date.

We regularly mentioned web services as an alternative approach to the migration tool or CLI-based operations during this chapter. The appendix will deal with Moodle Workplace-specific web services and also discuss the differences between the migration options that we covered in this chapter.

Appendix A – Moodle Workplace Web Services

In most enterprises, the LMS is rarely an isolated, standalone system; instead, the LMS is almost always part of a company-wide infrastructure containing several best-of-breed components. Web services facilitate the exchange and communication among these systems, and Moodle Workplace is no exception. At the time of writing, Moodle Workplace ships with over 700 web services functions, a number that is growing with every release.

First, we will be providing an overview of Moodle's built-in web service facility. You will familiarize yourself with what web services are, how they work, and when to use them. You will further learn how to configure web services in Moodle and Moodle Workplace. The process is identical in both systems; the only difference is that Moodle Workplace supports significantly more web service functions.

Second, we will describe the differences between migrations, as described in the previous chapter, and web services. Even though both mechanisms facilitate the exchange between external systems and Moodle Workplace, there are significant disparities between the two approaches.

Third, we will list all Moodle Workplace-specific web services to demonstrate that the majority of features covered in this book can also be controlled programmatically.

By the end of this appendix, you will know what web services are, how they are being configured, and which web services to use in a Moodle Workplace environment. This appendix comprises the following three main sections:

- Moodle web services overview
- Moodle Workplace migrations versus web services
- Moodle Workplace web services

Moodle web services overview

In this section, you will familiarize yourself with what web services are, how they work, and when to use them. You will further learn how to configure web services in Moodle and Moodle Workplace.

Introduction to Moodle web services

It has always been possible to extend Moodle via code (PHP and JavaScript). Due to Moodle's open source code base, there is no limitation to what code a developer can modify or extend. This is not a satisfactory situation, as you have no control over what parts of Moodle are being changed and, equally important, what data is being accessed or altered.

Moodle has various APIs that provide an abstract layer for specific functionalities. Examples of this are the Portfolio API, the Repository API, and the File API. These are great for developers as they reduce the amount of code that has to be re-written. In addition to these interfaces, Moodle also provides us with an ever-growing number of web services.

> **Important Note**
> Web services enable other systems to perform operations inside Moodle and vice versa.

Why would we want to use web services? Well, there are two main scenarios we can think of:

- Other systems in your organization, such as the HR system, have to trigger certain actions in your LMS. For example, once details of a new staff member have been added, an account has to be created in Moodle Workplace, and allocation to some compliance certifications has to occur.

- Certain information stored in Moodle Workplace might have to be transferred to external applications. Examples are course completions, program achievements, or certification statuses, which have to be recorded in the personnel file, or seminar participation, which will trigger invoicing for external attendees and cost allocation for internal staff.

Web services simplify these types of processes greatly. As a side note, internally, the Moodle Workplace app we covered in *Chapter 10, Mobile Learning*, also uses web services: all communication and data exchange between a mobile device and the actual Moodle Workplace backend takes place via web services.

Configuring Moodle web services

In this section, you will learn how to configure web services in Moodle and Moodle Workplace. The process is identical in both systems; the only difference is that Moodle Workplace supports significantly more web services and functions.

We will only cover the basics of Moodle web service configuration necessary to get you started with the topic. You can find an extended version of this section in *Chapter 15, Moodle Integration*, in *Moodle 3 Administration* by Packt Publishing.

> **Important Note**
> **A word of warning**: enabling web services comes with a potential security risk as you are granting access to Moodle to outside systems. The mantra should always be to open up as few services and functions as possible.

To get an overview of the tasks ahead, navigate to **Site administration | Plugins | Web services | Overview**, which acts as a dashboard to set up Workplace web services:

Step	Status	Description
1. Enable web services	Yes	Web services must be enabled in Advanced features.
2. Enable protocols	None	At least one protocol should be enabled. For security reasons, only protocols that are to be used should be enabled.
3. Create a specific user		A web services user is required to represent the system controlling Moodle.
4. Check user capability		The user should have appropriate capabilities according to the protocols used, for example webservice/rest:use, webservice/soap:use. To achieve this, create a web services role with protocol capabilities allowed and assign it to the web services user as a system role.
5. Select a service		A service is a set of web service functions. You will allow the user to access to a new service. On the **Add service** page check 'Enable' and 'Authorised users' options. Select 'No required capability'.
6. Add functions		Select required functions for the newly created service.
7. Select a specific user		Add the web services user as an authorised user.
8. Create a token for a user		Create a token for the web services user.
9. Enable developer documentation	No	Detailed web services documentation is available for enabled protocols.
10. Test the service		Simulate external access to the service using the web service test client. Use an enabled protocol with token authentication. **WARNING: The functions that you test WILL BE EXECUTED, so be careful what you choose to test!**

Overview
Allow an external system to control Moodle
The following steps help you to set up the Moodle web services to allow an external system to interact with Moodle. This includes setting up a token (security key) authentication method.

Figure A1.1 – Web services overview

The following steps are required to set up Moodle Workplace to interact with an external system:

1. First of all, you have to activate web services. Go to **Site administration | Advanced features** and turn on **Enable web services**.

2. Next, enable the web service protocol used in your company at **Site administration | Plugins | Web services | Manage protocols**. Supported protocols are REST, SOAP, and XML-RPC.

3. Create a web services user. Ideally, each external application should have a separate user account. This way, you can control the capabilities that each external system is going to use. You should also enable the web services authentication plugin (**Site administration | Plugins | Authentication | Manage authentication**).

4. Depending on the protocol you have selected, you have to allow the users' individual permissions. You achieve this by creating a new role with any of the three capabilities, `webservice/rest:use`, `webservice/soap:use`, or `webservice/xmlrpc:use`, and assign the role(s) to the web services user(s) in the **System** context.

5. A service is like a defined interface that an external application can connect to. It is a set of functions that have to be chosen. First, you need to add a custom service in **Plugins | Web services | External services**:

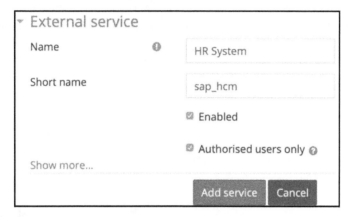

Figure A1.2 – Adding a web service

6. Next, you are asked to add web service functions. All Moodle Workplace-specific functions are listed in the last section of this appendix:

Figure A1.3 – Adding web services functions

Once you have added the selected functions, you will be shown the required capabilities that a user has to have to access the service. Make sure these have been allowed in the role assigned to the web services user.

7. The penultimate step is to add the earlier-created web service user as an authorized user, effectively connecting the user to the just-set-up web service. This takes place in **Plugins | Web services | External services,** where you need to select **Authorised users**.

8.   Finally, you need to create a token for your web services user. Web services use tokens for security. These are created for each user and can be added by going to **Plugins | Web services | Manage tokens**. To add a token, select your earlier-created web services user, select the web service to be accessed, and optionally specify an IP address (or range) and expiry date, as shown in the following screenshot:

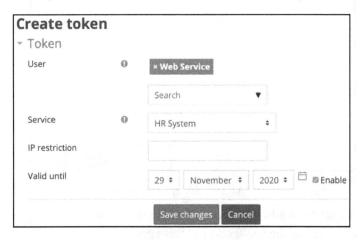

Figure A1.4 – Creating a web services token

There are two more optional steps, which are recommended to be set up:

9.   Moodle is able to generate documentation for developers for the selected functions in the format of the selected protocol (**Site administration | Plugins | Web services | Manage protocols**). Developers will then be able to see the documentation as part of their security keys.

10.   Once a web service has been set up, functions have been selected, and users have been assigned, it is highly recommended that you test the service to make sure that it works and, more importantly, that only the functionality that is required by the external system has been opened up. Navigation takes place from the web services dashboard, where you need to select the **Test the service** link. Be careful with executing functions via the test client as they are performed as though they are executed for real!

Now you are all set to go. Before we list all the Moodle Workplace-specific web service functions, let's compare migrations, as covered in the previous chapter, with web services.

Moodle Workplace migration versus web services

This section will describe the differences between migrations and web services. It is worth comparing the two approaches since both mechanisms facilitate data transfer from an external system to Moodle Workplace and vice versa. The discrepancies have been illustrated in the following diagram:

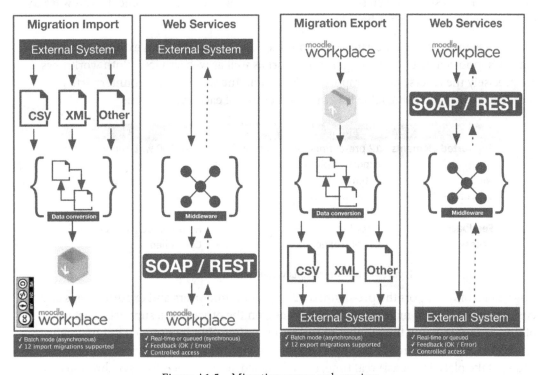

Figure A1.5 – Migration versus web services

The two leftmost columns represent the data workflow from any external system to Moodle Workplace; the two rightmost columns show the opposite data flow direction, namely from Moodle Workplace back to external systems.

We have already described the **migration import process** in detail in *Chapter 12, Migrations*: the external system generates output in CSV, XML, or any other proprietary format. An optional data conversion step might be necessary to transform the data into a Workplace migration-compatible format. This import file will then be used as input for Moodle Workplace's migration tool, either handled manually or scripted via its CLI.

The **web services** counterpart to the migration import process is effectively a series of web service calls. Moodle Workplace supports both popular protocols in commercial settings, namely **SOAP** and **REST**; the choice depends on the protocol being used in your organization. One advantage of using web services over migration tools is the fact that web services return feedback, whether the calls or transactions have been successful or not. For instance, if the user creation of a new employee has failed in the LMS for whatever reason, the HR system will be notified and can repeat the attempt after a pre-defined period. Most web services-based infrastructures require some **middleware** to facilitate queueing and error handling.

The reverse process—transferring data from Moodle Workplace to an external system—is equally supported by both the migration export as well as web services. Both workflows are precisely the reverse of the import workflow and the web services counterpart, respectively. The following table lists the key features of each mechanism:

Feature	Migrations	Web Services
Supported elements	12 pre-defined importers and exporters plus custom migrations	Over 700 web services
Mode	Batch	Real-time or queue
Synchronicity	Asynchronous	Synchronous
Handling	Manual or CLI	Code
Feedback	Error log at destination	Return code (OK / Error)
Access	Uncontrolled	Controlled

Figure A1.6 – Migrations versus web services features

Migrations only support the pre-defined 12 migration importers and exporters plus any custom or third-party migrations. Web services, on the other hand, support a vast array of features superseding the number of migrations. Migrations are carried out manually or via the CLI in batch mode and are therefore asynchronous; web services require coding, take place in (quasi) real time, or are queued, and are therefore synchronous. The only feedback available for migrations is the error log at the destination or the transfer progress; web services support a built-in mechanism of return codes for success and failure. Access via migrations is relatively uncontrolled; once permissions have been granted via import and export capabilities (`tool/wp:manageexportimport` or `tool/wp:useexportimport`), plus any tool-specific capabilities (for instance, to create programs), any data of that tool can be imported/exported. For web services, each function to be used has to be unlocked, giving the site administrator more control over what data leaves Moodle Workplace and what data is being changed.

The comparison should not be seen in terms of advantages or disadvantages as this depends heavily on the task at hand. For example, if you wish to perform a one-off migration from a staging site to the production environment, migrations might be your preferred option. However, if, on the other hand, you need to regularly synchronize competencies with a performance management system, web services appear to be your preferred choice.

Why do you have to care about web services when they have been designed for developers? Well, that's the other significant advantage of web services. The administrator can control which system is allowed to talk to your Moodle Workplace system and which service these systems are allowed to use. This way, you can control who has access to your system and limit what they can do.

Now that you are familiar with web services and can distinguish them from migrations, let's look into the Moodle Workplace-specific web services.

Moodle Workplace web services functions

Following the book's structure, we have grouped the web services functions in the same order as the chapters have been arranged in this book.

Tenants

The following web services functions are available for Moodle Workplace's **Tenants** tool (`tool_tenant_*`):

- `tool_tenant_allocate_users`
- `tool_tenant_assign_tenant_admin_roles`
- `tool_tenant_change_sortorder`
- `tool_tenant_delete_users`
- `tool_tenant_enable_shared_space`
- `tool_tenant_get_tenants`
- `tool_tenant_potential_tenant_selector`
- `tool_tenant_suspend_users`
- `tool_tenant_unassign_tenant_admin_roles`
- `tool_tenant_unsuspend_users`

Organizations

The following web services functions are available for Moodle Workplace's **Organisation structure** tool (`tool_organisation_*`):

- `tool_organisation_create_departments`
- `tool_organisation_create_positions`
- `tool_organisation_department_delete`
- `tool_organisation_department_move`
- `tool_organisation_is_jobs_tab_available`
- `tool_organisation_job_delete`
- `tool_organisation_position_delete`
- `tool_organisation_position_move`

Dynamic rules

The following web services functions are available for Moodle Workplace's **Dynamic rules** tool (`tool_dynamicrule_*`):

- `tool_dynamicrule_archive_rule`
- `tool_dynamicrule_can_enable_rule`
- `tool_dynamicrule_count_matched_users`
- `tool_dynamicrule_count_matching_users`
- `tool_dynamicrule_delete_condition`
- `tool_dynamicrule_delete_outcome`
- `tool_dynamicrule_delete_rule`
- `tool_dynamicrule_disable_rule`
- `tool_dynamicrule_duplicate_rule`
- `tool_dynamicrule_enable_rule`
- `tool_dynamicrule_potential_badge_selector`
- `tool_dynamicrule_potential_certificate_selector`
- `tool_dynamicrule_potential_competency_selector`
- `tool_dynamicrule_unarchive_rule`

Programs

The following web services functions are available for Moodle Workplace's **Programs** tool (`tool_program_*`):

- `tool_program_archive_program`
- `tool_program_deallocate_user`
- `tool_program_delete_course`
- `tool_program_delete_program`
- `tool_program_delete_set`
- `tool_program_duplicate_program`
- `tool_program_enrol_user_to_course`
- `tool_program_get_user_programs`
- `tool_program_move_program_item`
- `tool_program_potential_courses_program_selector`
- `tool_program_potential_program_selector`
- `tool_program_reset_program_progress`
- `tool_program_restore_program`
- `tool_program_submit_edit_program_set_completion_form`
- `tool_program_update_program_visibility`

Certifications

The following web services functions are available for Moodle Workplace's **Certifications** tool (`tool_certification_*`):

- `tool_certification_archive_certification`
- `tool_certification_certify_user`
- `tool_certification_deallocate_user`
- `tool_certification_delete_certification`
- `tool_certification_get_certification_user_log`
- `tool_certification_potential_certification_selector`
- `tool_certification_restore_certification`
- `tool_certification_revoke_certification`

Certificates

The following web services functions are available for Moodle Workplace's **Certificates** tool (`tool_certificate_*`):

- `tool_certificate_delete_element`
- `tool_certificate_delete_template`
- `tool_certificate_duplicate_template`
- `tool_certificate_regenerate_issue_file`
- `tool_certificate_revoke_issue`
- `tool_certificate_update_element`
- `mod_coursecertificate_update_automaticsend`

Reports

The following web services functions are available for Moodle Workplace's **Report builder** tool (`tool_reportbuilder_*`):

- `tool_reportbuilder_add_filter`
- `tool_reportbuilder_add_report_column`
- `tool_reportbuilder_add_report_condition`
- `tool_reportbuilder_delete_condition`
- `tool_reportbuilder_delete_report`
- `tool_reportbuilder_delete_report_filter`
- `tool_reportbuilder_delete_schedule`
- `tool_reportbuilder_get_report_sortable_columns`
- `tool_reportbuilder_get_reportbuilder`
- `tool_reportbuilder_remove_report_column`
- `tool_reportbuilder_reorder_columns_filter`
- `tool_reportbuilder_reorder_report_filters`
- `tool_reportbuilder_reorder_sortable_column`
- `tool_reportbuilder_reset_all_conditions`
- `tool_reportbuilder_reset_condition`
- `tool_reportbuilder_reset_filter`

- `tool_reportbuilder_reset_table`
- `tool_reportbuilder_send_schedule`
- `tool_reportbuilder_sort_table_by_heading`
- `tool_reportbuilder_toggle_column_sorting_direction`
- `tool_reportbuilder_toggle_report_sorting_column`
- `tool_reportbuilder_toggle_schedule`

Appointments

The following web services functions are available for Moodle Workplace's **Appointments** activity (`mod_appointment_*`):

- `mod_appointment_delete_session`
- `mod_appointment_get_session_details`

Migration

The following web services functions are available for Moodle Workplace's **Migration** tool:

- `tool_wp_delete_export`
- `tool_wp_delete_import`
- `tool_wp_export`
- `tool_wp_export_file_preview`
- `tool_wp_get_export_status`
- `tool_wp_get_import_status`
- `tool_wp_import`

Moodle HQ has announced more web services for Moodle Workplace's **Migration** tool, and it is expected that these will be released very shortly.

Miscellaneous

There are a small number of Moodle Workplace-related web services functions that cannot be allocated to any of the preceding sections:

- `tool_wp_get_tab_content`
- `tool_wp_modal_form`
- `tool_wp_potential_users_selector`

Summary

In this appendix, you learned what web services are, how they are configured, and which web services to use in a Moodle Workplace environment

First, we provided an overview of Moodle's web service facility. We explained what web services are, how they work, and when to use them. We also gave a brief overview of how web services are configured in Moodle and Moodle Workplace.

Second, we described the differences between migrations and web services. Both mechanisms facilitate the exchange between external systems and Moodle Workplace; we explained the disparities between the two approaches in terms of supported elements, mode, synchronicity, handling, feedback, and access.

Finally, we listed all Moodle Workplace-specific web services to demonstrate that almost all the features covered in this book can also be controlled programmatically.

Other Books You May Enjoy

If you enjoyed this book, you may be interested in these other books by Packt:

WordPress 5 Cookbook
Rakhitha Nimesh Ratnayake

ISBN: 978-1-83898-650-6

- Install and customize WordPress themes and plugins for building websites
- Develop modern web designs without the need to write any code
- Explore the new Gutenberg content editor introduced in WordPress 5 (Bebo)
- Use the existing WordPress plugins to add custom features and monetize your website
- Improve user interaction and accessibility for your website with simple tricks
- Discover powerful techniques for maintaining and securing your websites
- Extend built-in WordPress features for advanced website management

Mastering Adobe Captivate 2019 - Fifth Edition
Dr. Pooja Jaisingh , Damien Bruyndonckx

ISBN: 978-1-78980-305-1

- Learn how to use the objects in Captivate to build professional eLearning content

- Enhance your projects by adding interactivity, animations, and more

- Add multimedia elements, such as audio and video, to create engaging learning experiences

- Use themes to craft a unique visual experience

- Use question slides to create SCORM-compliant quizzes that integrate seamlessly with your LMS

- Make your content fit any device with responsive features of Captivate

- Create immersive 360° experiences with Virtual Reality projects of Captivate 2019

- Integrate Captivate with other applications (such as PowerPoint and Photoshop) to establish a professional eLearning production workflow

- Publish your project in a wide variety of formats including HTML5 and Flash

Leave a review - let other readers know what you think

Please share your thoughts on this book with others by leaving a review on the site that you bought it from. If you purchased the book from Amazon, please leave us an honest review on this book's Amazon page. This is vital so that other potential readers can see and use your unbiased opinion to make purchasing decisions, we can understand what our customers think about our products, and our authors can see your feedback on the title that they have worked with Packt to create. It will only take a few minutes of your time, but is valuable to other potential customers, our authors, and Packt. Thank you!

Index

www.ingramcontent.com/pod-product-compliance
Lightning Source LLC
Chambersburg PA
CBHW062053050326
40690CB00016B/3080